Modern Web Development with Go

Build real-world, fast, efficient, and scalable web server apps using Go programming language

by

Dušan Stojanović

First published: March 2023

Published by: Orange Education Pvt Ltd, AVA™

Address: 9, Daryaganj, Delhi, 110002

ISBN: 978-93-95968-36-2

www.orangeava.com

FOREWORD

The growth of web services has revolutionized the way businesses and organizations interact with the world. With the increasing demand for faster, more efficient, and scalable systems, there has been a growing interest in the development of robust and reliable web services.

Go has emerged as one of the leading programming languages for building web services due to its simplicity, performance, and scalability. Its clear and concise syntax, combined with efficient performance, makes it an ideal choice for developing web services that can handle heavy workloads and scale to meet growing demands.

I was incredibly excited when I heard that my colleague and friend, Dušan Stojanović, was writing a book on building web services with Go. As someone who has worked with him on various projects, I can attest to his expertise in web services development and his passion for teaching others. He has a unique ability to take complex concepts and break them down into simple, easily understandable terms.

In this book, Dušan not only provides a comprehensive guide to building web services with Go but also offers valuable insights into SQL and NoSQL databases. He covers the fundamentals of the language and the core concepts of web service development, including RESTful APIs, HTTP requests, and response handling, as well as the integration of databases. With practical examples and hands-on tutorials, he helps you understand the concepts and build your own web services from scratch.

I am confident that this book will become a valuable resource for anyone looking to gain a deeper understanding of web services development and expand their skill set in this exciting and rapidly growing field. I highly recommend this book to anyone looking to learn more about building web services with Go and integrating with both SQL and NoSQL databases.

Stefan Miletić,

Backend Software Engineer,

Glassnode

Dedicated to

My beloved parents:

Slađana Stojanović

Velmir Stojanović

and

My brother Nikola Stojanović

About the Author

Dušan Stojanović was born in Smederevo (Serbia) in 1989. He received a Master's degree in Computer Science from the University of Belgrade in 2013.

He has worked for several software companies on various projects, predominantly on backend components. A few of the projects include user administration, e-commerce, video streaming platforms, and advertising.

Since 2017, he has been developing software in Go, which is now his most preferred programming language. He was the presenter on the subject "How to write server-side applications with Go" in an internal company workshop. A few of the ideas from that workshop are also included in this book. In 2021, he published his first book "Building Server-side and Microservices with Go".

He currently lives in Belgrade (Serbia) and works as Senior Software Engineer.

Technical Reviewers

Stefan Miletic is a Senior Software Engineer with a decade of experience. Most of that experience is in backend development as he has an inclination towards tackling architectural and design problems.

He is always in quest of interesting challenges, thus, has experience in several domains of the software industry. He has worked in the communication, marketing, insurance technology, educational technology, and analytics sectors. This has allowed him to explore different architectures and designs, from classic monoliths to cutting-edge microservice architecture. He has a Bachelor's degree with Honors in Computer Science from Belgrade University.

Marijana Komatinovic is a DevOps engineer, co-founder of the DevOps Serbia Community, and part of G-Research's Open Source DevOps engineering team. While working as a developer in the past, she contributed to many projects and companies, mostly in developing OTT IPTV solutions, VoIP integrations and a private Cloud management platform. Marijana was born in Belgrade, the capital of Serbia in 1992 and graduated with a Master's degree in Information Systems and Technologies from the University of Belgrade in 2017. Since then, she has been building her knowledge and experience in developing software architectures and infrastructures with a focus on cloud services. Over the last few years, she has been working in AdTech as a DevOps engineer.

Acknowledgements

There are a few people I want to thank for the continued and ongoing support they have given me during the writing of this book. First and foremost, I would like to thank my parents and my brother for continuously encouraging me to write the book.

Special gratitude goes to two of my dearest friends, Marijana and Stefan, who were always there for advice and support. They also performed a technical review and made this book much better.

I am grateful to all of my friends and family. They were very understanding about my skipping our gatherings during work on this book.

My gratitude also goes to the team at Orange AVA for being supportive enough to provide me with quite a long time to finish the book. I thank them for their patience in all my breaking of agreed deadlines.

Finally, once again, thank you all!!!

Preface

This book covers the development of web server applications with state-of-the-art technology. Through this book, we will learn how to design, develop, deploy, and maintain web server applications, with various practical examples and code solutions. This book will introduce the importance of web server applications in the modern software industry and gives information about the usefulness of the Go programming language in the development of the same.

This book is divided into 12 chapters. They will cover the Go programming language basics and advanced concepts, the basics of web server applications and the complete development process. The first four chapters will serve as a preparation for the development process and will be more focused on an introduction to some important concepts and application design. Chapters 5 to 10 will concentrate on development, while the last two chapters will show how to deploy and maintain the application. The details are listed below.

Chapter 1 will focus on the basic concepts of Go programming language with some main advantages compared to other programming languages. Key features will be covered here, like keywords, variables, constants, packages, data types, control structures, and functions.

Chapter 2 will cover the advanced concepts of the Go programming language. Concepts introduced in this chapter will include methods, interfaces, generics, and modules. Panics as the main mechanism for handling unexpected errors will be presented here. This chapter will also cover concurrency in great detail.

Chapter 3 will cover the basics of Web servers. It will introduce the concept of servers, in general, with special reference to Web servers. REST architecture, HTTP protocol, JSON, and routing will be covered in detail here.

Chapter 4 will focus on how to set up a Go programming language project. It will explain how to install and set up all the necessary tools and write a small program. At the end of the chapter, standard and third-party libraries will be introduced.

Chapter 5 will cover the software development life cycle (and all its phases) and application design. It will introduce a couple of different design patterns, with deep dive into Layered design patterns.

Chapter 6 will focus on how to develop application layers of the web server application. It will explain how to organize code, create data models, configure the application, write the main() function, and initialize and start the HTTP server. Layers loosely based on databases will be covered in separate chapters.

Chapter 7 will cover relational databases and SQL. It will explain how to develop application layers related to the database. Two different database management systems will be used: PostgreSQL and MySQL. It will also explain how to install all tools and set up a database for each of them.

Chapter 8 will cover NoSQL databases and focus on how to develop application layers related to them. It will introduce MongoDB and DynamoDB with guidelines on installing tools, setting up a database, most important commands and development practices.

Chapter 9 will explain the fundamentals of application testing. It will explain the concepts of manual and automated testing and the differences between them. It will be shown how to execute the manual test and how to write and run automated tests with the Go programming language.

Chapter 10 will emphasize on how to make our application more secure. It will introduce concepts of authentication and authorization and explain how to implement them in an application developed through previous chapters.

Chapter 11 will focus on how to deploy the application. It will introduce concepts such as Docker and Docker Compose and describe how to use Google Cloud and Kubernetes for the deployment process.

Chapter 12 will describe the concepts of monitoring and alerting processes that follow deployment. It will explain how to use tools like Grafana and Prometheus to perform these processes.

Downloading the code bundles and colored images

Please follow the link to download the
Code Bundles of the book:

https://github.com/OrangeAVA/Modern-Web-Development-with-Go

The code bundles and images of the book are also hosted on
https://rebrand.ly/6c16c3

In case there's an update to the code, it will be updated on the existing GitHub repository.

Errata

We take immense pride in our work at Orange Education Pvt Ltd and follow best practices to ensure the accuracy of our content to provide an indulging reading experience to our subscribers. Our readers are our mirrors, and we use their inputs to reflect and improve upon human errors, if any, that may have occurred during the publishing processes involved. To let us maintain the quality and help us reach out to any readers who might be having difficulties due to any unforeseen errors, please write to us at :

errata@orangeava.com

Your support, suggestions, and feedback are highly appreciated.

DID YOU KNOW

Did you know that Orange Education Pvt Ltd offers eBook versions of every book published, with PDF and ePub files available? You can upgrade to the eBook version at www.orangeava.com and as a print book customer, you are entitled to a discount on the eBook copy. Get in touch with us at: **info@orangeava.com** for more details.

At **www.orangeava.com**, you can also read a collection of free technical articles, sign up for a range of free newsletters, and receive exclusive discounts and offers on AVA™ Books and eBooks.

Piracy

If you come across any illegal copies of our works in any form on the internet, we would be grateful if you would provide us with the location address or website name. Please contact us at **info@orangeava.com** with a link to the material.

Author with us

If you are interested in becoming an author

If there is a topic that you have expertise in, and you are interested in either writing or contributing to a book, please write to us at **business@orangeava.com**. We are on a journey to help developers and tech professionals to gain insights on the present technological advancements and innovations happening across the globe and build a community that believes Knowledge is best acquired by sharing and learning with others. Please reach out to us to learn what our audience demands and how you can be part of this educational reform. We also welcome ideas from tech experts and help them build learning and development content for their domains.

Reviews

Please leave a review. Once you have read and used this book, why not leave a review on the site that you purchased it from? Potential readers can then see and use your unbiased opinion to make purchase decisions. We at Orange Education would love to know what you think about our products, and our authors can learn from your feedback. Thank you!

For more information about Orange Education, please visit **www.orangeava.com**.

Table of Contents

CHAPTER 1

Basic Concepts of Go Programming Language

Introduction

This chapter will cover basic concepts of the Go programming language, which will help us to develop our web server application in the later chapters. We will talk and learn about variables, constants, data types (simple and complex ones), control structures, and functions. We will do a deep dive into these subjects and give some best practices. At the beginning of the chapter, we will give a short introduction and history of the Go programming language as well as some advantages compared to other programming languages.

Structure

In this chapter, we will discuss the following topics:

- Fundamentals of Go programming language
- Advantages of Go programming language
- Keywords
- Packages
- Basic data types
- Variables
- Constants
- Complex data types
- Control structures
- Functions

Fundamentals of Go programming language

Go is a *procedural programming language* based on concurrent programming. In procedural programming languages, procedures are stitched together to form a program. It is mainly used for the development of system and server software because it is designed to be performant.

Designed in *2007* by *Google* employees *Robert Griesemer*, *Rob Pike*, and *Ken Thompson* as a part of an experiment, with the idea to improve programming productivity. Designers wanted to eliminate bad practices from the programming language used inside *Google*, but keep the good ones, in order to create an efficient and elegant programming language that can be used for the development of complex software solutions.

Go was officially announced in *November 2009*, and the first *version (1.0)* was released in *March 2012*. As we can see Go is a relatively young and new programming language.

Go has the official logo and mascot. The official logo represents stylized italic *GO*, with trailing streamlines, which symbolize *speed* and *efficiency*. The official mascot is a *Gopher* (rodent from *North* and *Central America*) and was designed by *Renee French*, (*Figure 1.1*):

Figure 1.1: The official mascot of Go

(Designed by Renee French, licensed under Creative Commons 3.0 Attributions license)

The latest stable version of Go is 1.20 released in February 2023. Some of the companies where Go is represented are *BBC*, *Uber*, *Docker*, *Intel*, and of course *Google*.

Advantages of Go programming language

Go has become one of the most popular programming languages in the past couple of years, according to the site *Stack Overflow*. According to *LinkedIn*, there are more than *40,000* open positions for Go developers in the *United States* alone.

What makes Go so popular? Here are some main advantages of the Go programming language:

- **Easy and fast to learn**: Go is designed to be as simple as possible, so the basics can be learned in a few hours.
- **Good standard library**: We can execute all tasks and find solutions for usual problems without complex workarounds.
- **Fast build time**: Large projects can be compiled and built in less than *30 seconds*.
- **Performance**: Large-scale applications with a lot of input/output can be easily handled.

In this book, we will use these advantages to create a simple and efficient web application.

Go Playground

For all examples in this and the next chapter, we will use **Go Playground**. Go Playground represents a web service that can run programs written in Go. It can be opened in a web browser using the following link:

https://go.dev/play/

By default, Go Playground uses the latest stable version, but if necessary, we can lower it to one of the earlier versions.

Once we learn all the important concepts of the Go programming language and we are ready to start the development of our web application, we will learn how to install and set up the Go environment on our local machine. Until then, Go Playground is a good enough tool to get familiarized with the Go programming language.

But we must be aware of a couple of Go Playground's limitations:

- Go supports (through standard library) functionality for measuring and displaying time. In Go Playground, the current time will always be *2009-11-10 23:00:00 UTC* (the day when Go was officially announced).
- Execution time is limited.
- CPU and memory usage is limited.
- The program cannot access the external network host.
- Libraries (except the standard ones) are not available.

For the small code examples presented in this chapter, these limitations will not cause any problems.

Just for the test, we can copy this code example in Go Playground:

```
package main
import "fmt"

func main() {
        a := 2
        b := 3
        c := a * b
        fmt.Println("Result is: ", c)
}
```

If we click on the **Run** button, the following output should be displayed:

```
Result is:  6
Program exited.
```

In later examples, the declaration of the package and **main()** function may be omitted. If that is the case, code examples should be copied inside the body of **main()** function.

Keywords

Keywords are special words that help the compiler to understand and properly parse code. Currently, Go has *25 keywords* that can be classified into four categories:

- Keywords used for declaration: **const**, **func**, **import**, **package**, **type**, and **var**.
- Keywords used in composite type denotations: **chan**, **interface**, **map**, and **struct**.
- Keywords used for flow control: **break**, **case**, **continue**, **default**, **defer**, **else**, **fallthrough**, **for**, **goto**, **if**, **range**, **return**, **select**, and **switch**.
- Keywords specific for Go programming language: **go**.

In this and the next chapter, we will see how most of these keywords can be used.

Packages

Packages are basic building blocks for Go programs. All variables, constants, and functions are declared and defined in packages, and package definition is usually the first line in the file with code. This statement will define the new package with the name **country**:

```
package country
```

Each package can export things that can be used in other packages. In the Go programming language, there is no special keyword or complex syntax for export, everything inside the package that begins with a capital letter will be exported. Here is an example of exported and not exported integer constants:

```
const Exported = 27

const nonExported = 5
```

Everything exported from the package can be imported and used in other packages, these statements will import packages **`country`** and **`math`** (Go package with basic constants and mathematical functions):

```
import "country"
import "math"
```

Imports can be grouped in order to avoid writing the **`import`** keyword multiple times. This grouped import is equivalent to **`import`** statements from the previous example:

```
import(
        "country"
        "math"
)
```

All Go programs will start running from the **`main`** package (which must contain **`main()`** function).

Basic data types

Go basic data types can be separated into three categories:

- **Numerical data types**: These are used to represent different kinds of numbers. We can further classify numerical data types into more specific types:
    - **Integers**: Representation of whole numbers. Integers can be positive, negative, or zero. Examples of integers are *-27*, *0*, *21*, *1989*, *180192*, and so on. Based on the number of bits used to store integer values, the Go programming language supports the following types: **`int8`** (8 bits), **`int16`** (16 bits), **`int32`** (32 bits), **`int64`** (64 bits), and **`int`** (32 bits on 32-bit systems, 64 bits on 64-bit systems). A good practice is to use **`int`** unless we have some specific reason to use a specific size.

  - **Unsigned integers**: Positive whole numbers and zero. Based on the number of bits used to store unsigned integer values, the Go programming language supports the following types: `uint8` (8 bits), `uint16` (16 bits), `uint32` (32 bits), `uint64` (64 bits), `uintptr` (32 bits on 32-bit systems, 64 bits on 64-bit systems), and `uint` (32 bits on 32-bit systems, 64 bits on 64-bit systems). Type `uintptr` is an unsigned integer that is large enough to hold any pointer address (pointers will be explained later). Generally, `int` should be used whenever we need to use whole numbers and unsigned integers should be used only for some specific use cases.
  - **Floating point numbers**: Representation of whole numbers with a decimal point. Floating point numbers can be positive, negative, or zero. Examples of floating points are *-27.0589, 0.0, 21.1092, 1801.92, and so on*. Based on the number of bits used to store floating point numbers, the Go programming language supports two types: `float32` (32 bits) and `float64` (64 bits).
  - **Complex numbers**: Numbers that can be presented in the form *a + bi*, where *a* and *b* are real numbers and *i* is a solution of equation *x2 = -1*. Real numbers *a* and *b* are referred to as **real** and **imaginary** parts respectively. Based on the number of bits used to store floating point numbers, the Go programming language supports two types: `complex64` (64 bits) and `complex128` (128 bits).
- **Boolean data type:** A data type that has one of the two possible values, *true* or *false*. It is widely used for logical operations, we will see a lot of examples later in this chapter. Go programming language supports one Boolean data type: `bool`.
- **String data type**: Sequence of alphanumeric text or other symbols. Examples of strings are *Hello World!, DS27051989*, and *banicina@gmail.com*. Strings are mostly used for processing all kinds of textual data or to display different kinds of information to the users of the application (we will see more of that in this and the following chapters). Go programming language supports one type: `string`.

String is a sequence of characters, but Go has no data type that represents a single character (`char` in other programming languages). Characters are supported through two special aliases of integer types:

- **Byte**: Alias for `uint8`, represents ASCII character (by ASCII standard, each character is an *8-bit* code).
- **Rune**: Alias for `int32`, represents Unicode character encoded in *UTF-8 format*.

These aliases are introduced to make a clear distinction between characters and integer values. Generally, it will be hard to understand and maintain code where we use integer variables to store characters. **Rune** is a default type for characters, so if we do not explicitly declare the type for the variable with character value, Go will assign **rune** type to that variable (we will learn how to declare a variable soon).

All basic data types have a default value (this is often referred to in the documentation for Go programming language as *zero* value). The default value is *0* for numeric types, *""* (empty string) for strings and *false* for Boolean.

If we do not assign a specific value to the variable, the default one will be assigned. There is no *special* value for that situation (like undefined) and only pointers can have nil value. We will talk more about pointers later in this chapter.

Variables

Variables can be defined as containers for storing data values. The variable value can be changed after the initial value is set. The **var** statement can be used to declare a variable or list of variables, with the type at the end of it. This code sample will declare *four* integer variables and *one* Boolean variable:

```
var a, b, c int
var d bool
```

The **var** statement can include initializers; the number of initializers must be the same as the number of variable names. If the initializer is not present, the default value will be assigned to the variable. Here is the same code block from the previous example with initializers:

```
var a, b, c int = 1, 2, 3
var d bool = true
```

To see differences between initialized and uninitialized variables, we can execute this code in Go Playground:

```
var a int
var b bool
var c = 1
var d = true
fmt.Println(a)
fmt.Println(b)
fmt.Println(c)
fmt.Println(d)
```

As we can see, default values `0` and `false` will be assigned to uninitialized variables `a` and `b`, while specific values `1` and `true` will be assigned to initialized variables `c` and `d`.

If initializers are present, we can omit type and the variable will *inherit* type from the initializer. So, the previous example can be shortened:

```
var a, b, c, d = 1, 2, 3, true
```

Based on where they are declared, we have the following variables:

- **Local variables**: Declared and used inside functions. They cannot be accessed from outside of the functions in which they are declared.
- **Global variables**: Declared in a package or outside of functions. They can be accessed globally from other packages (must be exported).

In this example, `a` is global, while `b` is a local variable:

```
var a int

func main() {
        var b int
}
```

Variable can be declared and initialized with a short assignment statement. The following two statements are equal:

```
var i int = 1
i := 1
```

In the Go programming language, all statements outside the functions must begin with the keyword `var`, `func`, or `const`. So, short assignment statements can be only used for local variables.

Type conversion

Many programming languages support a concept called **implicit conversion**. If we have a numeric variable that is **floating point** type and try to assign value **7** (integer value), the programming language which supports implicit conversion will convert the value to **7.0** and assign it to a variable. Go does not support implicit conversion, so the value must be explicitly converted to a specific type.

If we try to execute the following statements, the compiler will report an error on the second one:

```
var a int32 = 7
var b float32 = a //fails
```

Expression *T(v)* will convert value *v* to type *T*. Conversion from our example (*integer* to *floating* point) can be executed with this statement:

```
var b float 32 = float32(a) //succeeds
```

Constants

Constants are values that cannot be changed once defined. Constants are declared like variables but with the **const** keyword instead of **var** and cannot be declared with a short statement. We can create constants from any basic data type, like integer constants, or floating-point constants. String constants are called **string literals**. Usually, constant names are written in capital letters with the underscore character used to separate words.

These statements will create string literal and floating-point constants:

```
const HELLO_WORLD = "Hello world!!!"
const GOLDEN_RATIO = 1.618
```

Very often, we want to assign successive integer values to constants, like this:

```
const (
        ZERO = 0
        ONE  = 1
        TWO  = 2
)
```

This can be done more elegantly with **iota** keyword. It represents successive integer constants (*0, 1, 2, …*), so the previous code segment can be written in the following way:

```
const (
        ZERO = iota
        ONE
        TWO
)
```

Value **0** is always the first one in sequence, but we can use arithmetic operators to start from another value, like in this example:

```
const (
        ONE = iota + 1
        TWO
        THREE
)
```

The **iota** will be reset to **0** whenever the keyword **const** appears in the source code. In the following example, value **0** will be assigned to constants **ZERO** and **TEST**:

```
const (
        ZERO = iota
        ONE
        TWO
)

const TEST = iota
```

Complex data types

Complex data types are composed of basic data types. Go supports the following complex data types: **pointers**, **structs**, **arrays**, **slices**, and **maps**. Now, we will take a look at each of them in detail.

Pointers

Pointers are complex data types that store the memory address of a value. Simply put, if we have a value stored in the memory address as **100** and a pointer to that value, the pointer value will be **100** (*Figure 1.2*). The default value for a pointer is *nil*. **Nil** pointer does not point to any value:

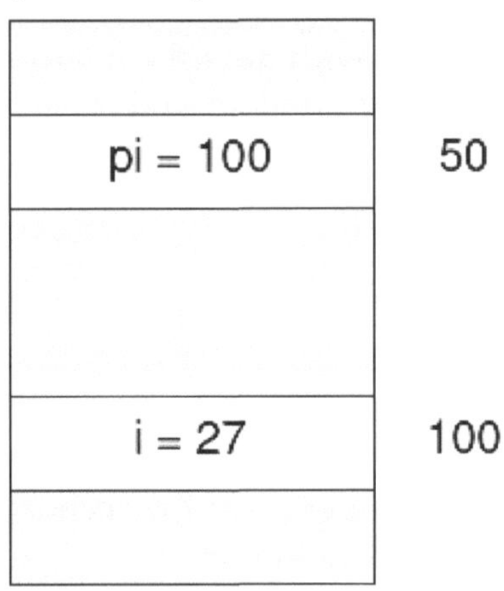

Figure 1.2*: Pointer and integer variable in memory*

To declare a pointer, we must add * (*asterisk*) before type. This will declare an integer pointer:

```
var pi *int
```

Go has two pointer operators:

- Operator **&** (*ampersand*) will get the address of the variable. We use this operator to initialize or assign a value for a pointer (**i** is an integer variable): **pi = &i**.
- Operator ***** (asterisk) will get us access to the pointed value. We can use it for the following operations:
    - Read value through pointer: **i := *pi**
    - Set value through pointer: ***pi = 27**

In the following example, we will use a pointer to change the value of the integer variable (value **27** will be displayed on the standard output at the end):

```
func main() {
        var i int = 18
        var pi *int

        pi = &i
        *pi = 27
        fmt.Println(i)
}
```

Some programming languages support *pointer arithmetic*. **Pointer arithmetic** allows us to perform simple arithmetic operations on pointers such as *increment*, *decrement*, *addition*, and *subtraction*. These operations will not change pointed values, but they will change the pointer value. Let's assume that the pointer points to memory address **100**. If we perform an increment arithmetic operation on a pointer, it will now point to address **101**. Designers of the Go programming language wanted to keep things as simple as possible. So, they decided that pointer arithmetic is too complex and is (currently) only supported through *unsafe package*. As the name suggests, usage of this package is *not recommended* and should be avoided (if possible).

Struct

Struct (shortened of structure) is a complex data type that can be defined as a collection of fields. Fields can be of different types. We use **type** and **struct** keywords to declare **struct**, with the name in between them. Fields are declared between curly brackets in classical *name-type declaration* style. Here is an example of **struct** person which has two fields, **name** and **age**:

```
type person struct {
        name string
        age int
}
```

We can access **struct** fields with the **.** (*dot*) operator. We can access the field in order to set, update, or read its value. This example will update the *age* of the created person:

```
p := person{
        name: "John",
        age: 27,
}
p.age = 30
```

We can declare a pointer to a **struct** and use the pointer to access fields. If we follow all pointer rules described in the previous section, the statement that will update the value of the field age should be (**pp** is *pointer to person*):

```
(*pp).age = 35
```

The previous statement is a little bit complex and unreadable. So, in Go, the design statement is simplified:

```
pp.age = 35
```

In the example where we created person, we provided values for all fields. In such situations, we can omit the field name from the definition. Also, we can provide values only for certain fields (in this case, we cannot omit field names) or omit values for all fields. Default values will be assigned to the omitted fields. Here are a couple of examples of how we can define **struct** variable:

```
p1 := person{"John", 27}
p2 := person{name: "Jake"}
p3 := person{}
```

One important thing, export rules are also applied to **struct** fields. Even if **struct** itself is exported, if the field is not exported, other packages will not be able to access it.

Arrays

Arrays are complex data types that can be defined as a collection of elements of the same type. Individual elements can be referenced by an *index* that corresponds to the position of the element in the array. The first element of the array will have the index **0**.

In order to declare an array, we must provide the *array length* (between square brackets) and the *type of element*. This is how we can declare an array of six integers:

```
var a [6]int
```

Elements of the array can be initialized. Without initialization, default values will be assigned to elements (in our case, all six elements of the array will be initialized with the value **0**). The next example will create and initialize an array of six integers:

```
a := [6]int{27, 5, 18, 1, 21, 10}
```

Arrays have one *critical* limitation. Length is a part of the array type, so the array cannot be resized. This means that we need to know the exact size of the array during the development of our program, but that is not always possible. Fortunately, Go provides a solution in the form of slices.

Slices

Slices are complex data types, loosely tied with arrays. As we mentioned before, arrays have fixed sizes. In order to provide a workaround for this limitation, *slices* are introduced. They do not store any data, they just point to an array. If we need a larger slice, a new *underlying* array will be initialized. Any change to the array will affect all slices that reference it.

Slice is defined with two attributes, **length** and **capacity**. Length represents the number of elements that the slice contains, while capacity represents the number of elements in the underlying array (counting from the first element of the slice). Length and capacity attributes can be obtained with **len(s)** and **cap(s)** functions, where **s** represents a **slice**.

This small block of code will create a slice where the *length* is equal to **5** and the *capacity* is equal to **7**:

```
a := [10]int{1, 4, 9, 16, 25, 36, 49, 64, 81, 100}
s := a[3:8]
```

We can use the **make()** function for slice creation. The function receives three arguments, **slice type**, **length**, and **capacity**. Capacity can be omitted and in that case, the length value will also be assigned to capacity. When we use a **make()** function, a new array will be created, initialized with default values for the specified type, and returns a slice that refers to an array. Here is a simple example of how to create an integers slice with the **make()** function:

```
s = make([]int, 10)
```

It is possible to create a slice from another slice. The new slice will reference the same array as the *original* slice.

Slices are defined with two indexes which represent *low* and *high* bound, respectively. Element of the original array with index defined with *low* bound will be included in the created slice. On the other hand, the element of the original array with an index defined with a *high* bound will be excluded from the created slice. In the next example, a new slice will be created and will include elements with indexes from **1** to **5** of the underlying array:

```
var s []int = a[1:6]
```

Bounds can be omitted, although *colon* must be present. When some of the bounds are omitted, the default value will be used. The default value for the low bound is **0**, while the default value for the high bound is equal to the length of the underlying slice. So, for the array of length **5**, these slice expressions are equivalent:

```
var s1 []int = a[0:5]
var s2 []int = a[:5]
var s3 []int = a[0:]
var s4 []int = a[:]
```

We can initialize slices, similar to arrays. This expression will create an array of length **5** and a slice that references that array:

```
s := []int{1, 4, 9, 16, 25}
```

We can use the **append()** function to add elements at the end of the slice. The function receives two arguments, a **slice** and a **list of elements to append**. The **append** function will return a slice that contains all elements of the original slice and new values. If the underlying array is too small for all new elements, a new bigger array will be allocated. We should be very careful with the **append()** function in order to avoid unnecessary memory allocation. This expression will add two elements to the integer slice:

```
s = append(s, 18, 27)
```

It is also possible to append one slice to another in the following way:

```
s1 := []int{1, 2, 3}
s2 := []int{4, 5, 6}
s1 = append(s1, s2...)
```

The default value for a slice is *nil*. Nil slices have no underlying array and have a length and capacity equal to *zero*.

It's important to point out that slices can contain any type, including other slices.

Maps

Maps are complex data types used to store *key-value* pairs. Each key can appear only once on the map and can be used to find the value paired with that key. The default value for the map is *nil*. A nil map has no keys and keys cannot be added.

Function **make()** will create and initialize a map of the given type. The *key* type is defined between square brackets and the *value* type is defined at the end. The returned map will be empty. This statement will create and initialize the map with a string key and string value:

```
var countryMap = make(map[string]string)
```

Without **make()** function, the **var** statement will define a *nil* map which will be more or less useless.

The following operations can be executed on maps:

- **Insert and update elements**:

  ```
  countryMap["fr"] = "France"
  ```

- **Get element**:

  ```
  country = countryMap["fr"]
  ```

- **Delete element**:

  ```
  delete(countryMap, "fr")
  ```

- **Test if the key is present**:

  ```
  country, ok = countryMap["fr"]
  ```

  If the key is in the map, the value *true* will be assigned to variable **ok** and the element value will be assigned to **country**, otherwise, the value *false* will be assigned to variable **ok** and *nil* will be assigned to **country**.

The following example shows map creation and usage of described operations:

```
var countryMap = make(map[string]string)
countryMap["fr"] = "France"
country := countryMap["fr"]
fmt.Println("Country in map is:", country)
delete(countryMap, "fr")
if _, ok := countryMap["fr"]; ok {
        fmt.Println("Country is still in map")
} else {
        fmt.Println("Country is not in map")
}
```

If the code is successfully executed, the following output will be displayed:

```
Country in map is: France
Country is not in map
```

If we use integers for keys, they don't have to be in order (*0, 1, 2, 3, 4 …)*. For example, if we have a map that represents the basketball team (*five* players), we can use shirt numbers as *keys*, and player names as *values*. It is a regular situation that we use these keys: *3, 9, 10, 12, 32*. If we need ordered keys, maybe map is *not* a good solution for our problem and we should use a slice instead.

Control structures

A **program** can be defined as a set of commands. It is not necessary that these commands will be executed sequentially. Sometimes, a certain block of code should be skipped or executed multiple times. For that reason, all programming languages have control structures that can be used to control execution flow. Go programming language is not an exception; so, we will discuss about Go control structures in the following part of this chapter.

If statement

If is the most common conditional statement in programming languages. If the result of the condition calculation is *positive (true)*, the code inside **if** statement will be executed. In the next example, value **a** will be incremented if it is less than **100**:

```
if a < 100 {
        a += 1
}
```

We can add a short statement before the condition. This statement will be executed before the condition, and the declared variable will be visible only in the scope of **if** statement. Here is an example, where variable **a** will be incremented, only if the previously calculated value for variable **b** is less than **100**:

```
if b := a * a; b < 100 {
        a += 1
}
```

We can add the **else** statement to **if** statement. Code inside the **else** statement will be executed if the result of the condition execution is *negative (false)*. In the next example, if the value of variable **a** is less than **100**, the value for **a** will be incremented, otherwise value **a** will be multiplied by **5**:

```
if a < 100 {
        a += 1
} else {
        a *= 5
}
```

Additionally, we can append **if-else** statements, but that code will not be readable. If we have a need to create such a construct, it is better to use the **switch** statement (we will see this statement later). Here is an example of an **if-else** statement that will return the **country** name based on the country **code**:

```
if code == "fr" {
        country = "France"
} else if code == "uk" {
        country = "United Kingdom"
} else {
        country = "India"
}
```

Switch statement

The **switch** statement is an elegant way to avoid the usage of **if-else** sequences. The sequence of **if-else** statements from the previous example can be replaced with the **switch** statement:

```
var country string
switch code {
case "fr":
        country = "France"
case "uk":
        country = "United Kingdom"
default:
        country = "India"
}
```

The first **case** statement whose value is equivalent to the condition expression will be executed. If the value of the code variable is equal to **fr**, the first **case** statement will be executed. In some programming languages, all following **case** statements will be executed unless we put the **break** keyword at the end of the **case** statement. In the Go programming language, only the selected **case** statement will be executed (**break** is provided automatically). If none of the **case** statements match the condition, the **default** statement will be executed.

Usually, **switch** cases must be constants and all involved values must be integers. Go programming language is much more flexible. We can even use a function call in **case** statements! It is possible to omit a condition from the **switch** statement and move it to the **case** statement. In that situation, the **case** statement whose condition is fulfilled will be executed. This condition-less **switch** statement will determine if the number is *even* or *odd*:

```
switch {
case number%2 == 0:
	fmt.Println("Even Number")
case number%2 == 1:
	fmt.Println("Odd Number")
default:
	fmt.Println("Invalid Number")
}
```

For loop

Often, we need to execute a specific block of code multiple times. **Loops** are constructs that help us to do that. We can find multiple loops in various programming languages, but to keep things as simple as possible, the Go programming language has only one loop, **`for`** loop.

The **`for`** loop consists of three statements separated with a *semicolon*, which comes after **`for`** keyword, as we can see in the following code example:

```
for i:=0; i<10; i++ {
	a[i] = i*2
}
```

The first statement, the **init** statement, will declare and initialize variables that will be visible in the scope of the loop (integer variable **`i`**). Init statement will be executed before the first iteration.

The second statement, **condition**, has the same role as the condition in **`if`** statement. The condition will be evaluated before every iteration and if the result of the evaluation is *positive (true)*, the next iteration will be executed.

The third statement, the **post** statement, will update conditional and local variables. The post statement will be executed at the end of every iteration. In our example, operator **`++`** will increment the value of the variable.

The **`for`** loop from our example will initialize an integer array with ten elements.

Init and **put** statements are *optional* and they can be omitted (in that case, semicolons can be also omitted). We often omit these statements when there is no need to use local variables. This for loop will update the value of the variable result:

```
for result < 500 {
	result *= sum*2
}
```

Technically, we can also omit conditional statement. But without it, the loop will never stop iterating. These kinds of loops are called **infinite loops**.

Range is a special form of **for** loop which is used to iterate over *slice* and *map*. For each iteration, two values will be returned, an *index* and a *value* (copy of the element at that index). In the next example, we will iterate through slice and sum-only elements on even indexes:

```
for i, v := range arr {
        if i%2 == 0 {
                sum += v
        }
}
```

The variable **v** is actually a copy of **arr[i]**, so any modification of variable **v** will not affect the original slice. We can test this with the following code example:

```
a := []int{1, 2, 3}

for _, v := range a {
        v = v * v
}

fmt.Println(a)
```

In order to modify the original slice, the element must be accessed through an index.

Variable v is allocated only once, it will not be allocated for each iteration, so we should be very careful. In the following example, all elements of the second slice will point to the same variable that holds the last assigned value (three in our case).

```
a := []int{1, 2, 3}
var b []*int

for _, v := range a {
        b = append(b, &v)
}

for _, v := range b {
        fmt.Println(*v)
}
```

The Go compiler does not allow the declaration of unused variables, but sometimes we do not need *index* or *value*. They can be ignored by assigning them to the _ (*underscore*) operator. This operator is also known as a **blank identifier**.

In this example, we decided to ignore the index:

```
for _, v := range arr {
	sum += v
}
```

There are situations when it is not necessary to execute all iterations. With the **continue** statement, the remaining part of the current iteration will be skipped, and the next iteration will be executed. In the following example, all slice elements, except one on index **3** will be printed on standard output:

```
a := []int{1, 2, 3, 4, 5}
for i := 0; i < 5; i++ {
	if i == 3 {
		continue
	}
	fmt.Println(a[i])
}
```

The **break** statement will terminate the execution of the current loop. This can be useful when we are looking for the index of an element with a specific value. When we find that element, we can stop the search and there is no need to execute the remaining iterations. In the next example, the loop will be terminated when the value of variable **i** is equal to **3**:

```
for i := 0; i < 5; i++ {
	if i == 3 {
		break
	}
	fmt.Println(a[i])
}
```

Defer

The **defer** statement will delay the execution of a function until the surrounding function is completed. Although execution is postponed, function arguments will be evaluated immediately.

Defer is quite useful in situations when we should execute a specific function call after the execution of the surrounding function. It is often used to close files, streams, or connections to a database because **defer** will be executed even if the function fails; so, we do not need to handle all situations when something goes wrong, one simple defer statement will take care of it.

In the following example, the execution of **fmt.Print(2)** will be postponed until **main()** function is concluded:

```
func main() {
        fmt.Print(1)
        defer fmt.Print(2)
        fmt.Print(3)
}
```

Value **132** will be displayed on the standard output.

We can have more than one **defer** statement inside a function. The function call will be pushed onto a stack. The **stack** can be defined as a collection of elements, where the most recently added element will be removed first. This principle is called **LIFO – Last in, first out**.

The following code snippet will print **1342** on standard output. The *first* print will be executed, the *second* one (under defer) will be pushed onto the stack, the *third* print will be executed, and the *fourth* one will be pushed onto the stack. Deferred function calls on the stack are presented in *Figure 1.3*. Since the *fourth* print is pushed onto the stack last, it will be executed first:

```
func main() {
        fmt.Print(1)
        defer fmt.Print(2)
        fmt.Print(3)
        defer fmt.Print(4)
}
```

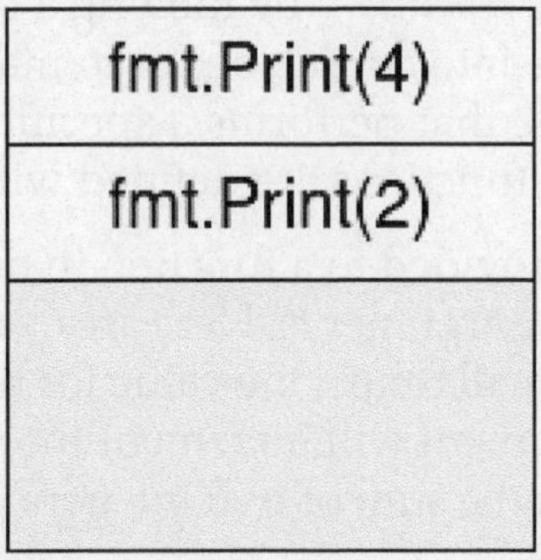

Figure 1.3*: Deferred function calls on the stack*

If **defer** is declared after **return**, the function call will not be executed, because **defer** statement will not be executed, and the function call will not be pushed into the stack. In the following example, *first* call of the **testDefer()** function will execute all *four* calls of the **Print()** function, and the *second* call will not execute the *fourth* one:

```
func testDefer(val int) {
	fmt.Print(1)
	defer fmt.Print(2)
	fmt.Print(3)

	if val == 5 {
		return
	}

	defer fmt.Print(4)
}

func main() {
	testDefer(3)
	testDefer(5)
}
```

Value **1342132** will be displayed on the standard output.

Functions

Functions are named sections of programs that perform specific tasks. We usually write functions to avoid *code repetition* (by moving a block of code that is repeated through a project or package into a function) or to make the code *more readable* (by moving a huge block of code that performs a specific task into a function). In the Go programming language, functions are defined with the keyword **func**.

Arguments are the values provided to a function in order to obtain the result. The function can have *zero* or *more* arguments. Here are examples of three functions, the *first* one without arguments will return the value for the mathematical constant **pi**, the *second* one with one argument will increment the value of the integer variable, and the *third* one will return the sum of two integers passed as arguments:

```
func pi() float64 {
	return 3.14159
```

```
}

func inc(a int) int {
        return a + 1
}

func add(a int, b int) int {
        return a + b
}
```

The return value type is at the end of the declaration after arguments and before the function body that is between the curly brackets.

If we have multiple arguments of the same type (like, in the *third* example with **add()** function), we can shorten the argument declaration by omitting the type for all variables except the *last* one (we see a similar thing for the declaration of variables, where we had a list of variable names before type). Here, is **add()** function with shortened declaration:

```
func add(a, b int) int {
        return a + b
}
```

In all previous examples, functions returned *one* result. But functions can return *multiple* results. Here, is an example of a function that returns two results:

```
func swap(a, b int) (int, int) {
        return b, a
}
```

We can also create functions that do not return any results. For these functions, we just need to omit the result type at the end of the declaration. The **main()** function is a good example of a function without a *return* value.

We can also name return values. Named return values will be treated as variables declared on the top of the function. With named return values, we can use return without arguments, which will return values assigned to named return values. Argument-less return is often referred to as a *naked return*. Here, is the **add()** function from previous examples with named return values:

```
func add(a, b int) (c int) {
        c = a + b
        return
}
```

Functions are the values, so they can be passed around like all other values. We can use functions as arguments in other functions or as return values. Here, is an example where we pass one function as an argument of another function:

```
func calc(fn func(int, int) int) int {
	return fn(7, 18)
}

func main() {
	add := func(a, b int) int {
		return a + b
	}

	fmt.Println(calc(add))
}
```

This example will display the sum of numbers **7** and **18** on standard output. As we can see, the function is assigned to a variable name, but we do not define the function name. These functions are called **anonymous functions**.

In the next example, function **multiply()** will return a function based on the value of **param** argument. If the passed value is an *even* number, a function that duplicates the integer value will be returned, otherwise, a function that triples the integer value will be returned:

```
func multiply(param int) func(int) int {
	if param%2 == 0 {
		return func(a int) int {
			return a * 2
		}
	} else {
		return func(a int) int {
			return a * 3
		}
	}
}

func main() {
	double := multiply(2)
```

```
        triple := multiply(3)
        fmt.Println(double(5), triple(5))
    }
```

In the previous example, values **10** and **15** will be displayed on the standard output.

Arguments are *passed by value*, so each time a function is called, a new copy of the passed argument is created. The function will work with that copy, so if we forgot to return the updated copy, changes will have no effect. But if we pass a *pointer as an argument*, a copy of the memory address will be created so that all changes will take effect on the original variable, pointed by the original pointer. It's good practice to use pointer arguments, especially for large structures in order to avoid unnecessary copying and memory consumption.

The following example shows the difference between *value* and *pointer* arguments. Function with value argument **double()** will multiply copy of the passed argument, so the first **Println()** will display value **5** on standard output. On the other hand, the function **doublePointer()** will multiply the value stored on the address referenced by the pointer, so the second call of **Println()** will display value **10**:

```
func double(a int) {
        a = a * 2
}

func doublePointer(a *int) {
        *a = *a * 2
}

func main() {
        a := 5
        double(a)
        fmt.Println(a)

        doublePointer(&a)
        fmt.Println(a)
}
```

If we slightly modify functions **double()** and **doublePointer()** with the addition of **Println()** call as the last expression in each function, the following values will be displayed on standard output: **10 5 10 10**

As we can see, a copy of the value will be properly updated, but that result will be lost. Here are the modified functions:

```
func double(a int) {
        a = a * 2
        fmt.Println(a)
}

func doublePointer(a *int) {
        *a = *a * 2
        fmt.Println(*a)
}
```

Functions with *slice* arguments are interesting ones. Slices have pointers to underlying arrays which means that the content of the slice can be changed even if the slice is *passed as value*, but *capacity* and *length* cannot. In the following example, the call of **Println()** inside **modify()** function will display a slice with the modified *first* element and new element appended at the *end*, while the second **Println()** inside the **main** function will display a slice only with the modified *first* element:

```
func modify(s []int) {
        s[0] = 4
        s = append(s, 5)
        fmt.Println(s)
}

func main() {
        s := []int{1, 2, 3}
        modify(s)
        fmt.Println(s)
}
```

Functions can reference a variable from outside their body, these functions are called **closures**. Each function value has its own copy of referenced variable and can access it and assign values to it. We can say that closure is bound to a variable. Here is an example of the function that returns a closure. As we can see, the anonymous function is bounded with variable **a**:

```
func calc() func() int {
        a := 0
        return func() int {
```

```
            a += 1
            return a
        }
    }
```

Conclusion

Now we are familiar with the basic concepts of the Go programming language. With the knowledge collected in this chapter, we can develop some simple applications. But our final goal is to develop something a little more complex. The next chapter will level up our knowledge by introducing some advanced concepts of the Go programming language.

References

- **http://reneefrench.blogspot.com/**
- **https://creativecommons.org/licenses/by/3.0/**
- **https://insights.stackoverflow.com/survey/2021#most-popular-technologies**
- **https://www.linkedin.com/jobs/go-developer-jobs?position=1&pageNum=0**
- **https://www.toptal.com/back-end/server-side-io-performance-node-php-java-go**

Points to remember

- Go is a relatively young and easy-to-learn programming language with good support for most common programming problems through the standard library.
- A package is a basic unit for Go programs. Everything inside the package that starts with a capital letter will be automatically exported and can be used in other packages.
- The array has a fixed size; when this is not flexible enough, we should use a slice.
- Defer will put function calls on the stack. The function will be executed when the surrounding function returns in the **Last In First Out** (**LIFO**) order.
- We should use pointer arguments, especially for large structures in order to avoid unnecessary copying and memory consumption.

Multiple choice questions

1. Which animal is the official mascot of the Go programming language?
   a. Lion
   b. Turtle
   c. Meerkat
   d. Gopher
2. What is not a keyword from the Go programming language?
   a. `for`
   b. `func`
   c. `while`
   d. `var`
3. What is the default value for bool type?
   a. nil
   b. true
   c. "false"
   d. false
4. Which two pointer operators do we have in Go?
   a. & and *
   b. * and <-
   c. ! and <-
   d. ! and &
5. Which values will be displayed on the standard output when the following code segment is executed?

```
a := [10]int{7, 13, 14, 20, 12, 32, 2, 10, 27, 9}
s := a[2:8]
fmt.Println(len(s))
fmt.Println(cap(s))
```

   a. **2** and **8**
   b. **6** and **8**
   c. **2** and **10**
   d. **8** and **10**

6. Which statement is not true for functions in the Go programming languages?
    a. A function can be passed as an argument to another function.
    b. A function can be returned from another function.
    a. A function can be assigned to a variable.
    b. All of the above.

Answers

1. d
2. c
3. d
4. a
5. b
6. d

Questions

1. Which numerical types are supported by the Go programming languages?
2. How can we export functions or constants from the package?
3. Why aliases **`byte`** and **`rune`** are introduced?
4. What are the differences between local and global variables?
5. Does Go support implicit conversion?
6. When will the default statement be executed in **`switch`** statement?
7. How many arguments can a function have?
8. How many values a **`fun`** can return?
9. What is an anonymous function?
10. What are closures?

Key terms

- **Keywords**: Special words that help the compiler to understand and properly parse code.
- **Packages**: Basic building blocks for Go programs where all variables, constants, and functions are declared and defined.
- **Variable**: Container for storing data values.
- **Constants**: Values that cannot be changed once defined.
- **Pointer**: Complex data type that stores the memory address of a value.
- **Struct**: Complex data type that represents a collection of fields.
- **Array**: Complex data type that represents a collection of elements of the same type.
- **Slice**: Complex data type that does not store any data, it just points to an array.
- **Map**: Complex data types used to store *key-value* pairs.
- **If**: Conditional statement. The code inside the statement will be executed only if the condition is fulfilled.
- **Switch**: Control statement that executes a specific logic based on the condition.
- **Defer**: Statement that will delay the execution of a function until the surrounding function is complete.
- **Functions**: Named sections of programs that perform specific tasks.

CHAPTER 2

Advanced Concepts of Go Programming Language

Introduction

This chapter will cover advanced concepts of the Go programming language, which will help us to develop our web server application in later chapters. We will get ourselves familiar with methods and interfaces and take a deep dive into panics and concurrency. At the end of the chapter, we will explain the concept of the Go modules.

Structure

In this chapter, we will discuss the following topics:

- Methods
- Interfaces
- Generics
- Panics
- Concurrency
    - Goroutines
    - Channels
    - Mutex
    - WaitGroup
    - Go Scheduler
    - Garbage collector
- Go modules

Methods

As you probably noticed, there are no classes in the Go programming language, but we can mimic this by declaring functions on types. The type which declares functions is called the **receiver argument** and the function declared on the type is called the **method**. The receiver argument is placed between `keyword` function and method name. This code block will declare type `Circle` and two methods for that type:

```
type Circle struct {
        r float64
}


func (c Circle) Perimeter() float64 {
        return 2 * c.r * math.Pi
}


func (c Circle) Area()  float64 {
        return c.r * c.r * math.Pi
}
```

We use operator **.** (*dot*) to call a method defined on type:

```
func main() {
        c := Circle{5.0}
        fmt.Println(c.Perimeter())
        fmt.Println(c.Area())
}
```

There is no explicit way to declare a method on basic types, but there is a catch on how to override this restriction. The receiver must be in the same package as the method, so if we have a need to define a method on an integer, we must *re-declare* the integer type inside our package:

```
type CustomInt int


func (ci CustomInt) Double() int {
        return int(ci * 2)
}
```

Technically, the previous method is not declared on basic type but the *re-declared* type has all the characteristics of the base type from which it was derived.

A method with receiver argument will act the same as function with it as an argument. The method from the previous example is identical with the following function:

```
func Double(ci CustomInt) int {
        return int(ci * 2)
}
```

We can also declare a method on pointers. Pointer receivers are quite common for two reasons:

- Method can modify the value to which the receiver points.
- Method will operate on a copy of the original receiver value. With a pointer receiver, we will avoid copying of whole value, only the memory address will be copied.

When we declare methods for the concrete type, we should decide which receiver we will use, value or pointer. It is *not* a good practice to combine them.

Interfaces

The **interface** can be defined as a set of method signatures. We define interface with keywords **type** and **interface**, between which we specify the *name of the interface,* followed by *method signatures* between curly brackets. This code block will declare interface **Geometry** with two methods, for the calculation of *perimeter* and *area* of different shapes:

```
type Geometry interface {
        Perimeter() int
        Area() int
}
```

Most programming languages have keywords dedicated to interface implementation. But that is not the case with the Go programming language. Any type that implements all interface methods will automatically implement the interface.

Here we can see how type **Square** implements **Geometry** interface:

```
type Square struct {
        a int
}

func (s Square) Perimeter() int {
        return s.a * 4
}
```

```
func (s Square) Area() int {
        return s.a * s.a
}
```

Now, we can create a **Square** whose side is equal to **5** and execute methods on it:

```
func main() {
        s := Square{5}
        fmt.Println(s.Perimeter())
        fmt.Println(s.Area())
}
```

If we have a function with interface type as an argument, we can pass any type that implements that *interface to function*. Here is an example of that kind of function:

```
func Details(g Geometry) {
        fmt.Println("Perimeter:", g.Perimeter())
        fmt.Println("Area:", g.Area())
}
```

This function will display details about *perimeter* and *area*. Inside the **main()** function, we can create a **Square** and pass it to the **Details()** function. The code will be executed successfully and proper information will be displayed:

```
func main() {
        s := Square{5}
        Details(s)
}
```

Under the hood, the interface can be examined as a pair consisting of a *type* and *value*. Following the previous example, the type is **Square** and the value is newly created **Square**, where *a (side)* is **5**. It is interesting that the value can be *nil*. This situation is not irregular but should be handled in order to avoid incorrect execution of the program.

We can declare a variable with the interface as a type. This variable will be interpreted as an interface that contains neither *type* nor *value*, called a **nil interface**. If we try to call any method on a nil interface, a *run-time error* will occur:

```
var g Geometry
g.Perimeter() // <- this line will cause run-time exception
```

An *empty interface* is an interface without methods and can hold values of any type. *How is this possible?* Type will implement the interface if it implements all methods from the declaration of interface; an empty interface has zero methods, so technically every type implements it.

The empty interface is a very useful thing. Each time we need to handle an unknown type in our code, we can use the empty interface. One good example of usage is the **Print()** function from the **fmt** package. The function takes any number of type **interface{}** so that we can pass different types (**strings**, **numbers**, **Boolean**, and so on) and values of that type will be printed on standard output. The empty interface will be surpassed by generics.

If we declare a variable of interface type, we can assign a value of any type that implements that interface. This can put us in a situation where we are not sure what is assigned to a variable. Fortunately, there is a concept known as **type assertion** that can help us. This is how we can check if the interface variable holds the value of a **Square** type:

```
var g Geometry = Square{5}
v, ok := g.(Square)
```

As we can see two values will be returned, the underlying value and Boolean (variables **v** and **ok** in the previous example). If a variable holds a **Square** type (which was the case in the previous example), **v** will hold the actual value of the interface variable (**Square** whose side is equal to **5**), and **ok** will be *true*. Otherwise, the default value for concrete type will be assigned to **v** (**Square** with default values assigned to all fields), and *false* will be assigned to **ok**. The second value (**ok**) can be omitted, but this can cause an error in case of an unsuccessful assertion, so it is *not* recommended to do so.

We can use a special **switch** to determine the underlying *value* and *type* for the interface variable. This **switch** is called a **type switch**. In type switches, **case** statements will specify specific types (not values like in regular switches):

```
switch g.(type) {
case Square:
        fmt.Printf("Square")
case Rectangle:
        fmt.Printf("Rectangle")
default:
        fmt.Printf("Unknown type")
}
```

Here is one interesting example for the end of interface section. This function will check if the provided value is equal to **nil**:

```
func IsNil(a interface{}) bool {
        return a == nil
}
```

In our **main()** function, we will just declare **Square** and pass it to the **IsNil()** function:

```
func main() {
	var s *Square
	fmt.Println(IsNil(s))
}
```

What is an expected output? It would be logical that **IsNil()** function returns *true*, but actually, it will return *false*! As we mentioned before, interface has two fields *type* and *value*. Even if we assign **nil** pointer to the interface, a value will be assigned to type (in our case, type will be ***Square** and the value will be **nil**). An interface will be **nil** only when both the *type* and *value* are **nil**.

Go programming languages have a couple of interfaces that are widely used. Some of the popular ones are **Stringers**, **Errors**, **Readers**, and **Images**.

Generics

Generics are new concepts added in Go *version 1.18*. Designers have long fought against adding support for generics, citing that it would break the simplicity of the design, and the empty interface can be used instead of it.

When can we use generics? If we want to have a function that checks if an element is present in the array, we must declare a function for each type (integer arrays, string arrays, and so on). Generally, these functions will have the same code base, iterate through the array, and check if the current element is the one we are looking for.

We can create a generic function by introducing the *type* parameter (in square brackets between the function name and function arguments), and use it in the function signature. Here is an example of **Contains()** function implemented with generics:

```
func Contains[T comparable](arr []T, x T) bool {
	for _, v := range arr {
		if v == x {
			return true
		}
	}
	return false
}

func main() {
	intArr := []int{18, 27, 21, 1}
```

```
        stringArr := []string{"apple", "banana", "pineapple",
                "orange"}
        fmt.Println(Contains(intArr, 27))
        fmt.Println(Contains(stringArr, "lemon"))
}
```

`T` can be any type that fulfills comparable constraints (all types that support equality operators `==` and `!=`).

Besides function generics, we can declare **generic types**. In the next example, we will define a type for the node which can be used in the implementation of a binary tree. In binary trees, each node can reference at most two other nodes (usually called **left** and **right** child) and hold value:

```
type Node[T any] struct {
        leftChild *Node[T]
        rightChild *Node[T]
        value T
}
```

Constraint any is basically an alias for the empty interface, so any type can be used in place of `T`.

Panics

Panic is a built-in function that stops the regular flow, similar to the concept of runtime exceptions from other programming languages (Java). When it is triggered, the message printed on standard output and function execution will be terminated.

Panic is often triggered by unexpected errors. Some examples of the most common unexpected errors are:

- Invalid memory address or nil pointer difference
- Divide by zero
- Index out of range

In the following example, **`panic`** *Index out of range* will be triggered:

```
func main() {
        s := []int{1, 2, 3}
        fmt.Println(s[3])
}
```

Panic can be explicitly triggered in code by calling **`panic()`** function. This is often used for error handling, like in the following example:

```
func checkName(name string) {
        if name == "" {
                panic("Invalid name!!!")
        }
}
```

It is *not* a good practice to use panics for normal error handling.

Concurrency

Concurrency is a paradigm where different parts of the program can be executed in parallel without impact on the final result. Go programming supports several concurrency concepts related to concurrent execution and communication between concurrent executions.

Goroutines

A **thread** is a small sequence of instructions that can be processed by a single CPU core. Modern hardware architectures have multiple cores, so we can execute multiple threads in parallel.

Go programming language offers its own solution for concurrent execution, called **goroutines**. Goroutines can be defined as lightweight threads (because they are very small, only a couple of KB will be used to store all thread-related data on the stack) managed by Go runtime.

If we use the **go** keyword in front of a function call, that function will be executed in a new goroutine, but the evaluation of arguments will be executed in the current goroutine. Here we have two function calls, the first one will be executed in the current goroutine and for the second one, a new goroutine will be created:

```
sendMessage(message1)
go sendMessage(message2)
```

Goroutines run in the same address space so, in certain situations, goroutines must synchronize memory access and communicate with each other.

Channels

We can define the channel as a construct through which we can *send* and *receive* values. In order to send or receive value, we will use the **<-** (*arrow*) operator in the following way:

- *ch* <- *v* will send value *v* to channel *ch*.
- *v* = <- *ch* will receive value *v* from channel *ch*.

As can be seen, the data flow is determined by the direction of the arrow.

We have two types of channels:

- **Unbuffered** without buffer for message storage.
- **Buffered** with buffer for message storage.

By default, the channel is unbuffered with send and receive as blocking operations. The *sender* will be blocked until the *receiver* is ready to pick up the variable from the channel and vice versa. The *receiver* will be blocked, waiting for the value until the *sender* sends it to the channel. This can be very useful because there is no need for any additional synchronization.

Traditionally, we use the **make()** function to create a channel. This will create a new channel that allows us to send and receive string variables:

```
ch := make(chan string)
```

Through the channels which we have dealt so far, we can send only one value. But in practice, this is *not* an acceptable solution, for example, if the *sender* is faster than the *receiver*, the *sender* will be blocked too often. We can avoid that by defining a buffer, now we can accept more variables. Channels with buffers are called **buffered channels**.

A buffered channel will be created by adding buffer size as a second parameter in the **make()** function:

```
ch := make(chan string, 100)
```

With the buffered channel, the *sender* will be blocked only when the buffer is full and the *receiver* will be blocked only when the buffer is empty. In the next code example, we will use the buffered channel to send two messages from new goroutines and receive those messages in the **main** goroutine:

```
func sendMessage(message string, ch chan string) {
        ch <- message
}

func main() {
        ch := make(chan string, 2)
        go sendMessage("Hello", ch)
        go sendMessage("World", ch)
        fmt.Println(<-ch)
        fmt.Println(<-ch)
}
```

We cannot influence which goroutine will send the message first, words **Hello** and **World** will not always be displayed in that order on standard output.

The sender and only the sender can close the channel when there are no more values to send by calling the **close()** function:

```
close(ch)
```

The receiver should check if the channel is closed. In the following expression, variable **ok** will have the value *false* when the channel is closed:

```
v, ok <- ch
```

Constant checking can be tiresome, but *luckily*, a special kind of for **range** loop can be used. If we put the channel in **for range**, the loop will receive values until the channel is closed:

```
for v := range ch {
        fmt.Print(v)
}
```

If we try to send a message to a closed channel, panic will be triggered. When panic occurs, a message will be displayed on standard output and the function where panic has occurred will crash.

In all of our previous examples, the receiver waits on only one channel, but Go provides us with the concept that allows the receiver to wait on multiple channels: **select** statement. Syntactically, **select** statement is similar to the **switch** statement, with one difference, keyword **select** is used instead of keyword **switch**. The receiver will be blocked until one of the **case** statements can be executed:

```
select {
case <-ch1:
        fmt.Println("Channel One")
case <-ch2:
        fmt.Println("Channel Two")
default:
        fmt.Println("Waiting")
}
```

A **default** case will be executed if no other case is ready.

Mutex

Channels are mainly used for goroutines that need to communicate with each other, in order for them to exchange some values. In a situation when multiple goroutines need to update the same value, we must prevent simultaneous access to that value. This concept is known as **mutual exclusion**.

Why simultaneous access is important? Well, without it, concurrency concepts can be violated. Let us imagine a situation where two goroutines need to duplicate the value of a variable. The initial value of the variable is `5`, so the final result should be `20 (5 * 2 * 2)`.

Without mutual exclusion next scenario is possible. The *first* goroutine reads the value of variable (`5`), in the meantime, the *second* goroutine reads the value of variable (`5`) and updates the value, so now the value of variable is equal to `10`. The *first* goroutine will now duplicate the value, but it holds the old variable value (`5`), so the final result will *not* be `20`, it will be `10` which is *not* correct.

With mutual exclusion, the *first* goroutine will wait until the *second* one updates the variable, so the final result will be correct.

Go programming language provides mutual exclusion through the standard library with type `Mutex from sync package` and two methods: `Lock()` and `Unlock()`. Only one goroutine can access code between calls of these two methods at a time. Here is a mutex solution for the previously described problem:

```
type MutualExclusion struct {
        mutex sync.Mutex
        value int
}

func (me *MutualExclusion) Double() {
        me.mutex.Lock()
        me.value *= 2
        me.mutex.Unlock()
}

func main() {
        me := MutualExclusion{value: 5}
        go me.Double()
        go me.Double()

        time.Sleep(time.Second)
        fmt.Println(me.value)
}
```

Sleep method is called in order to prevent method **Print()** to be executed before both goroutines complete execution. If we use the **Lock()** method to *lock* a certain part of the code, we must use the **Unlock()** method to *unlock* it. If we leave the code *locked*, other goroutines cannot access them. It is a good practice to combine the call of **Unlock()** method with **defer**, so we can be sure that the code will be *unlocked* no matter what.

WaitGroup

Sometimes, we can divide the task into several smaller tasks, and give each of the sub-tasks to one goroutine. This will help us to execute our tasks fast and more efficiently. For example, we should multiply every element of an array by 3. If an array contains *five elements*, we can give each element to a specific goroutine.

But *how can we be sure that all goroutines have finished?* If we use the result before everything has been calculated, that result will not be valid. **WaitGroup** can help us.

The **WaitGroup** will block execution until all goroutines have been completed. With **Add()** method, we will set the initial counter value. The method **Wait()** will block until counter reaches *zero*. In order to accomplish that, method **Done()** should be called inside goroutine. This method will decrement *counter* value.

The following code will perform the task explained in the previous example, where each thread will update one element of an array:

```
func main() {
	a := []int{5, 8, 4, 9, 3}
	wg := &sync.WaitGroup{}
	wg.Add(5)

	for i := 0; i < 5; i++ {
		go func(i int) {
			a[i] *= 3
			fmt.Println("Goroutine ", i)
			wg.Done()
		}(i)
	}

	wg.Wait()
	fmt.Println(a)
}
```

This specific function declaration will define and invoke the function in the same statement, that's why (`i`) is added at the end of the declaration. This synchronization method is called **barrier synchronization**, due to its similarity with physical barriers (structures used to block something).

Goroutines will not always be executed in the same order. The following output is displayed in two successive executions of the previous code example:

```
Goroutine  1
Goroutine  0
Goroutine  2
Goroutine  3
Goroutine  4
[15 24 12 27 9]
```

```
Goroutine  4
Goroutine  3
Goroutine  2
Goroutine  1
Goroutine  0
[15 24 12 27 9]
```

Go Scheduler

Goroutines will be executed on OS threads. Since they are *lighter*, multiple goroutines can be executed on one OS thread.

During the life cycle, goroutine can be in one of the following states:

- **Running**: goroutine currently running on OS thread
- **Runnable**: goroutine waiting for the OS thread to run
- **Blocked**: goroutine waiting on some resource (I/O, channel, mutex, and so on)

Go Scheduler can be described as *M:N scheduler*, which means that *M* goroutines can be distributed over *N* OS threads. In *Figure 2.1*, we can see a graphical representation of the *M:N scheduler*.

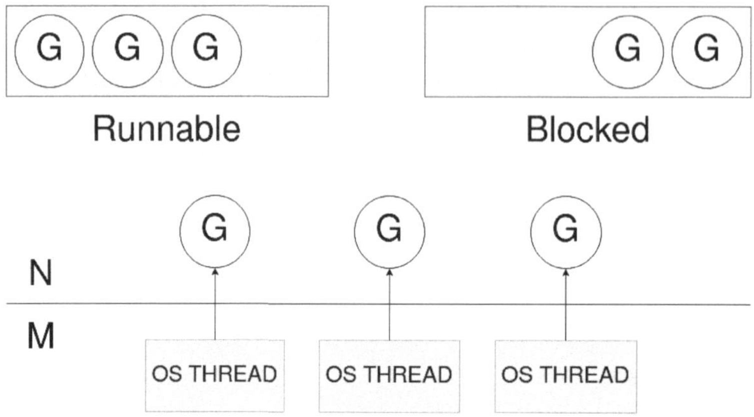

***Figure 2.1:** Go Scheduler*

The runnable queue will accept all newly created goroutines, from where they will be picked when the OS thread is available. When the goroutine needs to wait for any resource, it will be transferred to the *blocked* queue. When it is unblocked, the goroutine will be moved from the *blocked* queue to the *runnable* queue.

Garbage collector

During the execution of the program, space in memory will be allocated for variables, function stacks, and so on. But occupied memory space will not be needed throughout the whole execution time. For example, the variable defined in `for` loop will not be used after the last iteration, so we can free the memory occupied by that variable.

It will be too complicated for a developer to *de-allocate* memory space when it is no longer needed. Luckily, most programming languages offer **garbage collectors**, who will find and free memory occupied by unused objects. Related to garbage collection, the object is a dynamically allocated piece of memory that contains one or more Go values.

Go garbage collector is concurrent, it will run in parallel with the main program, without stopping or interrupting the main program.

The algorithm used for garbage collection in Go is **mark and sweep**, named after the two phases of the algorithm. The *first* phase (**mark**) will identify and mark unused objects, while the *second* phase (**sweep**) will free memory occupied by unused objects.

The object will be interpreted in a form of a graph (*Figure 2.2 a*). During the *mark* phase, the garbage collector will traverse the graph (starting from the root) and mark each object with one of three colors:

- **Black**: The object is still in use.

- **White**: The object is not used anymore and can be swept.
- **Gray**: The object cannot be categorized in the current execution of garbage collection.

When the *mark* phase is complete (*Figure 2.2 b*), the *sweep* phase will free the occupied memory marked with *white* color (*Figure 2.2 c*). The *swipe* phase will not start until the *mark* phase is completely finished:

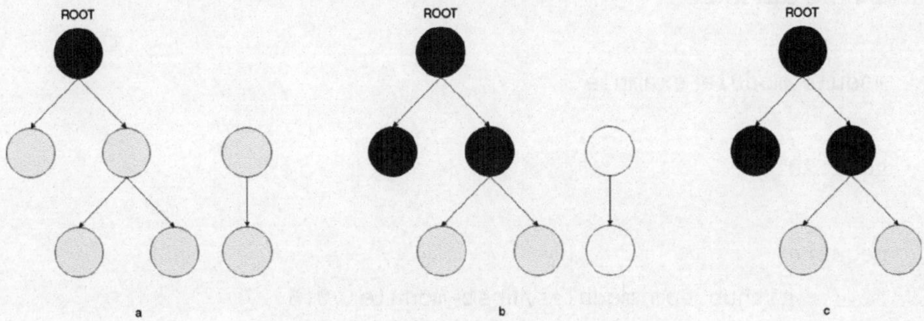

Figure 2.2: *Garbage collection algorithm*

Go modules

We will deal with Go modules in more detail in the next chapters when we are ready to write code outside Go Playground. Here, we will just give some basic information.

A **module** can be defined as a collection of packages that are versioned together as a single unit. Each module must contain two files inside the **`root`** directory:

- **`go.mod`**: Defines module name and dependency requirements (other modules used in our module).
- **`go.sum`**: Checksum for each dependency to confirm that none of them has been modified.

Support for the Go module is introduced in *version 1.11*, prior to that version **`GOPATH`** was used.

`GOPATH` is a directory path set through the environment variable where Go expects to find all of our source code files. Inside it we can find three directories:

- **`src`**: Contains all our projects and source code files.
- **`pkg`**: Contains packages used by Go.
- **`bin`**: Contains execution binaries.

`GOPATH` has two major flows:

- All our projects must be placed inside them.
- There is no built-in way for keeping track of the dependencies versions we are using.

The *version 1.13* module is the default mode for all developers, instead of **GOPATH** mode. With modules, we can put our source code outside **GOPATH**, and we can easily control which version of dependencies will be used. Here is an example of how a **mod** file can look:

```
module module-example

go 1.20

require(
        github.com/modules/first-module v0.5.27

        github.com/modules/second-module v0.1.18
)
```

As we can see, the version for each dependency is after its name. We will see in more detail how we can create modules and update dependencies versions in the following chapters, for now, it is just enough to familiarize ourselves with the concept of modules.

Conclusion

Now we are familiar with all concepts of the Go programming language. We possess knowledge that can be used for the development of all kinds of applications. Before we can develop our web application, we should get familiar with some concepts related to it. The next chapter will introduce and present some interesting concepts.

Points to remember

- We can mimic class behavior by defining methods on concrete types.
- With interfaces, we can define a set of methods (behavior) that can be reused by multiple concrete types.
- It is *not* a good practice to use panics for normal error handling.

- Go supports concurrency concepts, which we can use to execute some parts of code concurrently and provide communication between executions.
- Go modules provide us with a convenient way to group our packages.

Multiple choice questions

1. Which operator do we use to call a method defined on type?
   a. `<-` (*arrow*)
   b. `.` (*dot*)
   c. `*` (*asterisk*)
   d. `&` (*ampersand*)
2. Constraint any is an alias for:
   a. Nil interface
   b. Any type that supports equality operators (`==` and `!=`)
   c. Empty interface
   d. Empty struct
3. Who can close the channel?
   a. Sender
   b. Receiver
   c. No one
   d. Both sender and receiver
4. Which operation cannot be performed on channels?
   a. Receive
   b. Close
   c. Send
   d. Cancel
5. Which color is not used during the mark phase of garbage collection?
   a. White
   b. Blue
   c. Gray
   d. Black

6. Which directory we cannot find inside **`GOPATH`**?
    a. **`bin`**
    b. **`src`**
    c. **`sum`**
    d. **`pkg`**

Answers

1. b
2. c
3. a
4. d
5. b
6. c

Questions

1. Can we declare methods on basic type?
2. What are the differences between pointer and value receivers?
3. How to implement the interface in the Go programming language?
4. What are the differences between an empty interface and a nil interface?
5. Which type will fulfill compatible constraints?
6. What are goroutines?
7. When we should use the channel and when should we use the mutex?
8. What is a go module?
9. What is defined inside the **`go.mod`** file?
10. What is a **`GOPATH`**?

Key terms

- **Methods**: Functions declared on types.
- **Interfaces**: Set of method signatures.
- **Generics**: Function or type which can work with multiple different concrete types.

- **Goroutines**: Go implementation of lightweight threads.
- **Channel**: Construct through which we can send and receive values from one goroutine to another.
- **Mutex**: Go support for mutual exclusion.
- **WaitGroup**: Blocks execution until all goroutines have been completed.
- **Module**: Collection of packages.
- **Go Scheduler**: Simple scheduler in charge of managing the goroutines.
- **Garbage collector**: Process which will find and free memory spaces which are no longer used.

CHAPTER 3

Web Servers

Introduction

This chapter will cover the basics of web servers, which will be a good basis for the application that we plan to develop in the following chapters. We will introduce the concept of servers, with special reference to web servers. After that, we will do a deep dive into REST architecture and HTTP protocols. At the end of the chapter, we will explain JSON and routing.

Structure

In this chapter, we will discuss the following topics:

- Servers
- Web servers
- Proxies
- REST
- HTTP
  - HTTP flow
  - HTTP messages
  - HTTP methods
  - Additional functionalities
  - HTTP and REST
- JSON

- JSON and Go
- Routing

Servers

A **server** can be defined as software or hardware that provides certain functionality for other programs or devices (*clients*). Since we have two sides in communication (*clients* and *servers*), this communication model is called the **client-server model**.

The client is usually responsible for handling user interactions, while the server will store and process data. The typical flow for *client-server communication* can be described in two steps:

- The client will send a message (often called a *request*) to the server.
- The server will receive that message, process it and return the message (often called *response*) to the client.

The client and server are connected to some kind of network (internet or local, internal, network). One server can serve multiple clients, and one client can use multiple servers. In *Figure 3.1,* we can see a graphical representation of the client-server model.

We can categorize servers based on purpose. Some of the most common servers are:

- **Database servers**: Provide database service, maintains, and share any form of a database.
- **Application servers**: Host application. Clients can run applications and access application resources through the application server.
- **File servers**: Provide shared storage where files and directories can be stored and shared between clients.
- **Mail servers**: Provide service for E-mail communication.
- **Game servers**: Host multiplayer games. Multiple clients (PC computers, mobile phones, or gaming consoles) can simultaneously play the game.
- **Media servers**: Share digital video and audio content through media streaming.
- **Web servers**: Host web applications (websites or web portals).

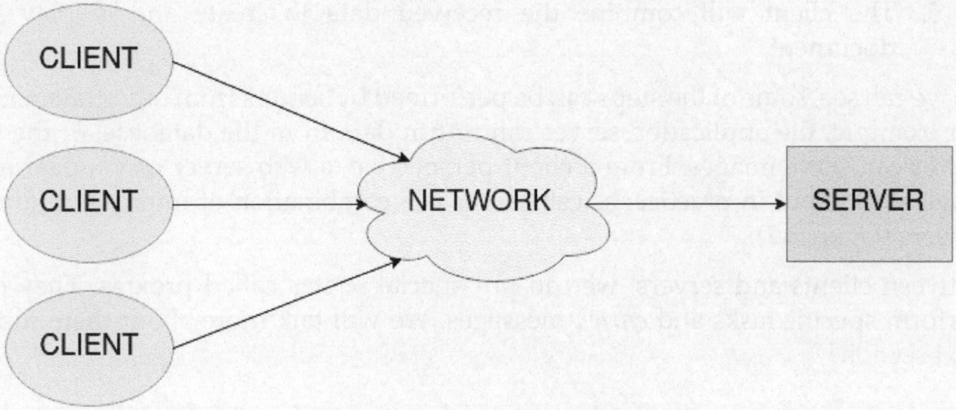

Figure 3.1: Client-server model

Some categories overlap, games, and web applications are only a specific type of application, so game servers and web servers are just a special type of application servers. But these servers are too common, so they are put into a separate category.

What we are most interested in are web servers, because we will deal with them in this book. Now we will take a closer look at web servers.

Web servers

Web servers are one of the most common servers used for hosting web applications. They provide all necessary data to clients (mainly, web browsers) so that clients can display content (website or web platform, we can use a collective term – **documents**).

The following steps represent a typical processing circle for web clients and servers:

1. The client will request an HTML page, and the server will return the HTML page. **HTML (Hypertext Markup Language**) is a language for documents designed to be displayed in a web browser.
2. The client will request a style sheet, and the server will return a CSS file. **CSS** stands for **Cascading Style Sheets**, a language used to define the appearance of a web page.
3. The client will request sub-resources (images, videos, audios, scripts, and so on), and the server will return proper files or links to that files.
4. The client will request data, and the server will get data from the database and send it to the client (usually in JSON format, which will be described in detail later).

5. The client will combine the received data to create and display the document.

As we can see, some of the steps can be performed by servers from other categories. For example, the application server can return data from the database, or the file server can serve images. From a client perspective, a web server can appear as a single entity, but in practice; a web server is a combination of multiple different servers (*Figure 3.2*).

Between clients and servers, we can put special *servers* called **proxies**. They can perform specific tasks and *enrich* messages. We will talk more about them in the next section.

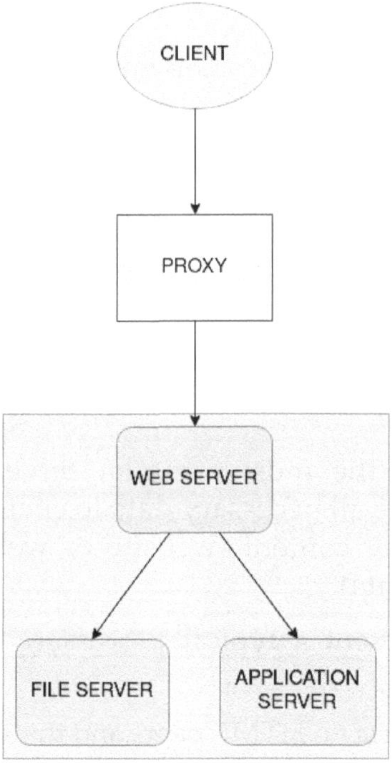

Figure 3.2*: Web server as a combination of multiple servers*

Modern web servers use HTTP protocol for communication and data exchange, so we will also take a deeper look at that subject.

A part of the web server that we are interested in, and which will be developed in this book, is one that reads and stores data in a database (*Step 4* in web client-server circle). In the following chapters, we will learn how to receive and process requests from the client and send a proper response.

Proxies

Proxy can be defined as a *machine* that can be placed between a client and a server. There are two types of proxies:

- **Transparent proxy** will just forward the message without any modification.
- **Non-transparent proxy** will modify the message before passing it.

Multiple actions can be performed with proxies. Some of the most common are:

- **Caching**: Messages related to a specific resource will be stored on a proxy. Next time, when that resource is required, the proxy will answer with a cached value instead of the server. This will prevent multiple identical database reads on the server side. Database operations are usually very slow, so this will boost the performance of the whole system.
- **Filtering**: Only messages that pass certain criteria will be forwarded to the server. For example, the server will only accept messages from a certain geographical area and all other messages will be rejected.
- **Load balancing**: When multiple instances of the same servers are presented, the proxy will try to forward the message to the least occupied instance.
- **Authentication**: Only messages from clients with proper permissions will be forwarded to the server.
- **Logging**: Information about messages will be stored in order to reconstruct communication in case of some errors or problems.

REST

REST (Representational State Transfer) is a software architectural style used to describe the interface between different components, often separated across the network. It was designed by *Roy Fielding* in *2000*.

The resource can be described as an abstraction of information in REST. Any information that we can identify and name can be considered a resource (documents, images, services, and so on). Each resource is determined by its state, known as **resource representation**. The resource representation consists of the following parts:

- Data
- Metadata is additional information that describes the data. Metadata can be used to control caching, detect transmission errors, negotiate appropriate representation format or perform authentication.

- Hypermedia links that can be used in transition to the next desired state

Hypermedia can be described as a concept where the server will inform the client about requests that the client can perform in the future. For example, the server will send an HTML page, where additional operations related to the resource will be available, like a button that will delete the resource. When the user clicks that button, a request to the server will be triggered and the actual representation of the resource will be deleted.

So, to sum up, the server will provide options, but the client will choose which option he wants.

The service interface must satisfy six guiding principles of REST and constraints. A service that fulfills this criterion is called **RESTful service**.

Here are the six guiding principles of REST:

1. **Uniform interface**: In order to archive this, we must follow a couple of concerns:
    - **Identification of resources**: Individual resources used in the interaction between client-server should be uniquely identified.
    - **Manipulation of resources**: Individual resources should have a unique uniform representation on the server side. The interface should use this representation to modify the resource state on the server.
    - **Self-descriptive messages**: Each message should carry enough information to describe how it should be processed. It can additionally provide information on actions that the client can perform on that resource.
    - **Hypermedia as the engine of the application state**: The client should only use the initial URL of the application. The client should use *server-provided links* dynamically to discover and access all available resources.
2. **Client–Server**: Concerns should be separated between the client and server. The *client* handles user interactions, while the *server* handles data storage and manipulation. The client is the one who initiates communication and dictates what will be done with the resources.

    The interface should be portable to different platforms so that different types of clients (web browsers, mobile phones, and so on) can use the same server. Client and server will evolve over time, we must be careful not to break the interface.

3. **Stateless**: Each request from the client must contain all necessary information that the client can use to understand and process the request. The server cannot use the information provided in any previous request to complete the current request.
4. **Cacheable**: Messages that the client receives from the server can be labeled as *cacheable* or *non-cacheable*. If the message is cacheable, the client can store it locally and reuse data for future equivalent requests. Data should be stored for a specific time period and deleted after that. Each reuse can extend that period.
5. **Layered system**: Architecture will be composed of hierarchical layers, where each layer will constrain certain behavior. Each component will not see beyond the immediate layer they are interacting with.
6. **Code on demand (optional)**: The client can extend his functionality by downloading and executing code from the server, usually in the form of scripts. This can simplify the client significantly, only a small number of functionalities should be implemented, and the server will provide all additional functionalities.

REST methods are used to perform the desired transition between states of any resource, while resources are accessed through **Uniform Resource Identifiers** (**URIs**).

HTTP

HTTP (Hypertext Transfer Protocol) was designed in the *early nineties* and represents the foundation for any data exchange on the web. It represents *client-server protocol,* where communication is initiated by the recipient (client, usually the web browser).

This protocol has two major advantages:

- It is *simple* and *human-readable* (which we will see in message examples, later in the chapter). We will very easily understand what the message is about by simply analyzing the message's content.
- HTTP is very *extensible*. We can introduce a new functionality by adding a new custom header or changing semantics. The client and server must be aware of these changes. The rule for how the client and server will communicate is often called an **agreement**.

By default, HTTP is *stateless,* there are no links between two successful requests performed over the same connection (context will not be shared between requests). But, we can use cookies (small blocks of data created by the server and placed on the client) to create a stateful session. Now, context can be shared between requests.

Context can be defined as local storage where data related to the current request can be stored (user id, authentication-related data, and so on). The context will be dropped when communication is completed, but we have seen it can be sealed and reused in further requests.

HTTP flow

When a client wants to communicate with the server, the following four steps will be performed:

1. The TCP connection will be opened and used for sending and receiving messages. The client can open a new connection or reuse an existing one.
2. The client will send a message to a server.
3. The client will read a message received from the server.
4. The TCP connection will be closed or reused for further communication.

TCP stands for **Transmission Control Protocol**, one of the main protocols for exchanging messages over the network.

HTTP messages

There are two types of HTTP messages:

- **HTTP Request**: Message sent by the client
- **HTTP Response**: Message sent by the server

An HTTP Request consists of the following elements:

- *Method* that defines the operation that the client wants to perform on a resource.
- *Path* is basically a URL without elements that are obvious from context, like protocol, domain, or port (URL: `http://national-library.org:8080/book/275`, path: `book/275`).
- *Version* of the HTTP protocol.
- *Headers* that provide servers with additional information (authorization permissions, format of data provided in the request body, and so on).
- *Body (optional)* that contains the resource sent by the client.

Here is a simplified example of one HTTP Request (without body) that can be used to get book information from the server:

Method: POST	Path: /book/275	Version: HTTP/1.1
Headers: Content-Type: application/json Accept-Language: en-US,en;q=0.5 Accept-Encoding: gzip		

An HTTP Response consists of the following elements:

- *Version* of the HTTP protocol
- *Status code* that indicates if the request was successful or not
- *Status message* that represents a short description of the status code
- *Header* that provides the client with additional information
- *Body (optional)* that contains resources sent by the server

Here is a simplified example of one HTTP Response with which the server will send book information to the client:

Version: HTTP/1.1	Status code: 200	Status message: OK
Headers: Content-Type: application/json Content-Encoding: gzip Server: Apache		

Body:
{
"name": "Alice's Adventures in Wonderland",
"author":"Lewis Carroll"
}		

HTTP methods

HTTP methods are used in HTTP requests to determine which operations will be performed on the resource. HTTP defines the following operations:

- `GET` is used for the retrieval of a representation of the requested resource. It's *not* a good practice to use `GET` for actions that can change the resource state.
- `HEAD` will receive an identical response as `GET`, but without a body.
- `POST` is used to send an entity of specified resource which will change the resource state. Mainly, it is used to create new resources or update existing resources.

- `PUT` will replace the current resource representation with one from the request. We should use it when we want to update a resource.
- `DELETE` will, obviously, delete specified resource representation.
- `CONNECT` will establish a tunnel to the server specified by the targeted resource.
- `OPTIONS` will describe communication options for the targeted resource.
- `TRACE` will perform a message *loop-back test* along the path to the resource.
- `PATCH` will perform *partial modification* on a resource. Can be used when only a part of the resource should be updated, for example, when we want to update only the password of the resource that represents the user account on the web platform.

HTTP status codes

Status codes are used in HTTP responses to indicate if the request was successful or *not*. Generally, we can separate status codes into five categories, defined by *standard*:

- **1xx Informational Responses**: The server informs the client that the request has been received with some provisional message while continuing to process the request. For example, the *client* should send a request with a large message body, so in the first message, only necessary headers will be sent. If the first message was valid, the *server* will inform *client* that it can send the next message, with a body. So, we will send a large amount of data through the network only if all prerequisites are fulfilled, and the network will not be overloaded.
- **2xx Successful**: Request was successfully received and processed. Some of the most common successful codes (with related HTTP status messages) are:
    - **200 OK**: Request was successful.
    - **204 Not Content**: Request was successful, but there will be no body in response.
- **3xx Redirection**: Additional actions should be performed for successful completion of the request (client should use another URL, change proxy, and so on).
- **4xx Client Errors**: Request contains bad syntax or cannot be processed. Some of the most common successful codes (with related HTTP status messages) are:

- **400 Bad Request**: Server cannot process the request due to invalid request (necessary field missed from the body, some field contains forbidden or invalid value, and so on).
- **401 Unauthorized**: The client must perform authentication before performing certain operations or invalid credentials are provided.
- **403 Forbidden**: Client has no permission to access certain resources or perform specific operations.
- **404 Not Found**: Requested resource could not be found by the server.

- **5xx Server Errors:** Server failed to process valid request:
  - **500 Internal Server Error**: Most common server error. The server has encountered a situation that it cannot resolve (server lost connection to the database, cannot reach other services, and so on).

Additional functionalities

We can use HTTP to control several common features related to client-server communication. Some of the features are:

- **Caching**: We can use HTTP to control what will be cached and for how long. Additionally, we can explicitly instruct cache providers to ignore stored data.
- **Origin constraint**: Web browsers enforce strict separation between websites. Only pages from the same origin can access all information on a web page. We can use HTTP to relax this strict separation on the server side, so other domains can access resources.
- **Authentication**: Some resources may be protected so only users with specific privileges can access them. Basic authentication can be provided by HTTP, either *through authentication-related headers* or by establishing a specific session using *cookies*.
- **Sessions**: With HTTP cookies, we can create a session in order to share context through multiple requests. This is often used for *e-commerce applications*, where the content of the shopping cart should be remembered through several different requests.

HTTP and REST

REST and HTTP are not the same! **REST** represents the software architectural style used for the designing system where the client and server will exchange representations of resources, while **HTTP** represents the actual protocol that performs that exchange. HTTP is the most widely used protocol in RESTful services, but it is not mandatory for REST, we can use other protocols instead.

REST methods are often (*wrongly*) related to HTTP methods. There are no recommendations on which HTTP methods should be used for resource method, the only rule is that we create a uniform interface.

If we decide that the `POST` method will create a new resource, we should use `POST` for the creation of all resources in our system. Other than that, there are no additional rules. If that suits us, we can use `POST` for all operations.

JSON

JSON (JavaScript Object Notation) can be described as a text format that can be used for storing and transporting data. It is specified by *Douglas Crockford* and exported from JavaScript.

One of the main advantages of the JSON format is that it is easy to understand. When we see text in JSON format, it is immediately clear to us what kind of object that text represents (we will see an example later).

Also, JSON is *language-independent*, although it was originally designed for JavaScript, all popular programming languages support it (Go is not an exception). JSON support is logical if we consider that it is just a special text format, and most programming languages can process text.

JSON syntax has a couple of simple rules:

- Data is represented as a *name-value pair*. The name must be a string while the value must be one of the following types: string, number (integer or float), object (must follow JSON syntax), Boolean, array (of any JSON-supported type), or null. The string must be surrounded with *double quotes*.
- Data is separated by a comma.
- Curly brackets hold an object.
- Square brackets hold an array.

Interestingly, there is no type for *Dates*. We must process them as strings.

Because it is just text, it is easy to send JSON from client to server and vice versa. To send it via HTTP, we should put it in the *body* and set `Content-Type: application/json header`.

The following example shows us a representation of a *person* in JSON format. Data about a spouse is listed as an *object*, while children's names are listed in an *array*:

```
{
    "name": "John Smith",
    "age": 33,
    "married": true,
    "spouse": {
        "name": "Julie",
        "age": 30
    },
    "children": [
        "Jack",
        "Jill"
    ]
}
```

Now that we are familiar with JSON format, we can see how it is supported by the Go programming language.

JSON and Go

Go programming language supports JSON by the standard library through **encoding/json** package. This package implements JSON encoding and decoding.

Decoding is a process in which JSON data will be converted and stored into a Go **struct**. Decoding will be performed by calling the **Unmarshal()** function:

```
err := json.Unmarshal(b, &s)
```

Function will accept two parameters, *JSON data* (**[]byte**) and *pointer to a struct*. If the bytes slice contains valid JSON, data from it will be stored in a **struct** and **err** will be **nil**. Otherwise, the error will be returned and partially decoded data will be stored in a **struct**.

The following structs represent the JSON from the previous example:

```
type spouse struct {
    Name string
    Age  int
}

type person struct {
    Name     string
```

```
        Age      int
        Married  bool
        Spouse   spouse
        Children []string
}
```

The **Unmarshal()** function will successfully decode JSON and map JSON data to **struct** fields only if **struct** field names start with a *capital letter*. Only fields that can be found on the destination type will be decoded. If our JSON contains, for example, **"pet":"dog"**, that information will be lost during decoding.

If we assume that the **jsonString** variable holds a string representation of a JSON from our example, the following code will perform decoding:

```
var p person
err := json.Unmarshal([]byte(jsonString), &p)
if err != nil {
        fmt.Println("Failed to decode JSON")
}
```

We usually perform decoding on the server side to extract data from the request sent to us by the client side.

Opposite to decoding, **encoding** is a process in which data stored in the Go **struct** is converted to JSON. Encoding can be executed with **Marshal()**:

```
err, b := json.Marshal(&s)
```

The function accepts the source **struct**. If encoding can be performed bytes slice that contains JSON will be returned and **err** will have the value **nil**, otherwise, an error will be returned. The error can occur in two cases, when an *unsupported type* is provided (channel, complex, and so on) or when *invalid values* are provided.

The following code will encode the variable of type *person* into JSON:

```
jsonByte, err := json.Marshal(p)
if err != nil {
        fmt.Println("Failed to encode JSON")
}
```

Encoding will be performed on the server side for the preparation of data for the response that will be sent to the client side.

Routing

Routing can be described as a process where it will be determined who will receive a specific request. The request receiver is usually referenced as a handler and can be defined as a function that will receive and process requests.

Requests are routed based on two parameters:

- HTTP method
- Request path

A combination of these two parameters and handler is called a **route**. Routes are usually created and added to the web server before the server is started and starts listening for the requests. Go programming language provides a couple of packages that can be used for routing, we will see how to use them in the following chapters.

Sometimes, the request path in the route can contain special symbols called **wildcards**, which can be used to replace one or more characters. Wildcards are usually used to route a group of paths to a single handler (for example, a single handler will be used for all reading operations).

Two wildcards are widely used:

- A single asterisk (*), which can occur anywhere in the path and represents one full component of the path.
- A double asterisk (**) or trailing wildcard must occur at the end of the path and represents any remaining portion of a path.

The following paths:

```
/person/test/id
/person/prod/id
```

Can be grouped with a single asterisk:

```
/person/*/id
```

Or with a trailing wildcard:

```
/person/**
```

And with the following path, we can route all requests to a single handler:

```
/**
```

It is important to stand out that some router implementations support wildcards, and some *do not*. We can also use them in the API documentation.

Conclusion

We are now familiar with all basics associated with servers and server applications. We know how to design our solution, and which protocols and data formats are widely used. With the knowledge gathered in this and previous chapters, we are ready to start the development of our web server application.

In the next chapter, we will finally install the Go programming language on our local machine and set up **IDE (Integrated development environment)**. After that, we will start developing and learning how to use standard and third-party libraries.

Points to remember

- In practice, web servers are a combination of different servers, where each will handle a specific task.
- The client will initiate communication and choose what operation will be performed on a resource.
- The client can use multiple servers, and the servers can serve multiple clients.
- REST and HTTP are not the same. REST is an architectural style, while HTTP is a resource exchange protocol often used in applications designed by REST guidelines.
- The JSON format is easy to understand; when we see text in JSON format, it is clear which object the text represents.

Multiple choice questions

1. Which category of HTTP status codes is nonexistent?
    a. 4xx
    b. 2xx
    c. 6xx
    d. 3xx
2. Which HTTP method does not exist?
    a. `TRACE`
    b. `PATCH`
    c. `GET`
    d. `REMOVE`

3. Which character is used to separate JSON data?
    a. Comma (,)
    b. Asterisk (*)
    c. Dot (.)
    d. Semicolon (;)
4. What is used to hold an object in JSON data?
    a. Square brackets []
    b. Brackets ()
    c. Curly brackets {}
    d. JSON cannot contains objects
5. What is used to hold an array in JSON data?
    a. Square brackets []
    b. Brackets ()
    c. Curly brackets {}
    d. JSON cannot contains objects

Answers

1. c
2. d
3. a
4. c
5. b

Questions

1. How can we categorize servers? Which are the most common servers?
2. What is a typical processing circle for web clients and servers?
3. What are the differences between transparent and non-transparent proxies?
4. What is the role of metadata?
5. Which service can be considered a RESTful service?
6. For what HTTP protocol is used?

7. JSON data is represented as a *name-value pair*. Which types can be used for name and which ones can be used for value?
8. Based on which two parameters requests are routed?
9. What is a route?
10. What are wildcards? Which wildcards can be used for request paths?

Key terms

- **Server**: Software or hardware that provides certain functionality for other programs or devices (clients).
- **Web server**: Serves the documents requested by the clients (web browsers).
- **Proxy**: Machine that can be placed between client and server in order to forward and additionally modify the message.
- **REST**: Software architectural style used to describe the interface between separated components (clients and servers).
- **HTTP**: Protocol used for data exchange over the web.
- **JSON**: Text format that can be used for storing and transporting data.
- **Routing**: Process for determining which handler will accept the request.
- **Handler**: Function that will receive and process requests.

CHAPTER 4

Setting up a Project With Go Programming Language

Introduction

In this chapter, we will do all the preparations for application development. First, we will install Go, and set up the **integrated development environment** (**IDE**). After that, we will write our first small program and learn how to build and run it. At the end of the chapter, we will learn how to use standard and third-party libraries, with additional details for some libraries which we will use.

Structure

In this chapter, we will discuss the following topics:

- Go installation
  - Linux
  - Windows
  - Mac
- Setting up a IDE
  - IDE installation
  - Visual Studio Code extension for Go
- Project creation
- Package creation
- Standard library
- Third-party libraries
- net/HTTP package

- Constants
- Variables
- Functions
- Types
- Simple HTTP server

Go installation

Until now, we used Go Playground for our small programs. Now is the time for more serious tools.

The first step on our journey is the installation of Go. All modern operating systems (Linux, Windows, and Mac) are supported. Installation files can be found on the following link:

https://go.dev/doc/install

A proper installation file for your operating system will be automatically offered, if that is not the case, all installation files can be found at **https://go.dev/dl/**.

Linux

After we successfully download the archive (**.tar.gz**) file and open the terminal, we should remove the previously installed Go version. Multiple Go versions on Linux operating systems can cause *collisions* and produce invalid installation:. The following command will remove the old version:

```
rm -rf /usr/local/go
```

If this is our first installation then we will not have this problem. We will use the following command to extract files from the archive (the command must be executed in the directory where the archive is):

```
tar -C /usr/local -xzf go1.20.linux-amd64.tar.gz
```

Depending on user settings, maybe we need to run the previous command in **sudo** mode, by simply adding the word **sudo** in front and entering the password when the dialog is prompted.

If we have an old Go version, maybe it is not stored inside /**usr/local** directory. The following command will show where Go is currently installed:

```
which go
```

Now we should add the Go installation path into the **PATH** environment variable. The following line should be added to **$HOME/.profile** file:

```
export PATH=$PATH:/usr/local/go/bin
```

We can find the exact value of the **HOME** environment variable with the command:

```
echo $HOME
```

Changes from the **profile** file will not be prompted immediately. We have two options for how changes will be applied:

- The next login will pull data from the **profile** file (including new ones), so we just simply log out and log in again.
- We can execute the command: **source $HOME/.profile**.

We can verify that the installation was successful by executing the version command:

```
go version
```

The command should print the installed version of Go *(Figure 4.1)*:

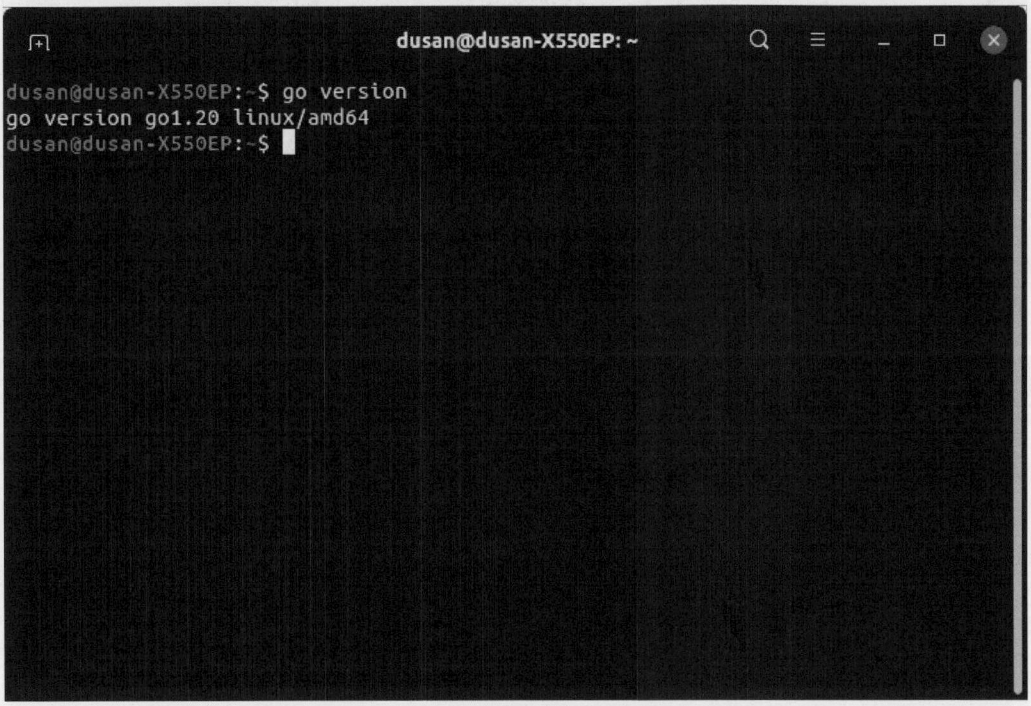

***Figure 4.1**: Checking the installed Go version on Linux*

Windows

When the download of the MSI file is complete, we just need to open it and follow the instructions. The installer will put Go into **Program Files** or **Program Files (x86)** folder (but we can change this during installation).

To verify installation, we can open the Command Prompt and execute the version command:

```
go version
```

The command should print the installed version of Go (*Figure 4.2*):

***Figure 4.2**: Checking the installed Go version on Windows*

Mac

In order to install Go on Mac operating system we just need to open the downloaded package file. The installer will put Go into the **/usr/local/go** directory and add it to the **PATH** environment variable. The effect may not be prompted immediately, so we should restart all opened Terminal sessions.

Installation can be verified with the execution of the version command in Terminal:

```
go version
```

As with previous operating systems, the command should print the installed version of Go (*Figure 4.3*):

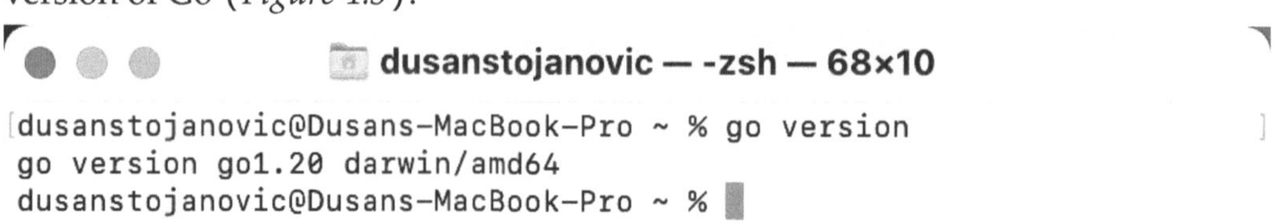

***Figure 4.3**: Checking the installed Go version on Mac*

Setting up an IDE

Now we have a programming language, but we need a tool for application development. Even though we can use an ordinary text editor, it is simpler and more practical to use **Integrated Development Environment** (**IDE**).

As a Go developer, multiple options are available. The two most popular are:

- **JetBrains GoLand**, IDE specialized for Go development. It is not free but offers *30 days free* trial. Can be downloaded from the following link:

  https://www.jetbrains.com/go/

- **Visual Studio Code** is a free solution that also can be used for other programming languages. The newest version can be downloaded from the following link:

  https://code.visualstudio.com/

For the development of our web server application, we will use the free solution.

IDE installation

The installation process for Visual Studio Code is quite easy. Depending on our operating system one of the following files will be downloaded:

- `deb` file for Ubuntu and Debian distributions of Linux
- `rpm` file for Red Hat and Fedora distributions of Linux
- `exe` file for Windows (we should pay attention to whether we need a 32-bit or 64-bit version)
- `zip` file for Mac

For Mac operating system, after the ZIP archive file is downloaded and extracted, an installation file will be provided. For other operating systems, the downloaded file is itself the installation file.

When the installation file is ready, we just need to open it and follow the instructions. Our IDE is installed, but we need one more step before we can develop Go applications.

Visual Studio Code extension for Go

Visual Studio Code is not a specialized solution for a specific programming language (like GoLand). In order to develop applications, proper extensions must be installed.

To install the extension, we should select **View**, then **Extensions** (*Figure 4.4*):

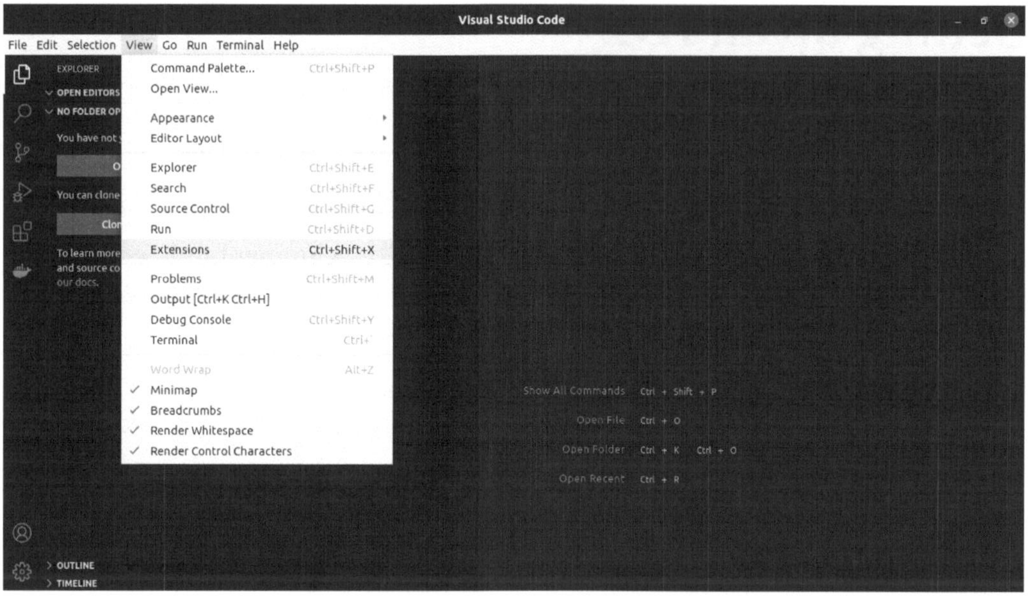

Figure 4.4: Visual Studio Code extensions

Inside the *Search* field, we can enter the phrase *go* and select one of the extensions from the top, **Go** or **Go Nightly** (*Figure 4.5*). After the extension is selected, simply click on the **Install** button will install it:

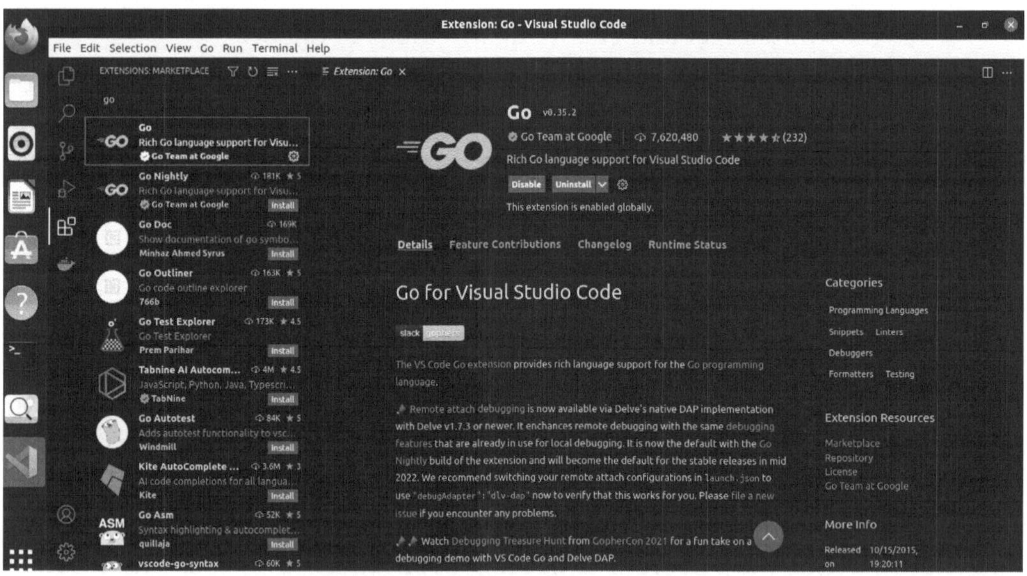

Figure 4.5: Installation of Go extension

We are now ready for development and we can write our first program.

Project creation

Our first program will be simple, it will just display some messages on standard output. Visual Studio Code does not offer the **Create Go Project** option, so we must do a few things manually.

First, we should create a folder where our project will be placed. A good practice is to create a **Project** folder, and all sub-folders will represent specific projects.

Our first project will be called `hello`, so we should create a folder with that name inside the **Projects** folder. Now we can start Visual Studio Code, and open the created folder by going to **File** and then to **Open Folder...** (*Figure 4.6*):

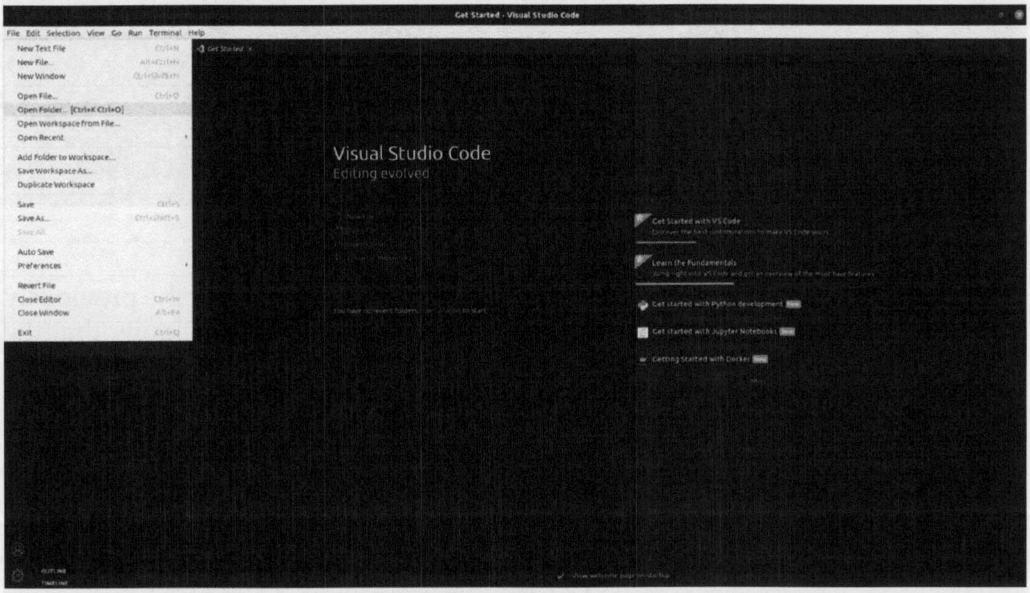

***Figure 4.6**: Folder opening*

Before we start coding, we should create a **go** module. The terminal can be opened by going to **Terminal** > **New Terminal**, and inserting the following command:

```
go mod init hello
```

The last word in the command (`hello`) represents the module name. This command will create a simple mod file that should look similar to this:

```
module hello

go 1.20
```

It's time for our first file that contains code written in the Go programming language. On the left side of the Visual Studio Code window, we can see **EXPLORER**, where folders and files of the currently opened project will be displayed. Inside it, we create a new file, by right-clicking and selecting **New File** (*Figure 4.7*):

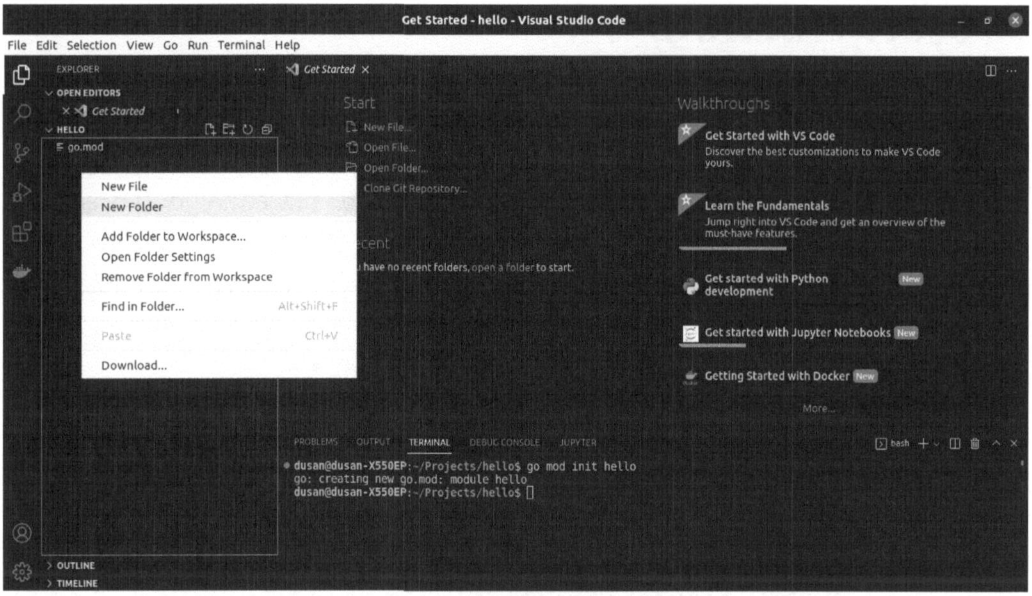

Figure 4.7: File creation

The file should be named **main.go**. The file extension .go will trigger the previously installed Visual Studio Go Extension, and from now on, IDE will know that the current project is actually a Go project. Some additional libraries can be missed, so if a dialog similar to one from *Figure 4.8* is prompted, we should click **Install** or **Install All**:

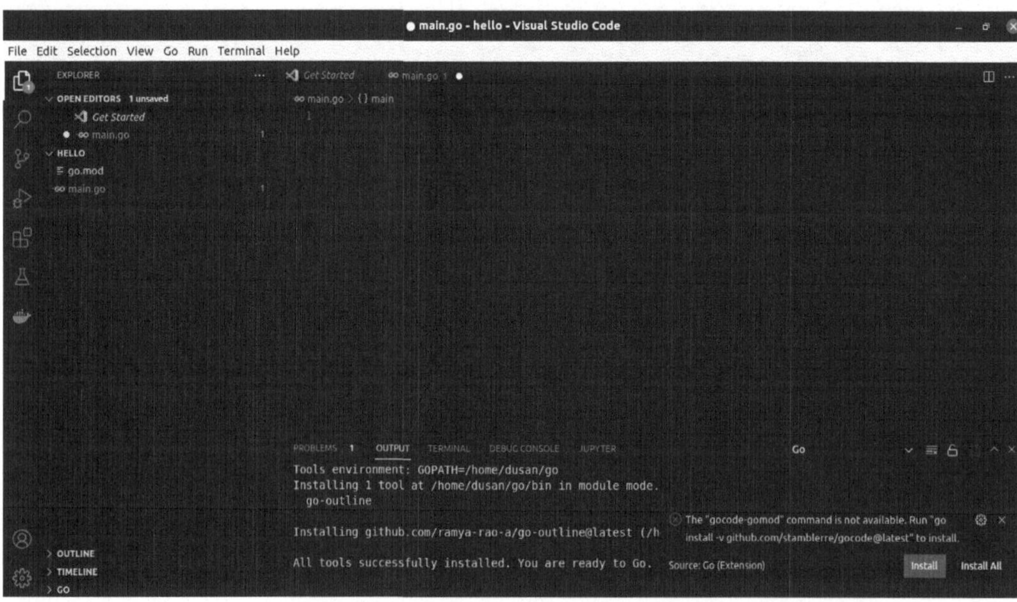

Figure 4.8: Installation of missing libraries

Inside the **`main.go`** file we will write the **`main()`** function where the text **`Hello World!!!`** will be printed on standard output. Visual Studio Code (and Go extension) should automatically import all packages used in the code:

```
package main

import "fmt"

func main() {
        fmt.Println("Hello World!!!")
}
```

Now we can build and run our code from the Terminal. The following command will build our project and create an executable file named **`hello`**:

```
go build hello
```

We can run the created file (if we are in the folder where the file is created) by executing the command:

```
./hello
```

It is possible to run our code without the creation of an executable file, with the run command. We must pass the file where the **`main()`** function is located as an argument. The following will compile and run our code:

```
go run main.go
```

We are familiar with the basics of Go projects, now let's create an additional package and make our small application a little bit more complex.

Package creation

Rarely will a project have only one (**`main`**) package. In this section, we will learn how to create a package inside our project. First, we will create a new folder, by right-clicking inside **EXPLORER** and selecting **New Folder** (*Figure 4.9*):

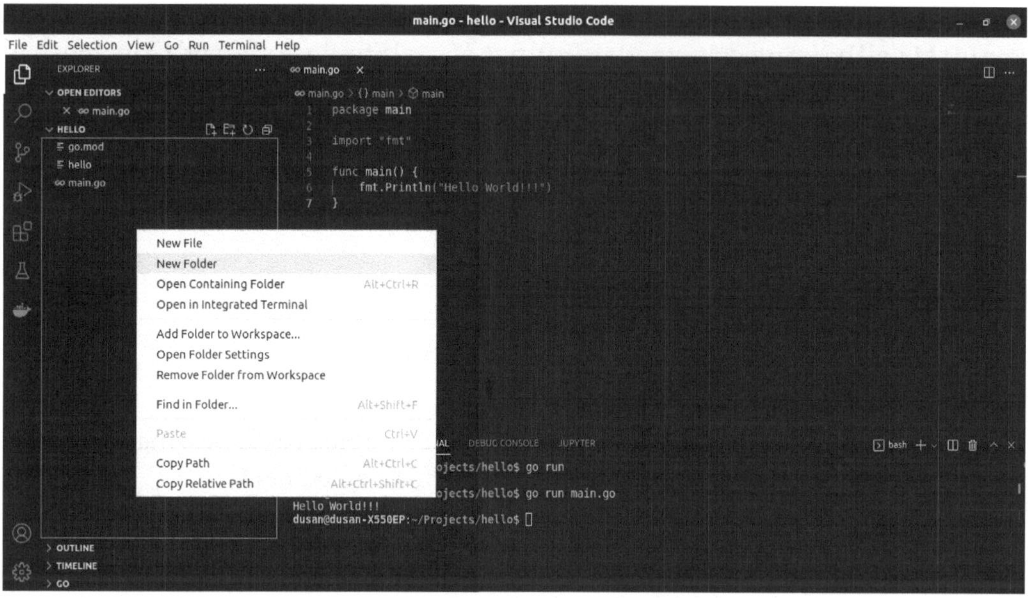

Figure 4.9: Creating a folder for the package

We will call our folder countries, and create file **countries.go** inside it. This file will contain an exported function that accepts two-letter country codes and returns the country name.

```
package countries


func GetCountry(code string) (country string) {
	switch code {
	case “FR”:
		country = “France”
	case “IT”:
		country = “Italy”
	case “IN”:
		country = “India”
	case “US”:
		country = “United States”
	default:
		country = “Unknown”
	}
	return
}
```

Now we can call a function from the countries package at the end of the **`main()`** function. When all imports are fixed (Visual Studio Code will probably fix this automatically), the content of the **`main.go`** file will now look like this:

```
package main

import (
        "fmt"
        "hello/countries"
)


func main() {
        fmt.Println("Hello World!!!")

        fmt.Println("Hello", countries.GetCountry("FR"))

}
```

When we execute this code with the run command, two messages will be displayed on the standard output (*Figure 4.10*):

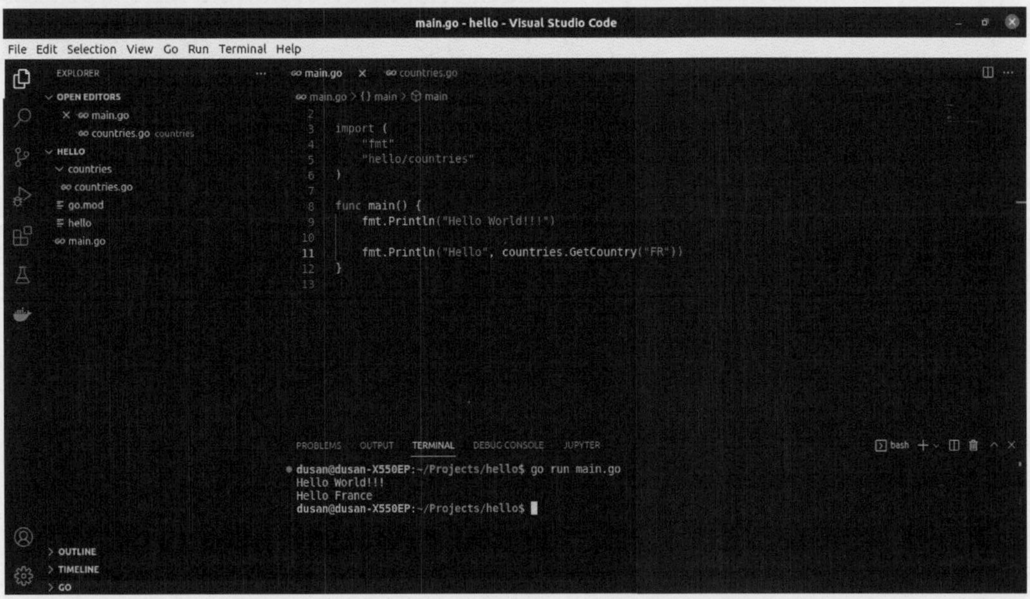

Figure 4.10: Project execution

If we run an executable file that we created with the **`build`** command, one message will be displayed, because the executable file is created before the creation of the countries package. If we want to run the Go application with an executable file, we must rebuild it with each change in order to keep it updated.

Now that we know how to create Go projects, it is time to see what standard library has to offer, and how to use third-party libraries.

Standard library

As an extension to standard language features, Go comes with a set of core packages that extends language functionality. These packages are a part of the standard library. With a standard library, we can perform a lot of usual tasks, like printing standard output or performing simple mathematical operations without the need to write our own implementation or download packages published by other developers.

Since the standard library is bounded by language, they come with several special guarantees:

- It will always exist, with all packages, for each minor release of the Go programming language.
- All packages will follow the backward compatibility rule (the newest version will support constants and methods from previous versions).
- The standard library is a part of the development, build, and release process for the Go programming language.
- Go contributors will maintain and review the standard library.
- All packages from the standard library will be tested and benchmarked with each new release of the Go programming language.

The following packages (and sub-packages) are part of the standard library (this list can be used as a reminder of what can be found in a specific package):

- **`archive`**: Support for archives (multiple files and folders compressed into a single file):
    - **`tar`**: Methods for reading and writing **`.tar`** archives.
    - **`zip`**: Methods for reading and writing **`.zip`** archives.
- **`bufio`**: Implementation of buffered I/O.
- **`builtin`**: Documentation for pre-declared identifiers (language constants and built-in methods).
- **`bytes`**: A set of functions for manipulations of **`byte`** slice.
- **`compress`**: A collection of different compression algorithms:
    - **`bzip2`**: Implementation of **`bzip2`** decompression.
    - **`flate`**: Implementation of **`DEFLATE`** compression data format.

- **gzip**: Methods for reading and writing of files compressed with **gzip** format.
- **lzw**: Implementation of *Lempel-Ziv-Welch* compression data format.
- **zlib**: Methods for reading and writing of files compressed with **zlib** format.

- **container**: Complex data structures, which are used to store collections of data:
  - **heap**: Methods for heap operations. Heap can be defined as a tree, where each node is the minimum valued node in its sub-tree (*Figure 4.11a*).
  - **list**: Methods for *double-linked list* operations. Double linked list can be defined as a set of sequentially linked nodes, where each node contains data, a pointer to the previous element, and a pointer to the next element (*Figure 4.11b*).
  - **ring**: Methods for circular list operations. A circular list is a variation of a double-linked list, where the last element points to the first one and vice versa (*Figure 4.11c*):

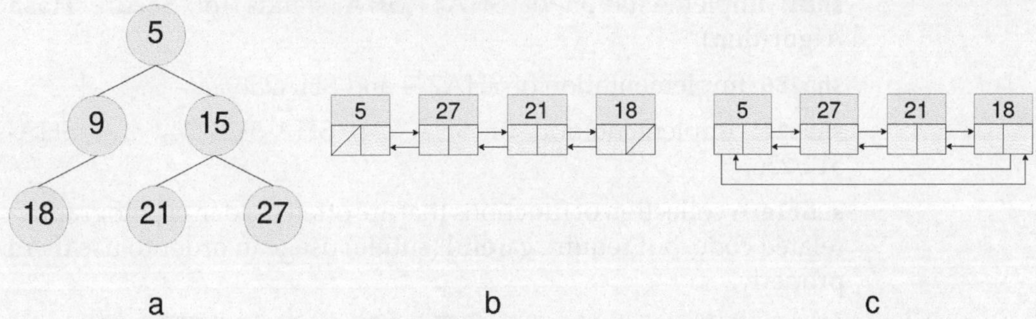

***Figure 4.11**: Data structures from container package*

- **context**: Context type is defined in this package. Context can carry deadlines, cancellation signals, and other similar request-scoped values across API boundaries and between processes.
- **crypto**: A collection of common cryptographic constants and methods:
  - **aes**: Implementation of AES encryption.
  - **cipher**: Implementation of standard block cipher modes (list of current modes can be found here:

    https://csrc.nist.gov/projects/block-cipher-techniques/bcm/current-modes)
  - **des**: Implementation of **Data Encryption Standard** (**DES**) and

Triple Data Encryption Algorithm (**TDEA**).

- `dsa`: Implementation of **Digital Signature Algorithm** (**DSA**).
- `ecdh`: Implementation of **Elliptic Curve Diffie-Hellman (ECDH)** key exchanges over NIST curves and Curve25519.
- `ecdsa`: Implementation of **Elliptic Curve Digital Signature Algorithm** (**ECDSA**).
- `ed25519`: Implementation of ED25519 Signature Algorithm.
- `elliptic`: Implements of the standard NIST P-224, P-256, P-384, and P-521 elliptic curves over prime fields. Safer and efficient packages crypto/ecdh should be used, if possible.
- `hmac`: Implementation of **Keyed-Hash Message Authentication Code** (**HMAC**).
- `md5`: Implementation of MD5 hash algorithm.
- `rand`: Cryptographically secure random number generator.
- `rc4`: Implementation of RC4 encryption.
- `rsa`: Implementation of **Rivest-Shamir-Adleman** (**RSA**) encryption.
- `sha1`: Implementation of SHA1 (**SHA** stands for **Secure Hash Algorithm**).
- `sha256`: Implementation of SHA224 and SHA256.
- `sha512`: Implementation of SHA-384, SHA-512/224, and SHA-512/256.
- `subtle`: A collection of functions that are often used in cryptography-related code, but require careful (subtle) usage in order to use them properly.
- `tls`: Partial implementation of TLS 1.2 and TLS 1.3 (**TLS** stands for **Transport Layer Security**).
- `x509`: Methods and functions for parsing of X.509-encoded keys and certificates.

- `database`: Interface for working with databases:
  - `sql`: Interface for SQL and SQL-like databases.
- `debug`: A set of tools, that can be used for debugging:
  - `buildinfo`: Provides access to building information embedded in Go binary.
  - `dwarf`: Provides access to DWARF debugging information, that is loaded from the executable file.
  - `elf`: Provides access to ELF object files.

    - `gosym`: Provides access to the Go symbol and line number. This information is generated by `gc` compiler and embedded in the Go binary.
    - `macho`: Provides access to *Mach-O object* files.
    - `pe`: Provides access to Microsoft Windows Portable Executable files.
    - `plan9obj`: Provides access to Plan 9 `a.out` files.
- `embed`: Provides access to the files embedded into the running program.
- `encoding`: Provides an interface that can be used for data conversion from byte to textual representation and vice versa:
    - `ascii85`: Implementation of `ascii85` data encoding, used in *Adobe PostScript* and *PDF* documents.
    - `asn1`: A method for parsing *DER-encoded ASN.1* data structures.
    - `base32`: Implementation of base32 encoding.
    - `base64`: Implementation of base64 encoding.
    - `binary`: A method for translation between number and byte sequences.
    - `csv`: A method for reading and writing **comma-separated values (CSV)** files.
    - `gob`: A method for managing stream of gobs. **Gobs** can be defined as binary values exchanged between the encoder and decoder.
    - `hex`: Implementation of hexadecimal encoding and decoding.
    - `json`: Implementation of encoding and decoding of JSON.
    - `pem`: Implementation of *Privacy Enhanced Mai*l encoding.
    - `xml`: Implementation of XML 1.0 parser.
- `errors`: A set of functions that can be used for error handling.
- `expvar`: Standardized interface for access to public variables. An example of a public variable is the operation counter in servers, which will be exposed via the HTTP endpoint.
- `flag`: Implementation of the command line flag parsing.
- `fmt`: Implementation of formatted input and output. We use functions from this package in our examples to display the value on standard output.
- `go`: A set of Go-specific packages:
    - `ast`: Declaration of types used to represent **abstract syntax trees (AST)** for Go packages.
    - `build`: Functions and methods that can be used to collect information related to Go packages.

- `constant`: Implementation of un-typed Go constants and related operations.
- `doc`: Extraction of source code documentation from Go AST.
- `format`: Implementation of standard formatting of Go source.
- `importer`: Gives access to data provided by importers.
- `parser`: Implementation of Go source file parser.
- `printer`: Printing of AST nodes.
- `scanner`: Scanner for Go source.
- `token`: Definition of constants that represents the lexical tokens of the Go programming language and basic operations on tokens.
- `types`: Declaration of GO data types and implementation of type-checking algorithms.

- `hash`: Interface for hash functions:
  - `adler32`: Implementation of Adler-32 checksum.
  - `crc32`: Implementation of 32-bit cyclic redundancy check.
  - `crc64`: Implementation of 64-bit cyclic redundancy check.
  - `fnv`: Implementation of FNV-1 and FNV-2 non-cryptographic hash.
  - `maphash`: Hash functions that can be performed on byte sequences.
- `html`: A set of functions that are used for escaping and un-escaping HTML text.
  - `template`: Implementation of data-driven templates for generating code injection safe HTML output.
- `image`: Implementation of basic 2D images:
  - `color`: Implementation of basic colors.
  - `draw`: A set of functions for basic image composition.
  - `gif`: Implementation of GIF image decoder and encoder.
  - `jpeg`: Implementation of JPEG image decoder and encoder.
  - `png`: Implementation of PNG image decoder and encoder.
- `index/suffixarray`: Indexed sub-string searching for data with in-memory usage.
- `io`: Interface to I/O primitives:

    - `fs`: Interface to a file system.
    - `ioutil`: I/O utility functions (reading file, writing file, reading directory, and so on).
- `log`: Implementation of logging functions:
    - `syslog`: Interface to the system log service.
- `math`: Mathematical constants and functions:
    - `big`: Implementation of arbitrary-precision arithmetic (big numbers).
    - `bits`: Function for manipulation on unsigned integer types.
    - `cmplx`: Constants and functions for manipulation of complex numbers.
    - `rand`: Implementation of *pseudo-random number generator*. This generator is not suitable for security-sensitive work, for that purpose we should use a generator from `crypto/rand` package.
- `mime`: Partial implementation of **Multipurpose Internet Mail Extensions** (**MIME**) specification:
    - `multipart`: Implementation of MIME multipart parsing.
    - `quotedprintable`: Implementation of quoted-printable encoding.
- `net`: Interface for network I/O. Network I/O includes **Transmission Control Protocol** (**TCP**), **Internet Protocol** (**IP**), **User Data Protocol** (**UDP**), domain name resolution, Unix domain sockets, and so on:
    - `http`: Implementation of HTTP client and server. We will explore this package with more details later.
    - `mail`: Implementation of mail messages parsing.
    - `netip`: Definition of a type that represents an IP address.
    - `rpc`: Provides access to exported methods of an object across the network or any other I/O connection.
    - `smtp`: Implementation of **Simple Mail Transfer Protocol**.
    - `textproto`: Provides support for *text-based request-responses* protocols.
    - `url`: Implementation of URL query escaping and parsing.
- `os`: Platform-independent interface to operating system functionality:
    - `exec`: Execution of external commands.

  - `signal`: Provides access to incoming signals.
  - `user`: Provides user account lookups by name or ID.
- `path`: Implementation of slash-separated paths manipulation:
  - `filepath`: Implementation of file path manipulation compatible with the targeted operating system.
- `plugin`: Implementation of loading and symbol resolution of Go packages.
- `reflect`: Implementation of *run-time reflection*. This will allow the program to manipulate objects with arbitrary types (for example to determine the actual type of `interface{}` variable).
- `regexp`: Implementation of regular expression search:
  - `syntax`: Functions for parsing regular expressions into parse trees and compiling parse trees into programs.
- `Runtime`: A set of operations for interaction with the Go runtime system. One usage example is controlling goroutines.
  - `cgo`: Support for code generated by the `cgo` tool.
  - `debug`: Facilities for programs to debug themselves while they are running.
  - `metrics`: Interface for accessing metrics exported by Go runtime (garbage collector, memory usage, and so on).
  - `pprof`: Exporting of runtime profiling data in a format expected by **pprof** visualization tool.
  - `race`: Implementation of data race detection logic.
  - `trace`: Facilities for programs to generate traces that can be used by GO execution tracer.
- `sort`: Methods for sorting slices and collections.
- `strconv`: Implementation of the conversion of basic types to and from a string representation.
- `strings`: Functions for manipulation of UTF-8 encoded strings. We saw the usage of this package in some examples.
- `sync`: Implementation of basic synchronization primitives. We saw examples of how to use **mutual exclusion locks** (**mutexes**).
  - `atomic`: Atomic primitives useful in synchronization algorithms.
- `syscall`: Interface to the operating system primitives:
  - `js`: Provides access to the **WebAssembly** host environment.

- **testing**: Go support for automated testing. We will see the usage of this package in a dedicated chapter:
    - **fstest**: Support for testing of file systems.
    - **iotest**: Implementation of readers and writers designed for usage in tests.
    - **quick**: Tools for black box testing.
- **text**: Methods for text manipulation:
    - **scanner**: Implementation of scanner and tokenizer for UTF-8 encoded text.
    - **tabwriter**: Implementation of a filter that transforms tabbed columns into aligned text.
    - **template**: Implementation of data-driven templates for textual output generation.
- **time**: Functions for measuring and displaying time:
    - **tzdata**: Provides a copy of the time zone database.
- **unicode**: Implementation of functions for testing Unicode code point properties:
    - **utf16**: Implementation of *UTF-16 sequences* encoding and decoding.
    - **utf8**: Implementation of *UTF-8 sequences* encoding and decoding.
- **unsafe**: Operations that can be used to override type safety of Go types.
- **internal**: Go internal tools. Some of the tools are accessed to build configurations, detection of processor features, detection of race conditions, and so on.

We already used some of the packages from the standard library (**fmt**, **math**, **encoding/json**). Here is an example of how we can use the **log** package. First, we must import the package. After that inside the **div()** function, we will use a log to display input parameters, results, and potential error (division by zero):

```
package main

import (
	“log”
)

func div(a, b float32) (c float32) {
```

```
        log.Println("Input parameters:", a, b)

        if b == 0 {
              log.Println("Division by zero")
              return 0
        }

        c = a / b

        log.Println("Division result:", c)
        return
}

func main() {
        div(6.0, 3.0)
        div(6.0, 0.0)
}
```

Each log line will contain a timestamp and specified log message. Code from this example will log the following output:

```
2022/09/14 07:44:44 Input parameters: 6 3
2022/09/14 07:44:44 Division result: 2
2022/09/14 07:44:44 Input parameters: 6 0
2022/09/14 07:44:44 Division by zero
```

Third-party libraries

Packages developed, maintained, and released by an entity (developer, company, and so on) other than the original vendor (Go contributors in our case) are considered *third-party libraries*. Usually, they contain some specific functionalities that are not widely used, bat can be reusable in multiple different situations.

Here is an example of the *missing functionality* of the Go programming language. Go includes multiple data types that represent some sort of collection (**array**, **slice**, **map**, and so on), but the set is not one of them. **Set** is a data type that can store unique values (no duplicates), without a specific order, and can be defined as an implementation of the mathematical concept of a finite set.

Luckily, someone developed a library that can be installed and used inside our Go programs. The first step is to download all packages included in the library. We will use the **go get** command for that task. The following command will download set related library:

```
go get github.com/deckarep/golang-set
```

If everything is executed successfully, output similar to the following should be displayed in the Console/Terminal (version can be different):

```
go: downloading github.com/deckarep/golang-set v1.8.0
go: added github.com/deckarep/golang-set v1.8.0
```

Now we can import library packages in the same way as packages from the standard library and packages that we created. We will use it to create two sets, one that includes *yellow fruits,* and the other one that includes *red fruits* and create a union of these two sets. Set can be created in two ways, *by creating an empty set and adding elements one by one,* or *by converting a slice into a set*:

```
package main

import (
	"fmt"

	set "github.com/deckarep/golang-set"
)

func main() {
	yellowFruit := set.NewSet()
	yellowFruit.Add("banana")
	yellowFruit.Add("lemon")
	yellowFruit.Add("pineapple")
	fmt.Println(yellowFruit)

	redFruit := set.NewSetFromSlice(
		[]interface{}{"apple", "cherry", "strawberry"})
	fmt.Println(redFruit)

	fruit := yellowFruit.Union(redFruit)
	fmt.Println(fruit)
}
```

If we execute this program, the following output will be displayed on the standard output:

```
Set{banana, lemon, pineapple}
Set{apple, cherry, strawberry}
Set{pineapple, apple, cherry, strawberry, banana, lemon}
```

The elements inside each set can be displayed in a different order because the set does not guarantee any specific order.

It's important to pinpoint that we should check *third-party libraries* before we use them. We should check if the library is commonly updated and maintained, and if support is provided by the author. Also, if we hesitate between a couple of similar libraries we should provide some performance tests and decide which best suits our requirements.

With **vendor** command, we can have our local copy of all packages used for **build** and **test**. All files will be stored inside **vendor** directory of the **main** module, so in case the internet connection is not available, or a certain package is no longer available, we can develop and run our application without any problem.

The following command will copy packages into the **vendor** directory:

```
go mod vendor
```

Now, when we know how to create our own packages, use packages from the *standard library*, and use packages from *third-party libraries*, we are ready for the development of our Web server application.

net/http package

Package **net/http** is one of the basic packages for the development of web-based applications. In previous sections, we saw that this package contains the implementation of the HTTP server and client. Now, we will see the content of this package with more details.

Constants

Package **net/http** contains constants for all HTTP methods and statuses (we saw some of them in the previous chapter):

```
const (
        MethodGet     = "GET"
        MethodHead    = "HEAD"
        MethodPost    = "POST"
        MethodPut     = "PUT"
        MethodPatch   = "PATCH"
        MethodDelete  = "DELETE"
```

```
        MethodConnect = "CONNECT"
        MethodOptions = "OPTIONS"
        MethodTrace   = "TRACE"
)

const (
        StatusContinue           = 100
        StatusSwitchingProtocols = 101
        StatusProcessing         = 102
        StatusEarlyHints         = 103

        StatusOK                   = 200
        StatusCreated              = 201
        StatusAccepted             = 202
        StatusNonAuthoritativeInfo = 203
        StatusNoContent            = 204
        StatusResetContent         = 205
        StatusPartialContent       = 206
        StatusMultiStatus          = 207
        StatusAlreadyReported      = 208
        StatusIMUsed               = 226

        StatusMultipleChoices   = 300
        StatusMovedPermanently = 301
        StatusFound            = 302
        StatusSeeOther         = 303
        StatusNotModified      = 304
        StatusUseProxy         = 305

        StatusTemporaryRedirect = 307
        StatusPermanentRedirect = 308

        StatusBadRequest                   = 400
        StatusUnauthorized                 = 401
        StatusPaymentRequired              = 402
        StatusForbidden                    = 403
```

```
StatusNotFound                      = 404
StatusMethodNotAllowed              = 405
StatusNotAcceptable                 = 406
StatusProxyAuthRequired             = 407
StatusRequestTimeout                = 408
StatusConflict                      = 409
StatusGone                          = 410
StatusLengthRequired                = 411
StatusPreconditionFailed            = 412
StatusRequestEntityTooLarge         = 413
StatusRequestURITooLong             = 414
StatusUnsupportedMediaType          = 415
StatusRequestedRangeNotSatisfiable  = 416
StatusExpectationFailed             = 417
StatusTeapot                        = 418
StatusMisdirectedRequest            = 421
StatusUnprocessableEntity           = 422
StatusLocked                        = 423
StatusFailedDependency              = 424
StatusTooEarly                      = 425
StatusUpgradeRequired               = 426
StatusPreconditionRequired          = 428
StatusTooManyRequests               = 429
StatusRequestHeaderFieldsTooLarge   = 431
StatusUnavailableForLegalReasons    = 451

StatusInternalServerError            = 500
StatusNotImplemented                 = 501
StatusBadGateway                     = 502
StatusServiceUnavailable             = 503
StatusGatewayTimeout                 = 504
StatusHTTPVersionNotSupported        = 505
StatusVariantAlsoNegotiates          = 506
StatusInsufficientStorage            = 507
StatusLoopDetected                   = 508
```

```
        StatusNotExtended                   = 510
        StatusNetworkAuthenticationRequired = 511
)
```

Additionally, we have a couple of configuration-related constants:

- **`DefaultMaxHeaderBytes`**: Definition of the maximum permitted size of the headers in the HTTP request. The constant value is set to **1 MB** but can be overridden with the setting of **`Serve.MaxHeaderBytes`**. The server type will be explained later.
- **`DefaultMaxIdleConnsPerHost`**: Definition of default value for field **`MaxIdleConnsPerHost`** from **`Transport`** type (this type will also be explained later).
- **`TimeFormat`**: Time format that will be used for time in HTTP headers.

Variables

The following variables are part of the **`net/http`** package:

- Errors used by the HTTP server. Errors are quite descriptive, so we will just list them here:

```
var (
        ErrBodyNotAllowed = errors.New("http: request method or
        response status code does not allow body")

        ErrHijacked = errors.New("http: connection has been
        hijacked")

        ErrContentLength = errors.New("http: wrote more than the
        declared Content-Length")

        // Deprecated
        ErrWriteAfterFlush = errors.New("unused")
)

var (
        ErrNotSupported = &ProtocolError{"feature not supported"}

        // Deprecated
```

```
        ErrUnexpectedTrailer = &ProtocolError{"trailer header
        without chunked transfer encoding"}

        ErrMissingBoundary = &ProtocolError{"no multipart boundary
        param in Content-Type"}

        ErrNotMultipart = &ProtocolError{"request Content-Type
        isn't multipart/form-data"}

        // Deprecated
        ErrHeaderTooLong = &ProtocolError{"header too long"}

        // Deprecated
        ErrShortBody = &ProtocolError{"entity body too short"}

        // Deprecated
        ErrMissingContentLength = &ProtocolError{"missing
        ContentLength in HEAD response"}
)
```

- **Default client** and default **ServerMux**:

```
var (
        DefaultClient = &Client{}
        DefaultServeMux = &defaultServeMux
)
```

- **Common errors**:

```
var (
        ErrAbortHandler = errors.New("net/http: abort Handler")
        ErrBodyReadAfterClose = errors.New("http: invalid Read on
        closed Body")
        ErrHandlerTimeout = errors.New("http: Handler timeout")
        ErrLineTooLong = internal.ErrLineTooLong
        ErrMissingFile = errors.New("http: no such file")
        ErrNoCookie = errors.New("http: named cookie not present")
        ErrNoLocation = errors.New("http: no Location header in
        response")
```

```
        ErrServerClosed = errors.New("http: Server closed")
        ErrSkipAltProtocol = errors.New("net/http: skip alternate
        protocol")
        ErrUseLastResponse = errors.New("net/http: use last
        response")
)
```

- **`NoBody: io.ReadCloser`** without body:

```
var NoBody = noBody{}
```

Functions

The following functions are part of the **`net/http`** package, for each of them we will see a declaration and a small description:

- **`func CanonicalHeaderKey(s string) string`**: This function will return the canonical format of header keys. In canonical format, the first letter and all letters after the hyphen (**`-`**) are in uppercase, and all other letters are lowercase. For example, the canonical format for *content-encoding* is **Content-Encoding**.
- **`func DetectContentType(data []byte) string`**: This function will determine the content type for provided data. Only the *first 512 bytes* will be checked.
- **`func Error(w ResponseWriter, error string, code int`**): We will use this function when a specific error message and HTTP code should be answered for a request.
- **`func Handle(pattern string, handler Handler)`**: A function that registers the handler in **`DefaultServeMux`** for a given pattern.
- **`func HandleFunc(pattern string, handler func (ResponseWriter, *Request)`**: A function that registers the handler function in **`DefaultServeMux`** for a given pattern.
- **`func ListenAndServe(addr string, handler Handler) error`**: This function will listen to the TCP network address (**`addr`**) and handle incoming requests by calling **`Serve()`** function with the handler.
- **`func ListenAndServeTLS(addr string, certFile, keyFile string, handler Handler) error`**: Similar to **`ListenAndServe()`** function, with couple of differences. This function will expect HTTPS connections and files with a certificate and a private key must be provided.
- **`func MaxBytesReader(w ResponseWriter, r io.ReadCloser, n int64) io.ReadCloser`**: The purpose of this function is to limit the size of bodies

for incoming requests. The client can send large requests (by accident or purposely through malicious requests) which can lead to the wasting of server resources.

- **func NotFound(w ResponseWriter, r *Request)**: We will use this function to respond to the requests with a **404 Not Found** response.
- **func ParseHTTPVersion(vers string) (major, minor int, ok bool)**: This function will parse a string that represents the HTTP version (**vers**). If we try to parse **HTTP/2.0** version string, the function will return the following results: **major = 2**, **minor = 0**, **ok = true**.
- **func ParseTime(text string) (t time.Time, err error)**: Function for parsing time header. All formats allowed by HTTP/1.1 are supported.
- **func ProxyFromEnvironment(req *Request) (*url.URL, error)**: This function will return the proxy URL. The proxy URL will be indicated by the environment variables **HTTP_PROXY**, **HTTPS_PROXY**, and **NO_PROXY**.
- **func ProxyURL(fixedURL *url.URL) func (*Request)(*url.URL, error)**: This function will return a **proxy** function that will always return the same URL.
- **func Redirect(w ResponseWriter, r *Request, url string, code int)**: We will use this function to respond to the requests with a redirect to the URL. Provided code should be from the *3xx group*.
- **func Serve(l net.Listener, handler Handler) error**: This function will accept incoming HTTP connections on the provided listener. A new Goroutine that reads the request and calls the proper header will be created for each connection.
- **func ServeContent(w ResponseWriter, r *Request, name string, modtime time.Time, content io.ReadSeeker)**: We will use this function to respond to the requests with content provided in **ReadSeeker**. If **Content-Type** is *not* set, the function will try to discover the type from the extension of the name file or by calling **DetectContentType()** function.
- **func ServeFile(w ResponseWriter, r *Request, name string)**: We will use this function to respond to requests with content from the name file or directory. The name should be sanitized before the function call.
- **func ServeTLS(l net.Listener, handler Handler, certFile, keyFile string) error**: Function similar to **Serve()** function. Unlike **Serve()** function, **ServeTLS()** expects HTTPS connections and we must provide files with a certificate and private key.

- **func SetCookie(w ResponseWriter, cookie *Cookie)**: This function will add a **Set-Cookie** header. The cookie name must be valid and invalid cookies will be dropped.
- **func StatusText(code int) string**: A simple function that will return a text message for provided status code. For example, for status code **404 function** will return **Not Found**.

Types

The following types are part of the **net/http** package:

- **Client**: HTTP client that is safe for concurrent use. The default (*zero*) value for the client is **DefaultClient** which is the client that uses **DefaultTransport**. Transport represents the mechanism by which individual HTTP requests are made. Transport has an internal state, so the client should be reused instead of created when needed.
- **CloseNotifier**: Interface used to detect when the underlying connection has gone away. This type is deprecated and **Request.Context** should be used instead, but we will mention it here for historical reasons.
- **ConnState**: State of client connection to a server.
- **Cookie**: HTTP cookie (**Set-Cookie** header in the HTTP response and **Cookie** header in HTTP request).
- **CookieJar**: Interface for managing storage and usage of cookies requests.
- **Dir**: Implementation of the file system (native file system will be used).
- **FileSystem**: Interface for accessing the collection of files. The file path must be separated by a slash (**/**) no matter which host operating system will be used.
- **File**: The type that will be returned by the **Open()** method from **FileSystem**.
- **Flusher**: Interface for flushing buffered data to the client.
- **Handler**: Interface for responding to HTTP requests. Contains one singular method **ServeHTTP(ResponseWriter, *Requests)** that should write response headers and data to **ResponseWriter** and return. We should only read requests and never modify them.
- **Header**: The map where the key represents the header name and value represents the header value.
- **Hijacker**: Interface implemented by **ResponseWriters**. It allows the HTTP handler to take over the connection.

- **`MaxBytesError`**: The type that will be returned by **`MaxBytesReader()`** function when the read limit is exceeded.
- **`Pusher`**: Interface implemented by **`ResponseWriter`**, supports *HTTP/2 server push*.
- **`PushOptions`**: Options for **`Push()`** method from **`Pusher`**. Options consist of **`Method`** (that represents HTTP method) and **`Header`** (that represents HTTP header).
- **`Request`**: Representation of HTTP request. HTTP requests are sent by the client and received by the server.
- **`ResponseController`**: Type used by HTTP handler to control response. Provides additional per-request functionality not handled by ResponseWriter interface.
- **`ResponseWriter`**: Interface used by HTTP handler to construct HTTP response.
- **`RoundTripper`**: Interface for the execution of a single HTTP transaction. The response will be returned for provided request.
- **`SameSite`**: Defines cookie attribute for prevention of *cross-site forgery attacks*. This cookie will not be sent along with cross-site requests.
- **`ServeMux`**: A multiplexer for HTTP requests. The incoming request will be matched with a list of registered patterns and the proper handler will be called.
- **`Server`**: Parameters for running an HTTP server. Valid configuration is the default (*zero*) value for the server.
- **`Transport`**: Implementation of **`RoundTripper`** that supports HTTP, HTTPS, and HTTP proxies, and is safe for concurrent usage by multiple Goroutines. The connection will be cached for future re-use. Responses with status codes from the *1xx group* will be automatically handled or ignored.

Simple HTTP server

At the end of this chapter, we will create one simple HTTP server with a **`net/http`** package. Inside **`main()`** function, we will use **`HandleFunc()`** function to register the handler function **`helloWorld()`** in **`DefaultServeMux`** for pattern **`/hello.`** Function **`helloWorld()`** is a simple function that will write the string **`Hello World`** and character for new in response.

At the end of the **`main()`** function, we will call **`ListenAndServe()`** to start listening for the incoming request. We will just pass the port number as the address because we will execute the application locally on our machine. Also, we will use **`DefaultServeMux`**, so we will pass **`nil`** for the handler:

```
import (
        "fmt"
        "net/http"
)

func helloWorld(rw http.ResponseWriter, req *http.Request) {
        fmt.Fprintf(rw, "Hello World\n")
}

func main() {
        http.HandleFunc("/hello", helloWorld)

        http.ListenAndServe(":8080", nil)
}
```

In order to test our small HTTP server, we will run it, open a new console/terminal, and enter the following command:

```
curl localhost:8080/hello
```

The string **Hello World** should be displayed in the terminal (*Figure 4.12*):

***Figure 4.12**: HTTP server call*

Conclusion

In this chapter, we learned how to install Go and set up IDE. After that, we created our first project and learned how to use the standard library, and third-party library. At the end of this chapter, we take a deep look into the `net/http` package from Go standard library and develop a simple application that utilizes it.

Now, we are familiar with all Go-related concepts related to web server application development. In the following chapter, we will concentrate more on application design, after that we can start with the actual development of our web server application.

References

- https://pkg.go.dev/std
- https://github.com/deckarep/golang-set

Points to Remember

- Go is supported by all modern operating systems.
- We can run the Go code without the creation of the executable file.
- The standard library will always exist, with all packages, for each minor release of the Go programming language.
- We should check if the third-party library is commonly updated, maintained, and supported by the author.

Multiple choice questions

1. On which operating system we can install Go?
    a. Mac
    b. Windows
    c. Linux
    d. All of above
2. Which command will create a new go module?
    a. `go mod`
    b. `go build`
    c. `go get`
    d. `go run`
3. What is an extension for the files with Go code?
    a. `mod`
    b. `sum`
    c. `go`
    d. `txt`
4. What collection structure is not a part of the container package from the standard library?
    a. heap

b. array

c. list

d. ring

5. Which command will download the third-party library?

a. `go mod`

b. `go build`

c. `go get`

d. `go run`

Answers

1. d
2. a
3. c
4. b
5. c

Questions

1. What command we can use to check if Go is installed properly?
2. What does IDE stand for?
3. Whit which guarantees Go standard library go comes?
4. Differences between the standard library and third-party libraries?
5. What packages are a basis for the development of web applications?

Key terms

- **Visual Studio Code**: Integrated development environment that can be used for the creation of Go applications.
- **Standard library**: Set of core packages that extends language.
- **Third-party libraries**: Packages developed, maintained, and released by an entity other than the original vendor.

CHAPTER 5

Design of Web Application

Introduction

In this chapter, we will introduce the concept of the **software development life cycle** (**SDLC**) and learn basic concepts of application design. We will learn how to separate and organize our code solutions. First, we will mention a couple of common application design patterns, and provide basic details for each of them. After that, we will take a deep dive into the layered design pattern and see the responsibilities of each individual layer. At the end of the chapter, we will plan and design our web server application.

Structure

In this chapter, we will discuss the following topics:

- Software development life cycle (SDLC)
- General approaches for application design
  - Micro-kernel (plug-in) design pattern
  - Command and Query Responsibility Segregation (CQRS) design pattern
  - Combine (hybrid) design pattern
- Layered design pattern
  - Controller (handler) layer: Handling HTTP requests
  - Service (core) layer: Business logic
  - Repository (data) layer: Queries and database operations

- Database layer
- Planning phase
  - Defining business requirements
  - Defining use cases
- Design phase
  - High-level system design
  - API design
  - Database design

Software development life cycle (SDLC)

The software development life cycle is often defined as a framework that defines tasks performed at each phase in the software development process. Usually, five phases are present as a part of SDLC (*Figure 5.1*):

- Planning
- Design
- Development
- Testing
- Maintenance

Figure 5.1*: Software development life cycle (SDLC) phases*

The phases are defined as follows:

- During the **planning phase**, all business requirements should be defined. Idea is to define what service our software solution should provide to future users. Based on those requirements, the main use cases should be defined. The final solution must properly execute all defined use cases in order to be released and used.

  In the planning phase, an overall draft plan on how and for how long the software solution should be completed can be created. Also, all potential risks should be identified during planning, in order to avoid future problems and delays in the release of the finished product.

- The end product of the **design phase** should be a high-level plan for the software solution. This plan can include:

  - Database design that will be used, with defined tables and relations.
  - Security processes and protocols (who and how can access certain data).
  - The technology stack that will be used during the development phase (programming languages, databases, and so on).
  - API design and potential integration with other software solutions.
  - Components that make up the solution.
  - Algorithm and architecture design (if needed).
- The high-level plan created during the design phase should be used during the **development phase** for solution development. The created solution must fulfill business requests defined during the planning phase.
- In the **testing phase**, developed software will be tested against use cases defined in the planning phases. In order for a software solution to get the *green light* for public release, all tests must *pass*. If some of the tests *fail*, the software must be fixed and tested again.
- When all previous phases are successfully completed, a software solution can be released and final phase **maintenance** can start. During this phase released solution is monitored to check if everything is working properly. If some users report any irregularity or problem, this should be investigated and fixed if the problem is related to the released solution. This phase is *active* until the software is alive.

We can include new features in the released software solution. It should also pass all phases of the software development life cycle.

The modern application development process is not straightforward as described here. All phases are still present, but they are often intertwined, with a link back to the previous phase. This approach is known as **agile methodology**.

To make things as clear as possible, in this and the following chapters, we will follow the process described in this section and pass through the complete software development process.

General approaches for application design

By general definition, design can be defined as a plan or specification for the construction of a certain object. In our case, the object is our web server application. Good software design should include most aspects listed in the previous section (database design, technology stack, and so on).

It is a good practice to spend more time on the actual design and try to cover most of the know issues. Starting development with a *bad design* can cause a lot of problems and delays in the release of the application. Rejection of a design, when development is already started demands the redesign of a solution and throwing away everything that has already been done.

There is another approach to this problem. We can release the application in its current state and redesign it on the fly. But here we must sacrifice time that can be used for the development of new features because time must be spent on redesign and code refactoring.

In development, we often solve similar problems. Some common *blueprints* are designed and can be used for specific problems. These *reusable* designs are known as **design patterns**.

The following design patterns are some of the most popular:

- Layered design pattern
- Micro-kernel (plug-in) design pattern
- Command and Query Responsibility Segregation (CQRS) design pattern
- Combine (hybrid) design pattern

The layered design pattern will be covered in detail in a separate section because we will use it to design and develop our web server application. Other patterns will be covered in this section with a smaller amount of detail.

For each of them, we will see basic ideas, examples of usage, and some advantages, and disadvantages.

Micro-kernel (plug-in) design pattern

In this design pattern we have two components (*Figure 5.2*):

- Micro-kernel (the core set of responsibilities)
- Plug-ins (interchangeable parts)

Micro-kernel is the entry point for the application and provides general flow. Plug-in will perform a specific task. The interesting part is that the micro-kernel does not know the role of the individual plug-in, but each plug-in must follow the API design defined by the *micro-kernel*. In other words, the plug-in must be compatible with the micro-kernel, in order to be able to connect with it:

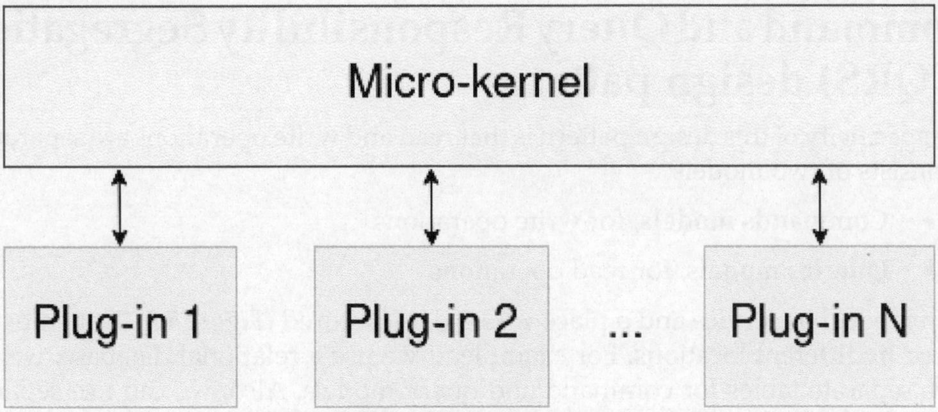

***Figure 5.2**: Micro-kernel (plug-in) design pattern*

A good example where this design pattern can be applied is a **simple task scheduler**. Micro-kernel will provide scheduling logic, while plug-ins will provides specific tasks. The scheduler does not need to know details about individual tasks, it just needs to schedule them.

This approach has a lot of *advantages*. One of the main ones is that new plug-ins can be added to the running application without any visible interruptions. This design pattern offers *high flexibility* and *extensibility*, all kinds of plug-ins can be added as long as they follow API specifications declared by the micro-kernel.

Micro-kernel and all individual plug-ins can be developed by separate teams (which do not have to be in the same physical locations). This can significantly speed up application development because the development of individual components can be parallelized.

Obviously, this approach has a lot of *disadvantages*. Predefined micro-kernel API may be appropriate at the time of initial application design, but may not be optimal for future plug-ins. Also, sometimes can be hard to separate what should be the responsibility of the micro-kernel and what should be the responsibility of plug-ins.

Whenever we have multiple components that provide certain functionality, integration test (where multiple components are tested as a group) can be complicated. Here can have a huge variety of different plug-ins, so multiple testing scenarios must be covered.

Micro-kernel design pattern is ideal for applications that process data from different sources, where the individual plug-in can handle one source. As we have already mentioned task scheduling applications are perfect to utilize this approach.

Command and Query Responsibility Segregation (CQRS) design pattern

The specificity of this design pattern is that read and write operations are separated. It consists of two models:

- **Commands models**, for write operations
- **Queries models**, for read operations

Each model has service and a place where data is stored (*Figure 5.3*). Data must be stored in different locations. For example, if we use a relational database, we can have separate tables for command and query models. Also, we can use separate databases for each model:

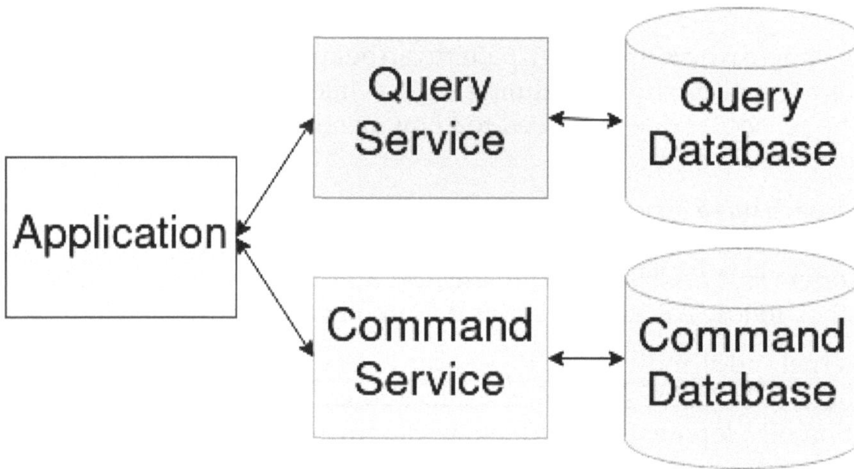

Figure 5.3*: Command and Query Responsibility Segregation (CQRS) design pattern*

As we can see in *Figure 5.3*, besides two models we have an additional component, a component called **Application**. Application is the entry point for our solution and will be called the proper model, based on the desired operation.

For a write operation, the following flow will be executed:

1. The application will send a command to command service.
2. The command service will receive data from the command database (table).
3. The command service will execute an action on received data.
4. Data will be stored in the command database (table).
5. The command service will send a notification to the query service.
6. The query service will update data in the query database (table).

Flow for a read operation is simpler:

1. The application will send a query to the query service.
2. The query service will receive data from the query database (table).

The biggest *advantage* of this approach is that we can use different data organizations in command and query databases. This will help us to avoid complex database queries for read operations. Also, *segregation* allows us to use the command model for business logic and the query model can be adjusted for specific scenarios.

The main *disadvantage* of this design pattern is synchronization between command and query databases. Without *synchronization,* the query database will have non-up-to-date data, so invalid information will be served to users. With different data organizations, synchronization can be too complex.

CQRS design pattern is ideal for applications with a high amount of reads. If we simplify the query model as much as possible, *read operations* will be quick and efficient. This can be crucial for better performance.

Combine (hybrid) design pattern

We can combine multiple design patterns in order to find the design that best suits our needs. This pattern is often referred to as a **combine** or **hybrid** design pattern. There are no strict rules about which patterns we can combine.

General idea is to combine patterns in order to use all advantages of a specific pattern. Also, a combination of patterns can cancel some disadvantages of individual patterns.

Feel free to combine and experiment with different patterns and combinations. Even if the initial solution is not perfect, do not be disappointed, just redesign the solution with knowledge collected from imperfect design in mind.

Layered design pattern

In this design, pattern code is split into layers (*Figure 5.4*) where each layer has a certain responsibility. This is one of the most popular design patterns and most developers are familiar with it.

One of the layers is an entry point for the application. General idea is that the higher layer will call the lower layer. The lower layer will perform a task related to layer responsibility and call the layer below it or return the result to the higher layer. In the ideal case (*happy path*), data will flow from the highest to the lowest layer and back:

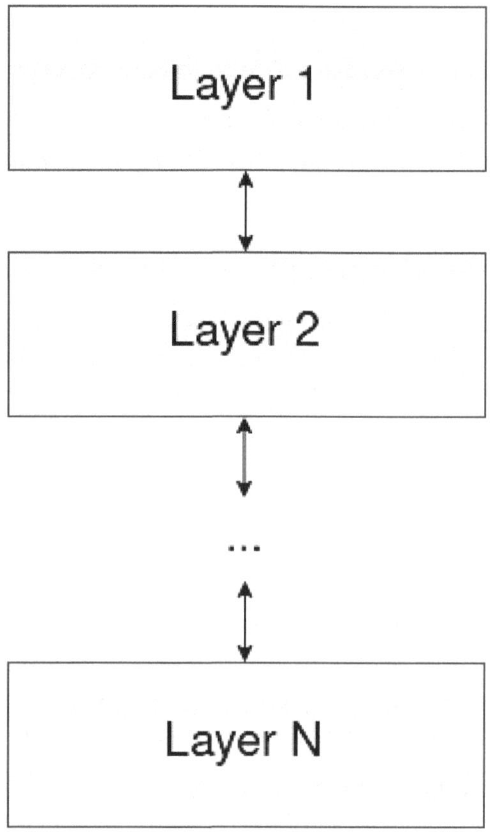

Figure 5.4: Layered design pattern

There is no predefined number of layers, we can have as many layers as we need. But there are some layers that are more common than others. Usually, one layered application has the following layers (*Figure 5.5*):

- Controller (handler) layer
- Service (core) layer
- Repository (data) layer
- Database layer

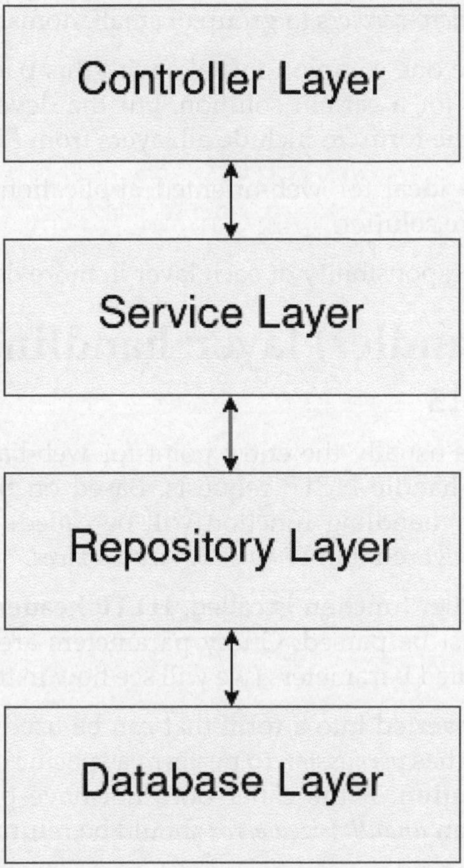

Figure 5.5: Most common layers

Layer names, *controller*, *service*, and *repository* are taken from **Spring** terminology, where these annotations are used to configure the behavior and role of a certain class. Handler, core, and data is the more common and neutral naming convention.

This approach has a lot of *advantages*. As was mentioned before, most developers are familiar with this pattern and know how to utilize it. This design pattern also provides a logical and easy way to organize code (we will see this in the following chapters).

Application designed with layered patterns is *easy to test*. Each layer can be tested separately (unit tests) and we can test all layers together (integration tests). We will talk more about testing in a dedicated chapter.

Like the other patterns, layered pattern also has some *disadvantages*. Because it is easy to separate code per layer, multiple domains can be placed inside a single application. This can drag development more toward *monolith* (single-tiered) applications. Monolith can be hard to maintain and support, so modern applications are more oriented to *micro-services* (a group of small, domain-separated services).

Developers often make one common mistake with this pattern. Sometimes some layer is not necessary for a certain solution, but the developer will write them anyway, just to fulfill the form (to include all layers from *Figure 5.5*).

This design pattern is ideal for web-oriented applications, so we will use this pattern for our software solution.

Now, we will see the responsibility of each layer in more detail.

Controller (handler) layer: handling HTTP requests

The **controller layer** is usually the entry point for web-based applications. This layer will accept and handle HTTP requests. Based on the HTTP method and request path, a proper handling function will be called. This process is called **routing** and we have covered it in *Chapter 3, Web Services*.

When the proper handler function is called, **HTTP headers**, **requests body**, and **query parameters** must be parsed. Query parameters are part of the URL that assigns values to specified parameters (we will see how in the following chapters).

Now when data is converted into a form that can be used in our code, it should be checked if the caller has *permission* to perform a specific operation. This process is known as **authorization**. If the caller does not have proper permissions for requested operations, an *unauthorized error* should be returned.

Here is a simple *authorization* example. We have a system with two types of user admin and regular user. Both types can read data, regular user can only update his/her data and admin can perform all operations. If a regular user tries to delete data, the request will be rejected with an unauthorized error. But if the admin tries to execute the same operation, it will be executed successfully.

If data is successfully parsed and authorization has passed, the service layer will be called.

Service (core) layer: business logic

Business logic can be defined as the implementation of real-world logic, which will determine how data will be created and changed. The **service layer** will handle it. Let us assume that we have an application that records the results of football matches and updates the league table based on results. In real life, the winner of the football match will receive three points, so the implementation of our application's service layer will get the current points of the winning team and increase it by three.

Before business logic is applied, received data should be validated. **Validation** can be defined as a process that will check if data satisfies the defined format. If the received data is invalid, the service layer must return the *validation error* to the *controller layer*. Validation can be considered a part of business logic, but due to its importance, it is often highlighted separately.

Here are some examples of invalid data:

- The numerical value that represents age as a negative value.
- The numerical value that represents months in a year as *greater than 12* or *less than 1*.
- The string value that represents the name of a person is empty.
- The length of the string value that represents three letter country code is *not equal to 3*.
- The string value that represents the email address is not in `prefix@domain` format or contains illegal characters.
- The value that represents the date of birth contains a date that is in the future.

If the received data is valid, business logic will be applied and data will be forwarded to the repository layer.

Repository (data) layer: queries and database operations

From the coding side, the **repository layer** is the simplest one. In this layer, queries that will be executed in the database layer are prepared. There is no additional work that should be done. Depending on the database technology, query preparation can differ, but the basic task is still the same.

When a query is ready, it will be forwarded to the database layer, where it will be executed. The repository layer will get data, or handle an error, depending on the result of the query execution.

Database layer

The **database layer** consists of the underlying technology (**SQL Server, MongoDB, DynamoDB**). This layer will execute queries received from the repository layer and returns a result or error.

Although we have executed every necessary validation, errors can occur. If our database is used to store system users, where each user has a unique integer identifier, we can try to delete a user with a specific identifier. Value **5** is a valid integer value, so it will pass validation in the service layer, but if there is no user with identifier **5**, the *error* will be returned.

Since this layer does not include any implementation, it is often excluded from the list of web application layers. Since we can consider it an integral part of the software solution, it will be included as one of the layers.

Planning phase

We are finally ready to start work on our web server application. As we previously mentioned, the first phase in the software development life cycle is the planning phase.

We will divide this phase into three sub-tasks:

- Defining business requirements
- Defining use cases
- Identification of potential risks

Since our application will not be too *complex*, and there are no deadlines for when the product should be developed, we can assume that there are no risks. The risks will be further reduced because there will be no communication or any job sharing between multiple teams of people.

With this assumption, the third sub-task is completed, so we can concentrate on others.

Defining business requirements

When a company, team, or individual has an idea for some software solution, a couple of things should be performed. Similarly, existing solutions should be analyzed in order to find out what our solution can additionally bring to users. Also, we should analyze, and listen to the requests, and wishes of potential future users. These *small* features and improvements which will distinguish our solution can push us to the top of the market.

The web server application that will be developed in this book is only used as an example, so performed analysis will be *fictional*.

The starting idea is an application for marathon runners. After analysis, the following business requirements are set:

- For each runner, the following information can be stored: *first name*, *last name*, *age*, and *nationality*. Age is *optional*, so we do not have to store them for each runner.
- For each runner, *personal best* and *season best* result will be saved, when they are set.

- For each result, the following information can be stored: *the runner who set the result, the time (race result), the location where the result is set,* and (optionally) *the runner's position in the race.*
- When the new result added is better than the personal best result, the new personal best result must be set. Similarly, if the added result is better than the season-best result, the new season's best result must be set.
- The runner can end his career (retire).
- The result can be canceled, as a result of doping, disqualification or any other penalty.
- The *top 10 active runners* in the *selected country* can be acquired.
- The *top 10 active runners* in the *selected season* can be acquired.

Now that we know how our application should work, we can move to the last sub-task and define use cases.

Defining use cases

Now that we know our business requirements, we can define some use cases. The following use cases can be created based on business requirements:

- Get the list of all runners
- Get a single runner with all results
- Get the top 10 runners for the selected country
- Get the top 10 runners for the selected season (year)
- Create a new runner
- Update existing runner
- Add (create) a new result
- Remove (delete) existing results
- Retire (delete) runner

With these use cases, we can create tests during the *testing phase* and run our solution against them. When all tests pass, our product is *ready for release.*

Now when business requirements and use cases are defined, all sub-tasks of the planning phase are completed. We can start the *design phase.*

Design phase

As we did for the *planning phase*, we will also divide the *design phase* into sub-tasks. We can define the following sub-tasks:

- High-level system design
- Defining technology stack
- Defining security procedures and protocols
- API design
- Database design

High-level system design is always the first step in the design phase. But because we already know what technologies we will use for development, we will complete that sub-task first.

Obviously, Go will be our programming language of choice. Since we mentioned the term *stored* multiple times in business requirements, we can conclude that we need some sort of database. For our first solution, **PostgreSQL** relational database will be used, but we will experiment with different types of databases in a separate chapter.

Security will also be covered in a separate chapter and will be introduced as a new feature. So, for now, we can skip this sub-task and create a *free* application where all operations are available to all users.

High-level system design

Our system will be quite simple, so we can (for now) put everything inside a single module. We can call that module a web service. We already said that a layered pattern is ideal for web-oriented applications. So, our code will be organized based on it.

Clients will call web service through web API, which will follow REST guidelines. HTTP protocol will be used for *client-server communication*.

Data will be stored in the dedicated database to which our web service will be connected. High-level system design can be seen in *Figure 5.6*:

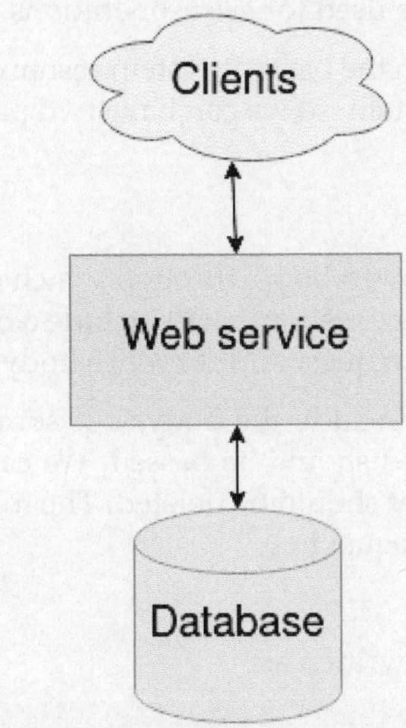

***Figure 5.6**: High-level system design*

With complete design, one of the most important tasks from the *design phase* is done. This is the actual point where the technology stack should be defined because we will be familiar with all the necessary information that can help us to choose the best-fitted technology. But we already explained our reasons to switch the order of sub-task executions.

API design

The first step in designing of API is to distinguish operations that can be performed from business requirements. Our web server will have the following:

- Four get operations (*get all runners, get single runners, get the top 10 runners from the selected country*, and *get the top 10 runners from the selected year*)
- Two create operations (*create runner* and *create result*)
- One update operation (*update runner*)
- Two delete operations (*delete runner* and *delete result*)

Now we can map HTTP methods to specific operations. The following mapping is most common:

- `GET` method will be used for *get* operations.
- `POST` method will be used for *create* operations.
- `PUT` method will be used for *update* operations.

- **DELETE** method will be used for *delete* operations.

The path is usually defined on the basis of system resources. Runner and result are the main resources of our system, so we can have two paths:

- `/runner`
- `/result`

POST and **PUT** requests will have a body, through which client data will be passed to the server. Vice versa, service response will include a body that will pass data to the client. Data passed in the request and response body will be in JSON format.

DELETE methods should not include the body, but somehow information about which resource will be deleted should be passed. We can include the resource id in path, so we can decide what should be deleted. The following path will be used to delete a **runner** with an id equal to **5**:

```
/runner/5
```

In API documentation this is written as:

```
/runner/{id}
```

For **GET** operations we can define four following paths:

```
/runner/all
/runner/{id}
/runner/top-ten-country
/runner/top-ten-year
```

But *this is not good practice!* Descriptions in the path are hard to understand and maintain. API path should be as simple as possible, but still readable and easy to understand. From our examples, only the second one follows the best API design practices.

So, we can use the second path to get a single runner, and the *plain* path to get all runners (**/runner**), but *what about the third and fourth get operations?* And *how to pass country and year parameters, when the GET method does not contain a body?*

We can use query parameters, one for the **country** and one for the **year**. Query parameters are presented in a *key-value format* and usually are placed after **?** (*question mark*). Character **&** (*ampersand*) is usually used to separate parameters.

So, the following path will solve our problems:

```
/runner?country=value&year=value
```

Proper operation will be performed based on path and combination of parameters.

Database design

Although we will have a chapter dedicated to databases, we must explain some basic concepts in order for us to understand how the database is designed. These concepts refer to relational databases:

- **Table**: Collection of related data held in table format. Each table has columns and rows. Columns define structures of data items that will be stored, while each row holds a single data item.
- **Primary key**: Column or a set of columns that uniquely specify a data item in a database table.
- **Foreign key**: Column or a set of columns that refers to the primary key of another database table.

We already identified two resources in our system, so for each of them, a separate table will be assigned (*Figure 5.7*):

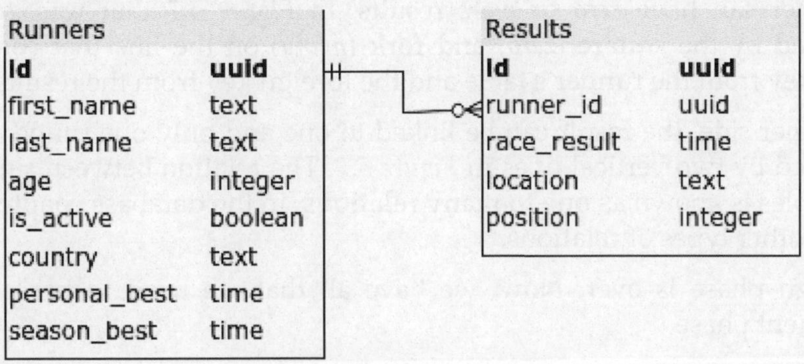

Figure 5.7: Database design

Based on business requirements, the runner table will contain the following columns:

- **id**: Unique identification for the runner. This column will serve as a primary key. Primary keys are usually bold in database design diagrams.
- **first_name**: First name of a runner.
- **last_name**: Last name of a runner.
- **age**: Age of a runner.
- **is_active**: A flag that indicates if the runner is still active. When the runner retires, the flag value will be set to *false*.
- **country**: The country that the runner represents.
- **personal_best**: Personal best carrier result of a runner.

- **season_best**: The best result of a runner in the current season.

The result table will have the following columns:

- **id**: The unique identifier of a result and the primary key for the result table.
- **runner_id**: Identifier of a runner who sets the result. This column will serve as a foreign key and will reference the primary key from the runner's table. In design diagrams, a line is used to connect keys, and mark relations between tables.
- **race_result**: Time set in the race.
- **location**: A place where the result is set.
- **position**: Runner's position in the race.
- **year**: Year when race result is set.

One runner can have *zero* or *more* results. In *Figure 5.7* that was graphically represented by the **square** (*zero*) and **fork** (*many*) on the line that connects the primary key from the runner's table and the foreign key from the results table.

On the other side, the result can be linked to one and only one runner, which is represented by two vertical lines in *Figure 5.7*. The relation between runners and results tables is known as **one to many relations**. In the database chapter, we will see some other types of relations.

The design phase is over. Now, we have all that we need to proceed to the development phase.

Conclusion

In this chapter, we learned how to design our applications. Our focus was mostly on web application design, but we covered some concepts that can be used in other types of applications. The most common and best-suited design pattern for web-based server applications is the *layered design pattern*, so we will use it as a base for our solution.

With the knowledge that we collected so far and with the high-level design prepared in this chapter, we are finally ready for development. In the following chapters, we will see how to develop layers of our application. Without further ado, *let's start coding!!!*

Points to remember

- All business requirements should be defined during the planning phase of the software development life cycle.

- It is a good practice to spend more time in the design phase. *Bad design* can cause a lot of problems in the future.
- Combining and experimenting with different design patterns and combinations can lead us to good and reliable solutions.
- A layered design pattern is ideal for web-oriented applications.
- High-level system design should be the first step in the design phase.

Multiple choice questions

1. Which is not a phase of the software development life cycle?
    a. Deploy
    b. Design
    c. Development
    d. Planning
2. How many phases are there in the software development life cycle?
    a. 6
    b. 7
    c. 4
    d. 5
3. How many layers the layered design pattern can have?
    a. Less than 4
    b. There is no predefined number of layers
    c. No more than 4
    d. 4
4. What layer is not one of the four common ones?
    a. Controller layer
    b. Repository layer
    c. Web layer
    d. Service layer
5. Which layer will perform data validation?
    a. Controller layer
    b. Repository layer

   c. Database layer
   d. Service layer
6. Which sub-tack cannot be performed in the planning phase?
   a. Defining technology stack
   b. Defining business requirements
   c. Defining use cases
   d. Identification of potential risks
7. Which sub-tack cannot be performed in the design phase?
   a. API design
   b. Defining business requirements
   c. High-level system design
   d. Defining security procedures and protocols

Answers

1. a
2. d
3. b
4. c
5. d
6. a
7. b

Questions

1. In which phase of the software development life cycle technology stack should be defined?
2. What are the roles of micro-kernel and plug-in in micro-kernel design patterns?
3. Which models are part of the CQRS design pattern?
4. How many design patterns can be combined in a combined (hybrid) design pattern? Are there any rules on which patterns can be combined?
5. Which layer will perform authorization?

Key terms

- **Software Development Life Cycle (SDLC)**: Framework that defines tasks performed at each phase in the software development process.
- **Design patterns**: Designs that can be used to design solutions for similar problems.
- **Micro-kernel (plug-in) design pattern**: Design pattern with two components micro-kernel (the core set of responsibilities) and plug-ins (interchangeable parts).
- **Command and Query Responsibility Segregation (CQRS) design pattern**: Design pattern where read and write operations are separated.
- **Combine (hybrid) design pattern**: Combination of multiple design patterns.
- **Layered design pattern**: Design pattern where code is split into layers.
- **Business logic**: Implementation of real-world logic.
- **Validation**: Process that will check if data satisfied the defined format.
- **Authorization**: Process that will check if the caller has permission to perform a specific operation.

CHAPTER 6

Application Layers

Introduction

In this chapter, we will start the development of our web server application. First, we will see how code can be organized, and after that, we will start with our `main()` function. Later, we will learn more about configuration and how web servers should be initialized. At the end of the chapter, we will develop application layers (controller and service). Implementation of the repository layer is loosely based on the database layer and selected technology, so it will be developed in the next chapter where we will talk about databases.

Structure

In this chapter, we will discuss the following topics:

- Code organization
- Models
- Main function
- Configuration
- HTTP server
    - Initialization
    - Start
- Development of controller layer
    - Runners controller
    - Result controller

- Development of service layer
    - Runners service
    - Result service

Code organization

We learned in *Chapter 4, Setting up a Project With Go Programming Language*, how to set up a Go programming language project and create modules, so we will skip these steps here. As we mentioned before, the Go application consists of packages, so the code for each package will be placed into a dedicated directory (*Figure 6.1*):

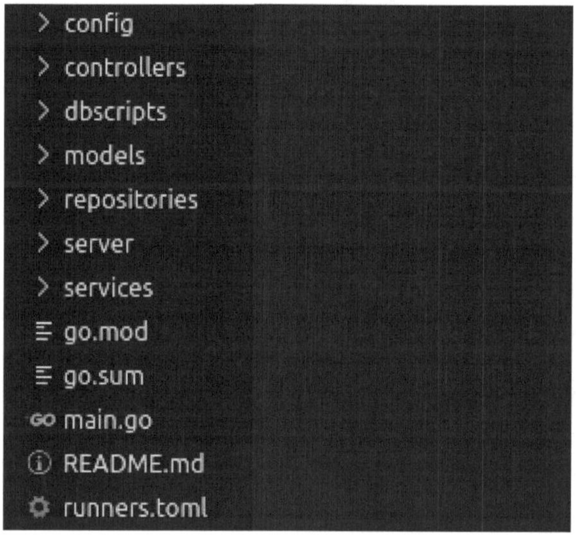

***Figure 6.1**: Code organization*

Our project will have the following packages:

- **`config`** package where functions for initialization and reading of configuration are placed.
- **`controllers`** package that contains the implementation of the controller layer.
- **`models`** package that contains **`structs`** that will be used in all layers (representation of runner or result).
- **`repositories`** package that contains the implementation of the repositories layer.
- **`server`** package that contains the initialization of HTTP and database servers.

- **service** package that contains the implementation of the service layer.

Directory **dbscripts** will not contain any code, only database scripts that will be used for the creation of tables, and potentially for data initialization. We will talk more about this in the next chapter.

Besides directories, in *Figure 6.1*, we can see five files. We explained the **go.mod** and **go.sum** files in *Chapter 4, Setting up a Project With Go Programming Language*, so we will concentrate on the other files:

- File **main.go** is the main file of our application, where the **main()** function is located.
- File **README.md** should contain instructions on how to run the application, and what should be installed for the application to work properly.
- File **runners.toml** contains application configuration, we will talk about it in the following sections.

You are free to organize your code differently, this is just an example. The only important thing is that, when we select our code organization pattern, we always stick to it.

Models

Package models will have three **structs**, one for the runner, one for the result, and one for custom errors (*Figure 6.2*):

***Figure 6.2**: Models package*

We can also put all **models** into a singular file, but it can be clearer if we separate them. It is a good practice to map all database columns to models that represents that entity. All files from *Figure 6.2*, must have this as a first line:

```
package models
```

It is also a good practice to separate models that usually represent database entities, from **Data Transfer Objects** (**DTOs**) that represent the body of the request. In our cases these will be identical, so to keep things as simple as possible we will only use models.

The following **struct** will be used to describe the runner:

```
type Runner struct {
	ID           string    `json:"id"`
	FirstName    string    `json:"first_name"`
	LastName     string    `json:"last_name"`
	Age          int       `json:"age,omitempty"`
	IsActive     bool      `json:"is_active"`
	Country      string    `json:"country"`
	PersonalBest string    `json:"personal_best,omitempty"`
	SeasonBest   string    `json:"season_best,omitempty"`
	Results      []*Result `json:"results,omitempty"`
}
```

Since the get single runner operation will return all runner's results in addition to standard data, we can include it in the model. Constructs **`json:"results,omitempty"`** are called **struct** tags. We will use them to control how JSON will be encoded to the **struct** and decoded from it. So, when we receive a JSON object that contains a field with the name **first_name**, that field will be mapped to the **FirstName** field of the **struct**, and vice versa.

Empty fields can be omitted, we usually use this for non-required fields in HTTP requests. In order to do this, we should add **omitempty** to the **struct** tag for a specific field (*age, personal best, season best,* and *results* in our case). We should be very careful with omitting because types with default values will be also considered *empty*.

Similarly, to the **Runner** model, we can define the **Result**:

```
type Result struct {
	ID         string `json:"id"`
	RunnerID   string `json:"runner_id"`
	RaceResult string `json:"race_result"`
	Location   string `json:"location"`
	Position   int    `json:"position,omitempty"`
	Year       int    `json:"year"`
}
```

The third model will be used for custom errors. Each error will have a message, and appropriate HTTP status. Controller layer will handle custom errors from lower layers and send a proper response to clients (we will soon see this in more detail).

Since HTTP status from custom error will be set as response status, there is no need to send it through the response body, so we can instruct the JSON decoder to ignore that field with the **`json:"-"` struct** tag.

The following **struct**, named **ResponseError**, will be used for custom errors:

```
type ResponseError struct {
        Message string `json:"message"`
        Status  int    `json:"-"`
}
```

Models can be defined later in development because, usually, we will not know which **struct** we will need at the start. But our application is not too complex, so we can define them now.

Main function

The **main()** function is the entry point for any Go application. It should be written as simply as possible. In the ideal case, the **main()** function should contain only calls to initialization functions/methods and the call of the function/method that starts the application. Additionally, logs can be added to make it easier to follow startup stages.

Here is the content of the **main.go** file, with a **main()** function that follows these guidelines:

```
package main

import (
        "log"
        "runners-postgresql/config"
        "runners-postgresql/server"

        _ "github.com/lib/pq"
)

func main() {
        log.Println("Starting Runners App")

        log.Println("Initializing configuration")
        config := config.InitConfig("runners")
```

```
        log.Println("Initializing database")
        dbHandler := server.InitDatabase(config)

        log.Println("Initializing HTTP server")
        httpServer := server.InitHttpServer(config, dbHandler)

        httpServer.Start()
}
```

This `main()` function has calls to three initialization functions and call to method `Start()` that will start the HTTP server which will listen for HTTP requests, and handle them. The following initialization functions will be called.

1. Function `InitConfig()` from `config` package will initialize the configuration. We will see details for this function in the next section.
2. Function `InitDatabase()` from the `server` package will initialize the database connection and provide `dbHandler`, which will be used in the repository layer for the execution of queries. We will see the implementation of this function in the next chapter when we talk about databases.
3. Function `InitHttpServer()` from the `server` package, will initialize all application layers and the HTTP server. This server will be started at the end of the `main()` function. Details and implementation will be provided in the following sections.

Now when our `main()` function is ready, we can handle application configuration.

Configuration

Before we see the implementation of configuration initialization, we will discuss a couple of potential solutions to how this problem can be solved. The following solutions are the most common:

- **Hard-coded configuration**: The whole configuration is set inside the code. Configuration is usually implemented as a group of constants and used in code when needed. This solution is the easiest, but it is not flexible. When the configuration must be changed, a new application version must be built and deployed. This is especially complicated if the change is *temporary*.
- **Configuration file**: The whole configuration is saved in a file. Application on start-up will read the file and set configuration parameters. Configuration change is quite simple, just update the file, and restart the

application. Potential problem is that application is down during restart. Some configuration solutions can have the option to monitor files and automatically read new configurations when the file is changed.

- **Configuration database or table**: Configuration is stored in a dedicated database or database table. The application will read the configuration on demand, so the update will take almost immediate effect. But there are some changes of configuration parameters that cannot take effect that fast. For example, database configuration is read on application start and never again. If we change the database and decide to use another one, we must change the configuration, but the application will still use the old database. In that case, a restart is *inevitable*.
- **Configuration service**: Similar solution as previous, but here special service will handle configuration for all services in the system.
- **Configuration from environment variables**: Configuration is stored within the environment variables of the system on which the application is running.

The last three solutions can be improved with some jobs that will read the configuration in a certain time interval (for example, every half hour). This way application will have an *up-to-date configuration*. But there would still be situations when a restart is necessary.

We will use the second approach, *configuration file*, for our solution, because it is easy to implement, and there is no need to strive for some complicated solutions for an application that is not overly complex.

For configuration handling, we will use **Viper**. It is a complete configuration solution for Go applications that can read configuration from different sources (configuration files, environment variables, command line, and so on) and convert them to *key-value pairs*.

Viper must be installed with the following command:

```
go get github.com/spf13/viper
```

Everything configuration related is stored in the `config` package (*Figure 6.3*):

Figure 6.3: Configuration package

The file `config.go` has only one function `InitConfig()`, which we call from `main()` function. This function receives one argument, the *name of the configuration file*. What is interesting is that it is not necessary to send the file extension, Viper will handle it by itself. Here is the complete content of the file:

```
package config

import (
	"log"

	"github.com/spf13/viper"
)

func InitConfig(fileName string) *viper.Viper {
	config := viper.New()

	config.SetConfigName(fileName)

	config.AddConfigPath(".")
	config.AddConfigPath("$HOME")

	err := config.ReadInConfig()
	if err != nil {
		log.Fatal("Error while parsing configuration file", err)
	}

	return config
}
```

At the start of the function, we will create a new configuration and assign a file name to it. After that, we will assign paths to the configuration file. In our case, Viper will try to find the configuration file in two locations, the current path where the execution file of the application is located (`.`) and the home directory of the hosting system **(`$HOME`)**.

When all parameters are set, we can try to read the file and place the configuration inside the **`config`** variable. If an error occurs during this operation, the **`Fatal()`** function from the **`log`** package will be executed. This function will log messages and terminate the execution of the application. It is logical to abort the execution of the application if the configuration is not valid because it will not work properly.

Viper supports multiple file formats, like **JSON**, **TOML**, **YAML**, and so on. We will use JSON for HTTP request and response bodies, and YAML for some deployment configuration files in the following chapters, so in order to be diverse, we will use TOML for the configuration file.

TOML is easy to read and write file format created especially for configuration files. Here, is the content of **runners.toml** configuration file from *Figure 6.1*:

```
########################################################################
# Database configuration

# Connection string is in Go pq driver format:
# host=<host> port=<port> user=<databaseUser>
# password=<databaseUserPassword> dbname=<databaseName>

[database]

connection_string = "host=localhost port=5432 user=postgres
password=postgres dbname=runners_db sslmode=disable"
max_idle_connections = 5
max_open_connections = 20
connection_max_lifetime = "60s"
driver_name = "postgres"
########################################################################
# HTTP server configuration

[http]

server_address = ":8080"
########################################################################
```

We will see the usage of these configurations in the next section of this chapter (HTTP server) and in *Chapter 6, Relational databases and repository layer*. Here is an example of how Viper will convert this file into *key-value pairs*, **http.server_address** will become key while **:8080** will become value.

HTTP server

The **server** package will contain two files, one will contain *HTTP server-related content*, other will contain *database server-related content* (*Figure 6.4*). We will study database servers in the next chapter, so for now we will concentrate only on the HTTP server:

***Figure 6.4**: Server package*

The HTTP server will represent the *heart* of our application. File **httpServer.go** will have the following elements:

- The **struct** that represents the HTTP server
- The initialization function **InitHttpServer()** that we call from **main()** function
- The method **Start()** that will start the HTTP server (called at the end of **main()** function)

Now we will examine the content of **httpServer.go** file. Function and method body will be omitted, for simpler display, and detailed in the next two sections:

```
package server

import (
	“database/sql”
	“log”
	“runners-postgresql/controllers”
	“runners-postgresql/repositories”
	“runners-postgresql/services”

	“github.com/gin-gonic/gin”
	“github.com/spf13/viper”
)

type HttpServer struct {
	config            *viper.Viper
	router             *gin.Engine
	runnersController *controllers.RunnersController
	resultsController *controllers.ResultsController
}
```

```
func InitHttpServer(config *viper.Viper,
        dbHandler *sql.DB) HttpServer {
        ...
}

func (hs HttpServer) Start() {
        ...
}
```

First, we will explain the **struct** that represents the HTTP server. It will contain configuration, a router that will accept requests, and pass them to the proper controller, and two controllers that forms the controller layer (one for runners and one for results).

For the router solution, we will use **gin**, an HTTP web framework written in Go. It is up to *40 times faster* than similar solutions and becomes very popular lately. The following command will install **gin**:

```
go get github.com/gin-gonic/gin
```

Now we can see how our HTTP server can be initialized.

Initialization

Before we see the concrete implementation of initialization functions, we should explain some design ideas. As we already saw, for each system resource (**runner** and **result**) we will have a dedicated controller. We will follow the same approach for the *server* and *repository* layer.

All controllers, services, and repositories will be represented with a **struct** that contains representations from lower layers. For example, controller representation will contain service representation, service representation will contain repository representation, and so on.

The **InitHttpServer()** function will receive two arguments, **configuration** and **database** handler. The **configuration** will be used to configure the HTTP server, while the **database** handler will be used in the repository layer to execute queries. Basically, we can observe the **database** handler as a representation of the database layer:

```
func InitHttpServer(config *viper.Viper,
        dbHandler *sql.DB) HttpServer {

        runnersRepository := repositories.NewRunnersRepository(
                dbHandler)
        resultRepository := repositories.NewResultsRepository(
```

```
        dbHandler)
    runnersService := services.NewRunnersService(
        runnersRepository, resultRepository)
    resultsService := services.NewResultsService(
        resultRepository, runnersRepository)
    runnersController := controllers.NewRunnersController(
        runnersService)
    resultsController := controllers.NewResultsController(
        resultsService)

    router := gin.Default()
    router.POST("/runner", runnersController.CreateRunner)
    router.PUT("/runner", runnersController.UpdateRunner)
    router.DELETE("/runner/:id",
        runnersController.DeleteRunner)
    router.GET("/runner/:id", runnersController.GetRunner)
    router.GET("/runner", runnersController.GetRunnersBatch)
    router.POST("/result", resultsController.CreateResult)
    router.DELETE("/result/:id",
        resultsController.DeleteResult)

    return HttpServer{
        config:            config,
        router:            router,
        runnersController: runnersController,
        resultsController: resultsController,
    }
}
```

At the start of the function, we will initialize application layers, by assigning proper elements. Because each layer is dependent on the lower layer, we will initialize the lowest layer first (repository in this case, because the representation of the database layer will be passed as the function's argument) and move upwards.

The interesting thing is that both repositories are assigned to each service, we will see why in the section dedicated to the service layer. Let it remain a secret, for now.

After the initialization of application layers, we can initialize the router. Based on the API design from the previous chapter, we will set the **HTTP method**, **HTTP**

path, and **controller** that will handle HTTP requests.

At the end of the function, we will return a new **`struct`** with values set for each field.

Start

Method **`Start()`** is quite simple. It will not receive any arguments, because everything that we need is already set in the previously initialized HTTP server. By calling the **`Run()`** method from our router, our HTTP server will start listening and serving HTTP requests.

The server address read by Viper from the configuration file will be passed to the **`Run()`** method. If we know the concrete type of value, we can use a method for that type (**`GetString()`** in this case). If we are not sure which is the value type, generic method **`Get()`**, that returns **`interface{}`** can be used:

```
func (hs HttpServer) Start() {
        err := hs.router.Run(hs.config.GetString(
                "http.server_address"))
        if err != nil {
                log.Fatalf("Error while starting HTTP server: %v",
                        err)
        }
}
```

It is important to mention that the **`Run()`** method will block the calling goroutine unless an error occurs. In case of an error, a log message will be logged and the application will be terminated.

Now, we can finally start with the development of application layers. The controller layer is the first one.

Development of controller layer

The controller layer will have two controllers, one for each resource (*Figure 6.5*). The **`runners`** controller will handle HTTP requests related to the runner's operations, while the **`results`** controller will handle operations related to results operations:

***Figure 6.5:** Controller package*

Methods from controller layers should be as simple as possible. They should only read data from the request and call methods from the service layer.

We can distinguish three operations of data reading from requests:

- Un-marshaling of data from the request body
- Reading parameters from the query string
- Reading parameters from the path

We will see the usage of all three operations in the following sub-sections.

Runners controller

First, we will start with the runner's controller. The whole code related to this controller is in **runnersController.go** file (*Figure 6.5*). Again, we will exclude method bodies in the first view and show them latter:

```
package controllers

import (
	"encoding/json"
	"io"
	"log"
	"net/http"
	"runners-postgresql/models"
	"runners-postgresql/services"

	"github.com/gin-gonic/gin"
)

type RunnersController struct {
	runnersService *services.RunnersService
}

func NewRunnersController(runnersService *services.
	RunnersService) *RunnersController {

	return &RunnersController{
		runnersService: runnersService,
	}
}
```

```
func (rh RunnersController) CreateRunner(ctx *gin.Context) {
        ...
}

func (rh RunnersController) UpdateRunner(ctx *gin.Context) {
        ...
}

func (rh RunnersController) DeleteRunner(ctx *gin.Context) {
        ...
}

func (rh RunnersController) GetRunner(ctx *gin.Context) {
        ...
}

func (rh RunnersController) GetRunnersBatch(ctx *gin.Context) {
        ...
}
```

The **struct** that represents the runner's controller (**RunnersController**) has only one field, a representation of the runner's service. It will be initialized through **NewRunnersController()** function, which we called in **InitHttpServer()** function from the **server** package.

All controller methods must receive **Context** as an argument. **Context** is the most important part of gin that allows us to pass variables, manage the flow, read the request body, read request parameters, and render a response.

At the start of the **CreateRunner()** method, we will use **Context** to read the request body and use **Unmarshal()** function from the json package to convert it to **Runner** defined in the **model** package. If any error occurs we will not use **Fatalf()** as we did in previous cases because our application runs correctly, the problem is in the received request.

Here we will use **Context** to control execution flow. Method **AbortWithError()** will stop the current chain responses with the status code and push the specified error to **Context**. This action will not stop the current handler, so we must add a return statement to accomplish this.

If the request is *valid*, the method **CreateRunner()** from the service layer will be called:

```
func (rh RunnersController) CreateRunner(ctx *gin.Context) {
	body, err := io.ReadAll(ctx.Request.Body)
	if err != nil {
		log.Println(
			"Error while reading create runner request body",
			err)
		ctx.AbortWithError(http.StatusInternalServerError, err)
		return
	}

	var runner models.Runner
	err = json.Unmarshal(body, &runner)
	if err != nil {
		log.Println("Error while unmarshaling " +
			create runner request body",err)
		ctx.AbortWithError(http.StatusInternalServerError, err)
		return
	}

	response, responseErr := rh.runnersService.
		CreateRunner(&runner)
	if responseErr != nil {
		ctx.AbortWithStatusJSON(responseErr.Status,
			responseErr)
		return
	}

	ctx.JSON(http.StatusOK, response)
}
```

All errors from lower layers will be wrapped in custom errors that we defined with the **`ResponseError struct`** in the **`model`** package. If any custom error occurs, we will use **`AbortWithStatusJSON()`** method to stop the flow. This method creates an HTTP response that has a JSON body, using the value of **`Status`** from returned error to set the **`response`** status and the error itself as a response body.

If everything went well, we will use context to send a response with the status **`OK`**, and representation of a runner (received from the service layer) as a response body.

Method **`UpdateRunner()`** is almost identical to **`CreateRunner()`** method with two minor differences. Method **`UpdateRunner()`** from the service layer will be called instead of **`CreateRunner()`** and the response will not contain a body, so we can use the **`Status()`** method from **`Context`** to create a response:

```
func (rh RunnersController) UpdateRunner(ctx *gin.Context) {
        body, err := io.ReadAll(ctx.Request.Body)
        if err != nil {
                log.Println("Error while reading " +
                        "update runner request body", err)
                ctx.AbortWithError(http.StatusInternalServerError,
                        err)
                return
        }

        var runner models.Runner
        err = json.Unmarshal(body, &runner)
        if err != nil {
                log.Println("Error while unmarshaling " +
                        "update runner request body", err)
                ctx.AbortWithError(http.StatusInternalServerError,
                        err)
                return
        }

        responseErr := rh.runnersService.UpdateRunner(&runner)
        if responseErr != nil {
                ctx.AbortWithStatusJSON(responseErr.Status,
                        responseErr)
                return
        }

        ctx.Status(http.StatusNoContent)
}
```

The next method **`DeleteRunner()`** is a little bit different. Delete requests do not contain a body, so we will read the runner's ID from the path. If we take a look at the API design or at **`InitHttpServer()`** function, we can see that path related to this controller method is **`/runner/:id`**. So, if the actual path is, for example, **`/`**

runner/5, value **5** will be assigned to the **runnerId** variable:

```
func (rh RunnersController) DeleteRunner(ctx *gin.Context) {
	runnerId := ctx.Param("id")

	responseErr := rh.runnersService.DeleteRunner(runnerId)
	if responseErr != nil {
		ctx.AbortWithStatusJSON(responseErr.Status,
			responseErr)
		return
	}

	ctx.Status(http.StatusNoContent)
}
```

At the end of the method, we will handle the response from the service layer. Like in **UpdateRunner()** this HTTP response will not contain a body.

Method **GetRunner()** will also receive the ID of a runner through the path. At the end of the function, we will handle the response from the service layer and set the proper status and body:

```
func (rh RunnersController) GetRunner(ctx *gin.Context) {
	runnerId := ctx.Param("id")

	response, responseErr := rh.runnersService.
		GetRunner(runnerId)
	if responseErr != nil {
		ctx.JSON(responseErr.Status, responseErr)
		return
	}

	ctx.JSON(http.StatusOK, response)
}
```

If we again take a look at the API design, we will see that requests for getting multiple runners can have two query string parameters, **country** and **year**. At the start of the **GetRunnersBatch()** method, **gin.Context** will be used to read them:

```
func (rh RunnersController) GetRunnersBatch(ctx *gin.Context) {
	params := ctx.Request.URL.Query()
	country := params.Get("country")
```

```
        year := params.Get("year")

        response, responseErr := rh.runnersService
                .GetRunnersBatch(country, year)
        if responseErr != nil {
                ctx.JSON(responseErr.Status, responseErr)
                return
        }

        ctx.JSON(http.StatusOK, response)
}
```

Again, in the end, the response from the service layer will be properly handled.

Results controller

There will be no new implementation details in the results controller, so we will just provide the entire content of the **resultController.go** file (*Figure 6.5*), in order to display a complete solution. This controller will have two methods **CreateResult()** and **DeleteResult()**:

```
package controllers

import (
        "encoding/json"
        "io"
        "log"
        "net/http"
        "runners-postgresql/models"
        "runners-postgresql/services"

        "github.com/gin-gonic/gin"
)

type ResultsController struct {
        resultsService *services.ResultsService
}

func NewResultsController(resultsService *services.
        ResultsService) *ResultsController {
```

```
	return &ResultsController{
		resultsService: resultsService,
	}
}

func (rh ResultsController) CreateResult(ctx *gin.Context) {
	body, err := io.ReadAll(ctx.Request.Body)
	if err != nil {
		log.Println("Error while reading " +
			"create result request body", err)
		ctx.AbortWithError(http.StatusInternalServerError,
			err)
		return
	}

	var result models.Result
	err = json.Unmarshal(body, &result)
	if err != nil {
		log.Println("Error while unmarshaling " +
			"creates result request body", err)
		ctx.AbortWithError(http.StatusInternalServerError,
			err)
		return
	}

	response, responseErr := rh.resultsService.
		CreateResult(&result)
	if responseErr != nil {
		ctx.JSON(responseErr.Status, responseErr)
		return
	}

	ctx.JSON(http.StatusOK, response)
}

func (rh ResultsController) DeleteResult(ctx *gin.Context) {
	resultId := ctx.Param("id")
```

```
	responseErr := rh.resultsService.DeleteResult(resultId)
	if responseErr != nil {
		ctx.JSON(responseErr.Status, responseErr)
		return
	}

	ctx.Status(http.StatusNoContent)
}
```

Development of service layer

The service layer will have two services (*Figure 6.6*). The **`runners`** service will handle business logic related to the runner's operations, while the **`results`** service will handle business logic related to results operations:

Figure 6.6: *Service package*

At the start of each method from the service layer, data received from the controller layer will be validated, and if the data is not valid, a proper error will be returned. After that operations business logic will be applied to that data and the proper method from the repository layer will be called.

Runners service

The code for the **`runners`** service is in the **`runnersService.go`** file (*Figure 6.6*). Here is the content of that file, without method bodies:

```
package services

import (
	“net/http”
	“runners-postgresql/models”
	“runners-postgresql/repositories”
	“strconv”
	“time”
)

type RunnersService struct {
```

```
	runnersRepository *repositories.RunnersRepository
	resultsRepository *repositories.ResultsRepository
}

func NewRunnersService(
	runnersRepository *repositories.RunnersRepository,
	resultsRepository *repositories.ResultsRepository)
	*RunnersService {

	return &RunnersService{
		runnersRepository: runnersRepository,
		resultsRepository: resultsRepository,
	}
}

func (rs RunnersService) CreateRunner(
	runner *models.Runner) (*models.Runner,
	*models.ResponseError) {
	...
}

func (rs RunnersService) UpdateRunner(
	runner *models.Runner) *models.ResponseError {
	...
}

func (rs RunnersService) DeleteRunner(
	runnerId string) *models.ResponseError {
	...
}

func (rs RunnersService) GetRunner(
	runnerId string) (*models.Runner, *models.ResponseError) {
	...
}

func (rs RunnersService) GetRunnersBatch(country string,
	year string) ([]*models.Runner, *models.ResponseError) {
```

```
    ...
}

func validateRunner(
    runner *models.Runner) *models.ResponseError {
    ...
}

func validateRunnerId(runnerId string) *models.ResponseError {
    ...
}
```

Here, the **struct** that represents runners service (**RunnersService**) has two fields, representations of both repositories. We will see why we need both repositories when we discuss the implementation of the **GetRunner()** method.

The runner service is initialized through **NewRunnersService()** function, which receives two arguments, one for each repository. The initialization function is called in **InitHttpServer()** function from the **server** package.

At the start of the **CreateRunner()** method, we will validate data about the runner. If data is not valid errors will be returned, otherwise, the method from the **runners** repository will be called:

```
func (rs RunnersService) CreateRunner(
    runner *models.Runner) (*models.Runner,
    *models.ResponseError) {

    responseErr := validateRunner(runner)
    if responseErr != nil {
        return nil, responseErr
    }

    return rs.runnersRepository.CreateRunner(runner)
}
```

Validation will be performed through the private function **validateRunner()**. Usually, an empty string is an *invalid* value for string data and numerical values should be set in some logical range. In our case, we have a value that represents the age of the runner. That value must be *positive,* and greater than or equal to 16 because the minimum age for participation in *marathon race is (usually) 16.* Additionally, we will set a high bound of *125. Why 125?* The oldest person whose age is documented was *Jeanne Calment* from *France* with a lifespan of *122 years* and

164 days. So, we can set a upper bound to a slightly higher value than that:

```
func validateRunner(
	runner *models.Runner) *models.ResponseError {

	if runner.FirstName == "" {
		return &models.ResponseError{
			Message: "Invalid first name",
			Status:  http.StatusBadRequest,
		}
	}

	if runner.LastName == "" {
		return &models.ResponseError{
			Message: "Invalid last name",
			Status:  http.StatusBadRequest}
	}

	if runner.Age <= 16 || runner.Age > 125 {
		return &models.ResponseError{
			Message: "Invalid age",
			Status:  http.StatusBadRequest,
		}
	}

	if runner.Country == "" {
		return &models.ResponseError{
			Message: "Invalid country",
			Status:  http.StatusBadRequest,
		}
	}

	return nil
}
```

If some validation fails, a proper error message will be set and returned status will be *400 Bad Request*.

Why we did separate validation into a separate function? The same fields will be checked during the update operation. It is a good practice to avoid code duplication and to put that kind of code into a separate function. Such code is more *readable* and *understandable*.

In **UpdateRunner()** method, we must check the value for the runner ID. This value will be generated by the database layer during creation and that is a reason why we did not check it inside **CreateRunner()** application.

In the end, the method from the **runners** repository will be called:

```
func (rs RunnersService) UpdateRunner(
        runner *models.Runner) *models.ResponseError {

        responseErr := validateRunnerId(runner.ID)
        if responseErr != nil {
                return responseErr
        }

        responseErr = validateRunner(runner)
        if responseErr != nil {
                return responseErr
        }

        return rs.runnersRepository.UpdateRunner(runner)
}
```

Validation of runner ID is simple, if has the value of the empty string, an error will be returned:

```
func validateRunnerId(runnerId string) *models.ResponseError {
        if runnerId == "" {
                return &models.ResponseError{
                        Message: "Invalid runner ID",
                        Status:  http.StatusBadRequest,
                }
        }

        return nil
}
```

Method **DeleteRunner()** is not too complicated, validate value for runner ID and call method from the **runners** repository:

```
func (rs RunnersService) DeleteRunner(
      runnerId string) *models.ResponseError {

      responseErr := validateRunnerId(runnerId)
      if responseErr != nil {
            return responseErr
      }

      return rs.runnersRepository.DeleteRunner(runnerId)
}
```

If we take a look at the business requirements in the previous chapter, our web server can return a single runner with all his results. This is a reason *why both repositories are needed!*

After runner ID validation, first, we will call the **runners** repository to get the runner and then call the **results** repository to get a list of results. Results will be assigned to the runner and returned to the controller layer:

```
func (rs RunnersService) GetRunner(
      runnerId string) (*models.Runner, *models.ResponseError) {

      responseErr := validateRunnerId(runnerId)
      if responseErr != nil {
            return nil, responseErr
      }

      runner, responseErr := rs.runnersRepository.
            GetRunner(runnerId)
      if responseErr != nil {
            return nil, responseErr
      }

      results, responseErr := rs.resultsRepository
            .GetAllRunnersResults(runnerId)
      if responseErr != nil {
            return nil, responseErr
      }
```

```
        runner.Results = results

        return runner, nil
}
```

The last method, **`GetRunnersBatch()`**, will cover all scenarios when multiple runners should be returned. Based on business requirements, we have three such scenarios:

- Get all runners.
- Get the *top 10 runners* from one country.
- Get the *top 10 runners* of a given year.

Based on described scenarios we can separate four cases:

- If the country parameter is passed, we will call **`GetRunnersByCountry()`** methods from the **`runners`** repository. It will handle the second scenario.
- If the year parameter is passed, we will call **`GetRunnersByYear()`** method from the **`runners`** repository. It will handle the third scenario.
- In no parameters are passed, we will call **`GetAllRunners()`** method from the **`runners`** repository. It will handle the first scenario.
- If both parameters are passed, validation will fail, because this is an illegal situation:

```
func (rs RunnersService) GetRunnersBatch(country string,
        year string) ([]*models.Runner, *models.ResponseError) {

        if country != "" && year != "" {
                return nil, &models.ResponseError{
                        Message: "Only one parameter can be passed",
                        Status:  http.StatusBadRequest,
                }
        }

        if country != "" {
                return rs.runnersRepository.
                        GetRunnersByCountry(country)
        }

        if year != "" {
                intYear, err := strconv.Atoi(year)
```

```
            if err != nil {
                return nil, &models.ResponseError{
                    Message: "Invalid year",
                    Status:  http.StatusBadRequest,
                }
            }

            currentYear := time.Now().Year()
            if intYear < 0 || intYear > currentYear {
                return nil, &models.ResponseError{
                    Message: "Invalid year",
                    Status:  http.StatusBadRequest,
                }
            }

            return rs.runnersRepository.
                GetRunnersByYear(intYear)
        }

        return rs.runnersRepository.GetAllRunners()
    }
```

There are a few more things to do if the year parameter is passed. Parameters country and year are query string parameters, so they are retrieved as string variables and passed as arguments of the **GetRunnersBatch()** method. We must convert the string representation of year into an integer, with **Atoi()** function from the **strconv** package. If the string does not represent a valid integer, an error will occur, so we will handle this situation.

The value that represents the year cannot be negative and cannot be the value that represents any future year. We can get the current year by calling the **Now()** function from the time package to get the current time and extract the year from it.

Results service

Results service contains slightly complicated methods that **runners** service. Here is a code from file **resultsService.go** (*Figure 6.6*):

```
package services

import (
```

```
        "log"
        "net/http"
        "runners-postgresql/models"
        "runners-postgresql/repositories"
        "time"
)

type ResultsService struct {
        resultsRepository *repositories.ResultsRepository
        runnersRepository *repositories.RunnersRepository
}

func NewResultsService(
        resultsRepository *repositories.ResultsRepository,
        runnersRepository *repositories.RunnersRepository)
        *ResultsService {

        return &ResultsService{
                resultsRepository: resultsRepository,
                runnersRepository: runnersRepository,
        }
}

func (rs ResultsService) CreateResult(
        result *models.Result) (*models.Result,
        *models.ResponseError) {
        ...
}

func (rs ResultsService) DeleteResult(
        resultId string) *models.ResponseError {
        ...
}

func parseRaceResult(timeString string) (time.Duration, error) {
        return time.ParseDuration(
                timeString[0:2] + "h" +
```

```
                    timeString[3:5] + "m" +
                    timeString[6:8] + "s")
}
```

The **struct** that represents the results service will have two fields, one for each repository (we will soon see why). This **struct** will be initialized through **NewResultsService()** function. So far, nothing is different than the **runners** service implementation.

Typical race result is formatted like **HH:MM:SS**, where **HH** represents hours, **MM** minutes, and **SS** seconds. Go has a **Duration** type (in package **time**) that represents *elapsed* time, so it is ideal for this use case, but it can interpret a different format: **HhhMMmSSs**. So, for example, result **02:15:32** must be converted to **02h15m32s**.

The private function **parseRaceResult()** will convert race results in a format that can be interpreted by **Duration**, and return a new **Duration** variable. We will use this function for validation and some calculations in business logic.

Like in all other service methods, first we will perform *validation*. The *bad requests error* will be returned if any string field is *empty* if the number that represents a position in the race is *negative* if the year is *not* valid (less than 0 and greater than the current year) and if the string that represents race results cannot be parsed to **Duration**.

If all checks are passed, a method that creates new results from the **results** repository will be called. But that is not the end. If the created result is the *personal best*, or *season best* for the runner, we must update that information. This is a reason why both repositories are required.

First, we must get a user. If the value for personal best is *empty*, the created result is automatically a *new personal best*. If the value is *not* empty, we should check if the new result is better than the *current personal best*, if that is the case, the created result will be set as a personal best.

Similar logic will be executed for *season's best*, with one additional condition. Season best should represent the result in the current season, so we must check if the newly created result is set in the current year. At the end of the function, the method from the repository layer that updates the runner's result is called:

```
func (rs ResultsService) CreateResult(
      result *models.Result) (*models.Result,
      *models.ResponseError) {

      if result.RunnerID == "" {
            return nil, &models.ResponseError{
                  Message: "Invalid runner ID",
```

```
                Status:  http.StatusBadRequest,
            }
        }

        if result.RaceResult == "" {
            return nil, &models.ResponseError{
                Message: "Invalid race result",
                Status:  http.StatusBadRequest,
            }
        }

        if result.Location == "" {
            return nil, &models.ResponseError{
                Message: "Invalid location",
                Status:  http.StatusBadRequest,
            }
        }

        if result.Position < 0 {
            return nil, &models.ResponseError{
                Message: "Invalid position",
                Status:  http.StatusBadRequest,
            }
        }

        currentYear := time.Now().Year()
        if result.Year < 0 || result.Year > currentYear {
            return nil, &models.ResponseError{
                Message: "Invalid year",
                Status:  http.StatusBadRequest,
            }
        }

        raceResult, err := parseRaceResult(result.RaceResult)
        if err != nil {
            return nil, &models.ResponseError{
                Message: "Invalid race result",
```

```
            Status:  http.StatusBadRequest,
        }
    }

    response, responseErr := rs.resultsRepository.
        CreateResult(result)
    if responseErr != nil {
        return nil, responseErr
    }

    runner, responseErr := rs.runnersRepository
        .GetRunner(result.RunnerID)
    if responseErr != nil {
        return nil, responseErr
    }

    if runner == nil {
        return nil, &models.ResponseError{
            Message: "Runner not found",
            Status:  http.StatusNotFound,
        }
    }

    // update runner's personal best
    if runner.PersonalBest == "" {
        runner.PersonalBest = result.RaceResult
    } else {
        personalBest, err := parseRaceResult(
            runner.PersonalBest)
        if err != nil {
            return nil, &models.ResponseError{
                Message: "Failed to parse " +
                    "personal best",
                Status:  http.
                    StatusInternalServerError,
            }
```

```
            }

            if raceResult < personalBest {
                runner.PersonalBest = result.RaceResult
            }
        }

        // update runner's season-best
        if result.Year == currentYear {
            if runner.SeasonBest == "" {
                runner.SeasonBest = result.RaceResult
            } else {
                seasonBest, err := parseRaceResult(
                    runner.SeasonBest)
                if err != nil {
                    return nil, &models.ResponseError{
                        Message: "Failed to parse " +
                            "season best",
                        Status:  http.
                            StatusInternalServerError,
                    }
                }

                if raceResult < seasonBest {
                    runner.SeasonBest = result.RaceResult
                }
            }
        }

        responseErr = rs.runnersRepository.
            UpdateRunnerResults(runner)
        if responseErr != nil {
            return nil, responseErr
        }

        return response, nil
    }
```

The second method will be used for the deletion of the result. At the start, we will check if the result ID is valid (*not* an empty string), and call the repository layer method for the deletion of a result if is. But here we come to a problem. *What if the deleted result is personal best or season best for a refereed runner?* We must check that before we return a response to the controller layer.

After we get the runner, if the deleted result is his personal best, we must get a new personal best result (by calling the repository layer method) and assign it to the runner. Same for the season's best result. There are concepts that can help us to overcome this obstacle, but we will talk more about that at the end of the next chapter. The results will be updated:

```
func (rs ResultsService) DeleteResult(
	resultId string) *models.ResponseError {

	if resultId == "" {
		return &models.ResponseError{
			Message: "Invalid result ID",
			Status:  http.StatusBadRequest,
		}
	}

	result, responseErr := rs.resultsRepository.
		DeleteResult(resultId)
	if responseErr != nil {
		return responseErr
	}

	runner, responseErr := rs.runnersRepository
		.GetRunner(result.RunnerID)
	if responseErr != nil {
		return responseErr
	}

	// Checking if the deleted result is
	// personal best for the runner
	if runner.PersonalBest == result.RaceResult {
		personalBest, responseErr := rs.resultsRepository
			.GetPersonalBestResults(result.RunnerID)
```

```
            if responseErr != nil {
                return responseErr
            }
            runner.PersonalBest = personalBest
        }

        // Checking if the deleted result is
        // season best for the runner
        currentYear := time.Now().Year()
        if runner.SeasonBest == result.RaceResult &&
            result.Year == currentYear {

            seasonBest, responseErr := rs.resultsRepository.
                GetSeasonBestResults(result.RunnerID,
                result.Year)
            if responseErr != nil {
                return responseErr
            }
            runner.SeasonBest = seasonBest
        }

        responseErr = rs.runnersRepository.
            UpdateRunnerResults(runner)
        if responseErr != nil {
            return responseErr
        }

        return nil
    }
```

But *these methods are not properly implemented! What will happen if an error occurs during the update of results, but the delete result operation is successful and deleted result is personal best for the refereed runner?* The system will be in an invalid state. *The runner will have canceled, non-existed result as personal best!*

In the next chapter, we will introduce the concept that can help us with this problem.

Conclusion

Two of the four layers are completed. Our application is slowly taking a shape of the complete product. In the next chapter, we will finish the development of our solution and after that see some alternatives that can be used for the database layer. Implementation of the repository layer is directly dependent on the chosen technology, and that is the main reason why these layers will be covered in the same chapter.

References

- https://github.com/spf13/viper
- https://github.com/gin-gonic/gin

Points to remember

- The code for each package should be placed in a dedicated directory.
- All models can be put into a singular file, but it is cleaner to keep them in separate files.
- The `main()` function should be as simple as possible.
- Duplicated code should be put into a function or method.

Multiple choice questions

1. Which `struct` tag will give the instruction to the JSON parser to ignore empty fields?
    a. `` ` json:"position"` ``
    b. `` ` json:"-"` ``
    c. `` ` json:"position,omitempty"` ``
    d. `` ` json:"position,ignore"` ``
2. Which `struct` tag will give the instruction to the JSON parser to completely ignore the field?
    a. `` ` json:"position"` ``
    b. `` ` json:"-"` ``
    c. `` ` json:"position,omitempty"` ``
    d. `` ` json:"position,ignore"` ``

3. What file formats for configuration files are supported by Viper?
    a. JSON
    b. TOML
    c. YAML
    d. All of the above

Answers

1. c
2. b
3. d

Questions

1. What is a `struct` tag and how can it be used?
2. Which operations should be performed in the controller layer?
3. Which operations should be performed in the service layer?

Key terms

- **Viper**: Complete configuration solution for Go applications.
- **TOML**: Easy to read and write file format for configuration files.
- **Gin**: HTTP web framework is written in Go.
- **Context**: The most important part of Gin that allows us to pass variables, manage the flow, read request body, read request parameters, and render a response.

CHAPTER 7

Relational Databases and Repository Layer

Introduction

In this chapter, we will introduce the basic concepts of relational databases and SQL. After that, we will learn more about the **PostgreSQL** database management system and how to implement the repository layer with it. At the end of the chapter, we will implement a repository layer with different technology, this time we will use MySQL.

Structure

In this chapter, we will discuss the following topics:

- Relational databases
- SQL
    - SELECT command
    - Modification commands
    - Aggregate functions
    - JOIN
    - Table definition commands
- PostgreSQL
    - Setting up a database
    - Repository layer
    - Database layer
- MySQL

    - Setting up a database
    - Repository layer
    - Database layer
- Improvements

Relational databases

Relational databases are databases based on the relational model. In the relational model, data is organized in tuples (finite sequences of attributes) grouped into relations (sets of tuples). In *Figure 7.1*, we can see a graphical representation of the relational model:

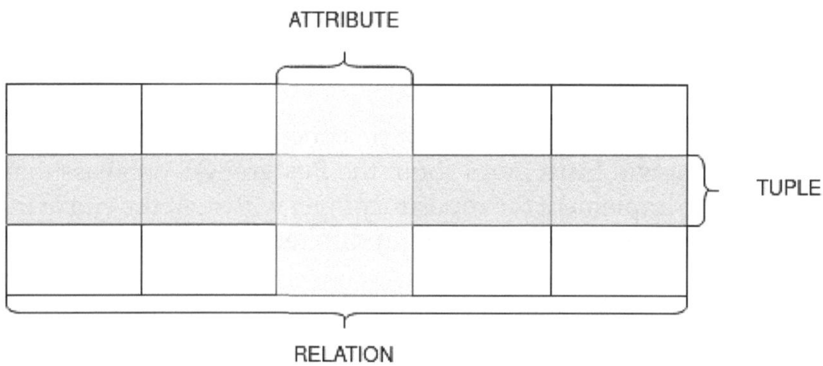

***Figure 7.1**: Relational model*

Databases that use different data models are called **NoSQL databases**. We will talk about them in the next chapter.

In *Chapter 5, Design of Web Application,* we mentioned some concepts of relational databases. Now, it is time to talk about more concepts:

- **SQL**: Language for data manipulation in databases.
- **Database**: Set of named relations (tables).
- **Database Management System (DBMS)**: Software solution for creating and managing databases.
- **Schema**: Structural description of relations in a database, described with some formal language.
- **Instance**: Data content at a given point in time.
- **Table**: Representation of relation, can be described as a set of named attributes (columns).

- **Column**: Representation of named attributes, with specified type.
- **Row**: Representation of tuples, has a value for each attribute (column).
- **NULL value**: Special value for *unknown* or *undefined*. Relational operators cannot be used to check if a column holds a *NULL* value, special operators **IS NULL** or **IS NOT NULL** must be used.
- **Primary key**: Column or set of columns, whose value is *unique* in a database table.
- **Foreign key**: Column or set of columns that refer primary key of another database table.
- **Indices**: Mechanism for improving performance on a database table; with them, data can be located faster and more efficiently. They are stored in the database and *not* visible to database users. Indices are created automatically for *primary keys* (and sometimes for unique columns) by the database management system. For systems where data will often be created than read, indices are not efficient.
- **Query**: Request for information retrieval from the database.
- **View**: Virtual table that contains rows and columns, like a real table. Columns in a view are from one or more real tables from the database.
- **Constraints**: Rules enforced on database columns. Primary keys, foreign keys, and indices are types of constraints. Besides them, the following constraints are used:
    - **NOT NULL**: Column cannot have a NULL value.
    - **UNIQUE**: All column values are different (unique).
    - **DEFAULT**: Sets the default value for a column, if the value is not specified.
    - **CHECK**: The value in a column must fulfill a specified condition.
- **Triggers**: Procedures stored in databases, which are automatically invoked when a specified event occurs. Idea is to move logic from the application into the database management system. For example, in the case of our application, the trigger can check and update the runner's personal and season best when a new result is created.
- **Transactions**: Sequence of multiple SQL commands treated as a single command. It will begin on the first SQL command and end on the `commit` command. If one of the commands fails, a *rollback* procedure will be triggered to undo the effects of successfully executed commands. This concept will help us to solve problems during the creation and deletion of results, mentioned in the previous chapter.

When we designed our database, we talked about the relationship between *runners* and *results* tables. We mentioned that one runner can have zero or more results. This relationship is called **cardinality**.

In our case, cardinality is *one-to-many*, where one side is *mandatory* and many sides is *optional*. It is often called **mandatory-one-to-optional-many**.

There are six *characteristics* that can be combined into different types of cardinalities:

- One
- Many
- Mandatory one (exactly one)
- Optional one (zero or one)
- Mandatory many (one or more)
- Optional many (zero or more)

Now that we are familiar with basic relational database concepts, we can introduce SQL and SQL commands that will be used in the repository layer for database data manipulations.

SQL

SQL stands for **Structured Query Language** and represents language designed for the manipulation of data from relational databases. It is **ANSI (American National Standard Institute**) and **ISO (International Organization for Standardization**) standardized and supported by all relational database solutions.

It should be noted that each database solution supports basic SQL commands, but has some *extensions*. This means that sometimes it is necessary to make small changes to the query, depending on the solution.

SQL can be divided into four sub-languages:

- **DQL (Data Query Language)** for performing queries on the data (getting data from the database)
- **DDL (Data Definition Language)** for creating and modifying database objects (tables, indices, and so on)
- **DCL (Data Control Language**) for controlling access to stored data
- **DML (Data Manipulation Language**) for creating and modifying database data

SELECT command

The first command that we will introduce is **SELECT**. This command is used to get data stored in a database. The following command will return selected columns from a table that fulfill the condition:

```
SELECT column_1, column_2, …, column_N
FROM table_name
WHERE condition;
```

The **WHERE** statement is *optional*, without it, all rows will be returned. Also, multiple conditions can be combined with logical operators (**AND**, **OR**, and **NOT**).

We can get all columns from the table with the asterisk (*) symbol:

```
SELECT *
FROM table_name
WHERE condition;
```

It is possible to sort returning result sets in ascending or descending order, with the **ORDER BY** statement:

```
SELECT column_1, column_2, …, column_N
FROM table_name
WHERE condition
ORDER BY column_1, column_2, …, column_N ASC|DESC;
```

Ascending order is the default one. If we use the **ORDER BY** statement without **ASC** or **DESC**, ascending order will be applied.

One interesting thing, it is possible to place another query (sub-query) in **WHERE** and **FROM** statements. This is often used for some complex queries, and we will see this when we talk about the implementation of the repository layer.

Here are some examples of conditions. Let us assume that we have *Products* table (*Table 7.1*), with the following columns and rows:

product_id	product_name	color	price
1	shirt	red	100
2	pants	blue	200
3	gloves	red	50

***Table 7.1:** Products table*

This query will return the *first* and *third* row because the condition matches only products with **red** color:

```
SELECT *
FROM products_name
WHERE color = 'red';
```

While the following query will return all products with prices greater than **75**:

```
SELECT *
FROM products_name
WHERE price > 75;
```

It is also possible to combine conditions, like in the following query:

```
SELECT *
FROM products_name
WHERE color = 'red' AND price > 75;
```

Modification commands

There are three basic modification commands: **INSERT**, **UPDATE**, and **DELETE**.

INSERT command is used to create a new database row. In the command, we should specify which columns will be filled, and with which values:

```
INSERT INTO table_name (column_1, column_2, …, column_N)
VALUES (value_1, value_2, …, value_N);
```

If we add values for all columns, we can omit columns from the query. In that case, we must be sure that the order of values is the same as the column order in the database table:

```
INSERT INTO table_name
VALUES (value_1, value_2, …, value_N);
```

It should be mentioned, that we can use the **SELECT** command instead of the **VALUES** statement. This is often used to copy data from one table to another.

The **UPDATE** command is used to modify existing rows in the database. The **SET** statement is used to specify which columns will be updated and with which values. The following command will modify all rows that fulfill the condition:

```
UPDATE table_name
SET column_1 = value_1, column_2 = value_2, …, column_N = value_N
WHERE condition;
```

Without a **WHERE** statement, all rows will be modified.

The **DELETE** command is used to remove rows from the database. The following command will remove all rows that fulfill the condition:

```
DELETE FROM table_name WHERE condition;
```

Without a **WHERE** statement, all rows will be deleted.

Aggregate functions

Aggregate functions perform calculations on a set of values and return a single value. We have the following functions:

- **MIN()**: Returns the smallest value of the selected column.
- **MAX()**: Returns the largest value of the selected column.
- **COUNT()**: Returns the number of rows that fulfills a condition.
- **AVG()**: Returns the average value of the numeric column.
- **SUM()**: Returns the sum of a numeric column.

All aggregate functions ignore *NULL* values, except **COUNT()**. The following examples show the syntax for aggregate functions:

```
SELECT MIN(column)
FROM table_name
WHERE condition;

SELECT MAX(column)
FROM table_name
WHERE condition;

SELECT COUNT(column)
FROM table_name
WHERE condition;

SELECT AVG(column)
FROM table_name
WHERE condition;

SELECT SUM(column)
FROM table_name
WHERE condition;
```

If the **WHERE** statement is omitted from the query, the aggregate function will be applied on all rows.

JOIN

The JOIN is a SQL clause that combines rows from two (or more) tables, based on related columns between tables. In our system, both tables (**runners** and **results**) have a column that represents the ID of a runner, so we can (and we will) join data by using this column.

There are several types of JOIN (*Figure 7.2*):

- **INNER JOIN**: Returns rows from both tables whenever there are matching values in fields common to both tables.
- **LEFT JOIN**: Returns all rows from the left table and the matched rows from the right table.
- **RIGHT JOIN**: Returns all rows from the right table and the matched rows from the left table.
- **FULL JOIN**: Returns all rows from both tables, whether is a match or not.

After JOIN, all columns from both tables are available for the **SELECT** command. The following example shows the syntax for **INNER** JOIN:

```
SELECT table_1.column_1, ..., table_1.column_N,
      table_2.column_1, ..., table_2.column_N
FROM table_1
INNER JOIN table_2
ON table_1.column_name = table_2.column_name;
```

The **ON** statement is used to define which related column data will be combined. For other JOIN types, another reserve word (**LEFT**, **RIGHT**, or **FULL**) can be used instead of **INNER**:

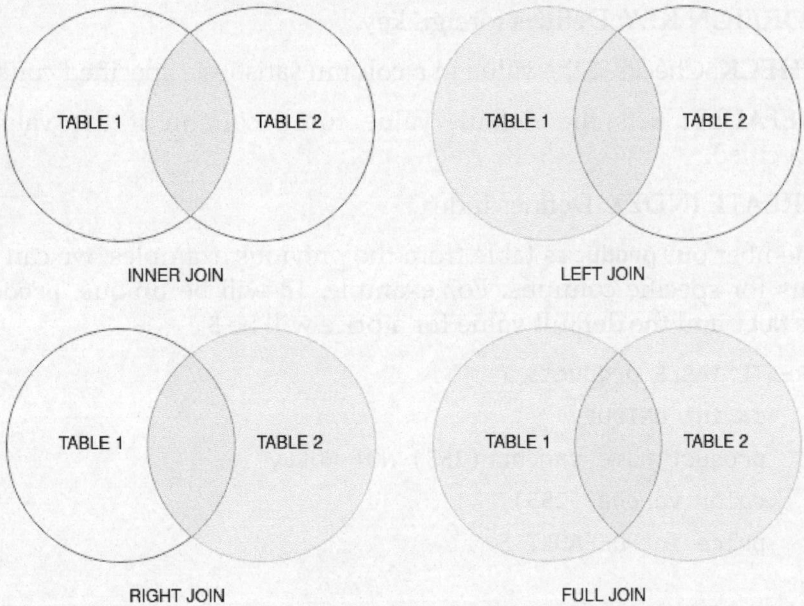

Figure 7.2: Types of JOIN

Table definition commands

Table definition commands are used for creating, modifying, and deleting database tables.

Command **`CREATE TABLE`** will create a new table in the database. For each column, we must specify the column name, data type, and, optionally, constraint. A **constraint** can also be defined at the end of **`CREATE TABLE`** command with the **`CONSTRAINT`** statement:

```
CREATE TABLE table_name (
    column_name_1 data_type constraint,
    column_name_2 data_type constraint,
    ...
    column_name_N data_type constraint
);
```

Some of the constraints are:

- **NOT NULL**: Column will not have NULL values.
- **UNIQUE**: All values in the column will be different (unique).
- **PRIMARY KEY**: Defines primary key, can be observed as a combination of **NOT NULL** and **UNIQUE**.

- **FOREIGN KEY**: Defines foreign key.
- **CHECK**: Checks if the value in a column satisfies a specified condition.
- **DEFAULT**: Sets the default value for a column if the value is not specified.
- **CREATE INDEX**: Defines index.

If we remember our **products** table from the previous examples, we can set some constraints for specific columns. For example, **id** will be unique, **product_name** cannot be **NULL** and the default value for a price will be **5**:

```
CREATE TABLE products (
    id int UNIQUE,
    product_name varchar(255) NOT NULL,
    color varchar(255),
    price int DEFAULT 5
);
```

Based on the database management system, types can be different (we will see this soon). Some systems use text instead of **varchar**.

Command **DROP TABLE** will delete a specified table from the database. It should be used very carefully because can cause major data loss:

```
DROP TABLE table_name;
```

The last command, **ALTER TABLE** can be used to add, remove, or modify columns. The column will be added with **ADD** statement:

```
ALTER TABLE table_name
ADD column_name data_type constraint;
```

The existing column can be modified with **ALTER COLUMN** or **MODIFY COLUMN** statements, depending on the database management system. For example, PostgreSQL uses **ALTER COLUMN**, while MySQL uses **MODIFY COLUMN**. The syntax is similar:

```
ALTER TABLE table_name
ALTER|MODIFY COLUMN column_name data_type constraint;
```

Statement **DROP COLUMN** is used to remove a specified column:

```
ALTER TABLE table_name
DROP COLUMN column_name;
```

Command **ALTER TABLE** can also be used to add or remove constraints.

It is also possible to define indices on a specified column from the table with **CREATE INDEX** command:

```
CREATE INDEX index_name
ON table_name (column_1, column_2, …, column_N);
```

Some database management systems (PostgreSQL) have a command for index deletion, while some (MySQL) uses **ALTER TABLE** for it:

```
DROP INDEX index_name ON table_name;
```

```
ALTER TABLE table_name
DROP INDEX index_name;
```

Now that we are familiar with basic SQL commands, we can develop our repository layer.

PostgreSQL

PostgreSQL is an open-source object-relational database management system. It supports all features of a standard relational database management system with some advanced *next-gen* features. Objects, classes, and inheritance are supported in the database schema and query language.

Setting up a database

PostgreSQL is available for multiple platforms. Installation files can be found on the official website:

https://www.postgresql.org/download/

PostgreSQL is included by default in most Linux distributions. The included version is one that was supported through the lifetime of that Linux version. It is possible to install the latest PostgreSQL version with the following commands:

- Red Hat Enterprise Linux (6 and 7):

  yum install postgresql-server

- Red Hat Enterprise Linux 8 and Fedora:

  dnf install postgresql-server

- Debian and Ubuntu:

  apt-get install postgresql

It is also possible to install a specific version, by adding a version (for example, **12**) at the end of the command, in the following way:

- Red Hat Enterprise Linux (6 and 7):

  yum install postgresql-server-12

- Red Hat Enterprise Linux 8 and Fedora:

```
dnf install postgresql-server-12
```

- Debian and Ubuntu:

```
apt-get install postgresql-12
```

PostgreSQL is not included in Windows and Mac. Installation is simple, we just need to download the installation file, and follow the instructions. Since version 11.7, PostgreSQL is not supported for *32-bit versions* of Windows.

We can execute SQL queries and manage our database in the terminal, but it is much easier to use some tools. One of the most popular administration and development platforms for PostgreSQL is **pgAdmin**. The **pgAdmin** is open-source and supports a lot of features that can help developers during database design and application development processes. Installation files can be found on the official website:

https://www.pgadmin.org/download/

For Linux distributions, **pgAdmin** can be installed with the following commands:

- Red Hat Enterprise Linux and Fedora:

```
sudo yum install pgadmin4
```

- Debian and Ubuntu:

```
sudo apt install pgadmin4
```

When the installation process is complete, the configuration script must be executed:

```
sudo /usr/pgadmin4/bin/setup-web.sh
```

For Windows and Mac, the installation file should be downloaded from the official website, and follow the instructions. Since *version 4.29, 32-bit versions* of Windows are not supported.

During the installation or execution of the configuration script, we can be asked to set up the admin *username* and *password*. A username and password will be used for connection to the database (in the configuration file).

When the installation is complete, we can start **pgAdmin**, it will probably be opened in the web browser. First, we should create a database server, by selecting **Object, Create,** and **Server** (*Figure 7.3*). Sometimes it is necessary to click on **Server Group** on the left side of the window (**Servers(1)** from *Figure 7.3*) in order to display the desired create options:.

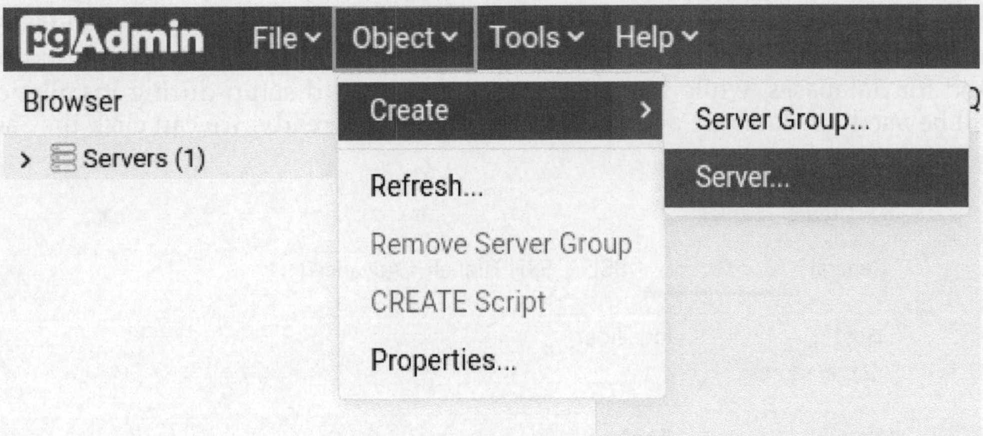

Figure 7.3: *Create a new server*

A new panel will be opened. In the **General** tab, we should enter the name. Since we will run the database on our local machine (computer), we can enter **localhost** as the server name (*Figure 7.4*):

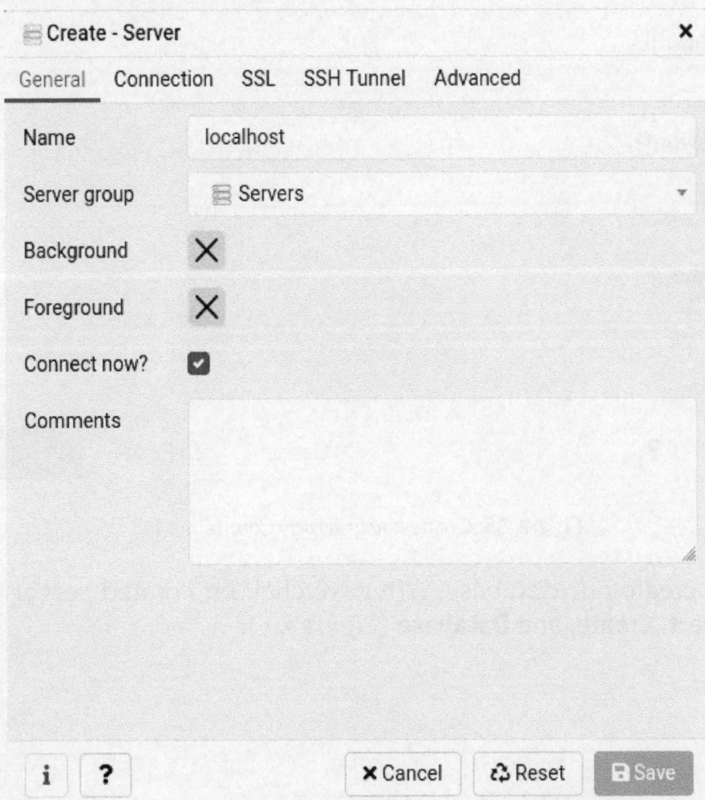

Figure 7.4: *Create a new server, General tab*

In the **Connection** tab, we will enter **`localhost`** for the host name/address, and leave everything else to the assigned settings (*Figure 7.5*). Port **5432** is the standard port used for databases, while the username and password setup during installation will be used for database access. When everything is ready, we can click the **Save** button:

***Figure 7.5**: Create a new server, Connection tab*

Now we can create our database. After we click on created server (**`localhost`**), we select **Object, Create,** and **Database** (*Figure 7.6*):

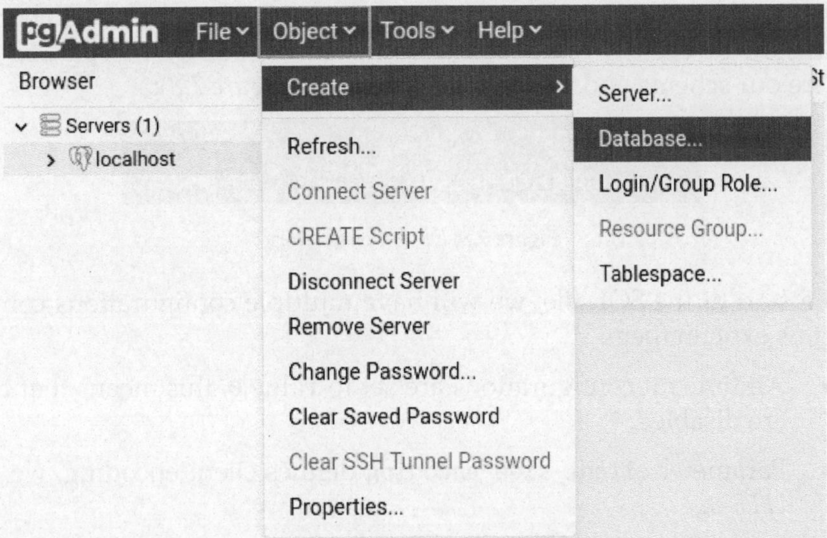

Figure 7.6: Create a new database

In the **Create - Database** panel, on the **General** tab, we will set the database name in **Database** field. We will enter `runners_db` (*Figure 7.7*). All other settings can remain on assigned values, so we can click on the **Save** button:

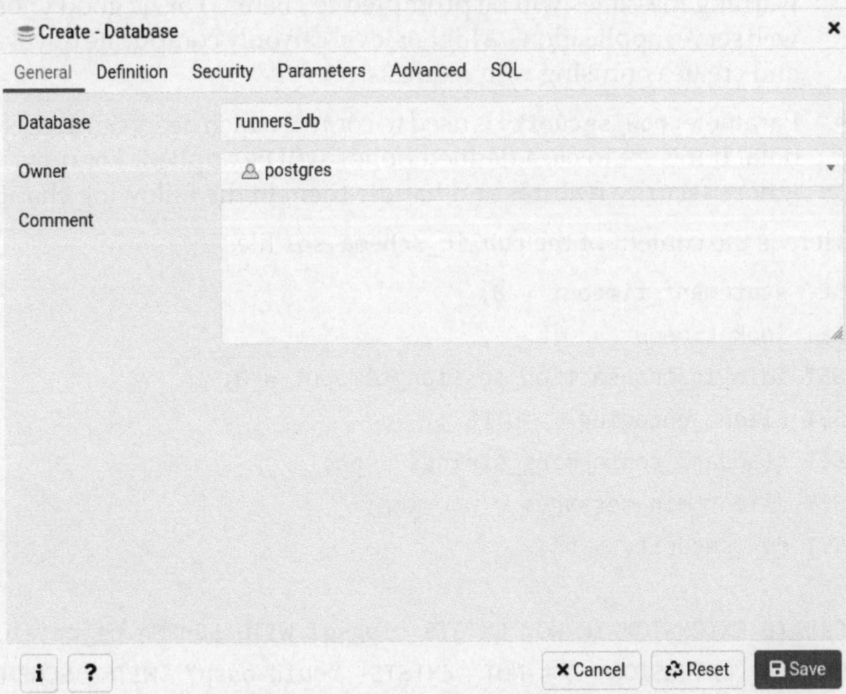

Figure 7.7: Create a new database, General tab

When the database is created, we can create our tables. It is time to go back to our project. Inside the **dbscripts** directory, we will have one SQL file, **public_schema.sql**, where our schema and tables will be defined (*Figure 7.8*):

***Figure 7.8**: Dbscripts directory*

At the start of the SQL file, we will have multiple configurations commands, so let us explain them:

- All timeout configurations are set to value **0**, this means that timeouts are disabled.
- Parameter **client_side_encoding** defines client encoding, we will use *UTF-8*.
- Parameter **standard_conforming_strings** controls how string literals will treat backslash (\) characters. If it is set to **on**, backslash will be treated literally. Since *PostgreSQL version 9.1*, **on** is the default setting.
- Parameter **client_min_messages** set the message level that will be sent to the client. We will use a *warning*. This means that all info, error and warning messages will be prompted to clients. This is good enough for web server applications, a higher level can only complicate development and create confusing web requests.
- Parameter **row_security** is used to control which users can access certain data. If it is set to **on**, a defined policy will be applied. For now, we will ignore security features and handle them in the following chapters.

Here is the content of the **public_schema.sql** file:

```
SET statement_timeout = 0;
SET lock_timeout = 0;
SET idle_in_transaction_session_timeout = 0;
SET client_encoding = ‘UTF8’;
SET standard_conforming_strings = on;
SET client_min_messages = warning;
SET row_security = off;

CREATE EXTENSION IF NOT EXISTS plpgsql WITH SCHEMA pg_catalog;
CREATE EXTENSION IF NOT EXISTS “uuid-ossp” WITH SCHEMA pg_catalog;
```

```
SET search_path = public, pg_catalog;
SET default_tablespace = '';

-- runners
CREATE TABLE runners (
        id uuid NOT NULL DEFAULT uuid_generate_v1mc(),
        first_name text NOT NULL,
        last_name text NOT NULL,
        age integer,
        is_active boolean DEFAULT TRUE,
        country text NOT NULL,
        personal_best interval,
        season_best interval,
        CONSTRAINT runners_pk PRIMARY KEY (id)
);

CREATE INDEX runners_country
ON runners (country);

CREATE INDEX runners_season_best
ON runners (season_best);

-- results
CREATE TABLE results (
        id uuid NOT NULL DEFAULT uuid_generate_v1mc(),
        runner_id uuid NOT NULL,
        race_result interval NOT NULL,
        location text NOT NULL,
        position integer,
        year integer NOT NULL,
        CONSTRAINT results_pk PRIMARY KEY (id),
        CONSTRAINT fk_results_runner_id FOREIGN KEY (runner_id)
            REFERENCES runners (id) MATCH SIMPLE
            ON UPDATE NO ACTION
            ON DELETE NO ACTION
);
```

After setting parameters, we have SQL command for the creation of the runners table. For each column, we have defined column name, data type and (for some columns) constraints (**NOT NULL** and **DEFAULT**). At the end of the command, we will use the **CONSTRAINT** statement to define the primary key. Here we will define the constraint name (**runners_pk**) and on which column the constraint will be applied (**id**). Function **uuid_generate_v1ms()** will generate a new UUID during the **INSERT** command.

As we will need to search runners by *country* and *year*, we can create indices on these two columns in order to improve database performance. Two simple **CREATE INDEX** commands from the SQL file will handle this. In each command, we define on which table and column index will be created.

The last command will define the results table. The only difference between this command and the command that creates the **runners** table is the definition of *foreign key constraint*. Here, we will define the constraint name (**fk_results_runner_id**), and on which table, and column the foreign key will referee.

Two statements **ON UPDATE NO ACTION** and **ON DELETE NO ACTION** defines what will happen if the row referenced by a foreign key is deleted. Since the runner will never be deleted (only active status will be changed from true to false) there is no need to handle this situation, but just in case we should define that no action will be performed. There is no update action that can affect the result, so the same here, no action will be applied.

There are two more options that can be used in these statements:

- **SET NULL**: Sets foreign key value to **NULL**.
- **CASCADE**:
  - o Removes all rows that refereed removed row from another table, for delete operation.
  - o If the primary key is changed, all foreign keys that refereed it will be updated.

Now we can go back to **pgAdmin**, click on **runners_db** and open **Query Tool**, by selecting **Tools** and then **Query Tool** (*Figure 7.9*):

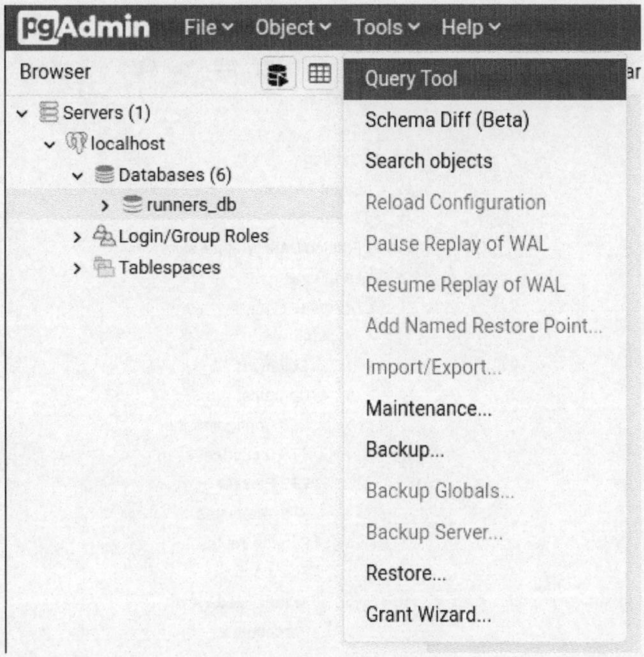

***Figure 7.9**: Query Tool*

Inside *Query Editor*, we will copy the content of the **`public_schema.sql`** file, and execute it by clicking on *Execute* button (*Figure 7.10*):

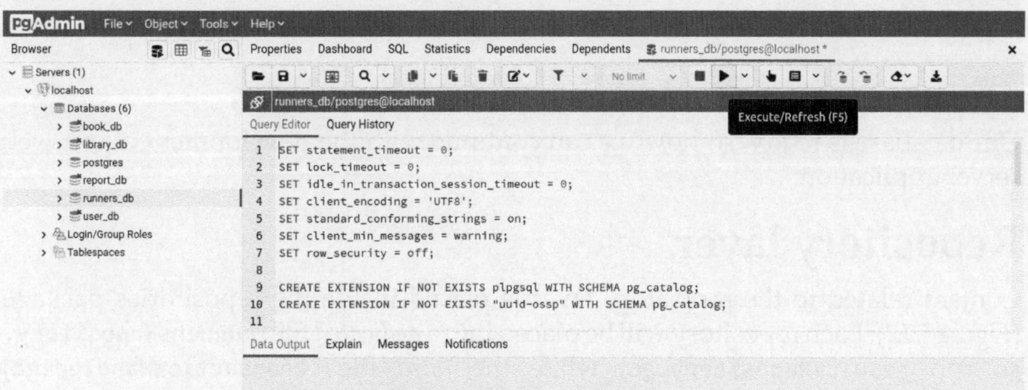

***Figure 7.10**: Query editor*

If the execution was successful, a *success message* will be displayed, and we should see our tables by clicking on **runners_db, Schemas, public,** and **Tables** (*Figure 7.11*):

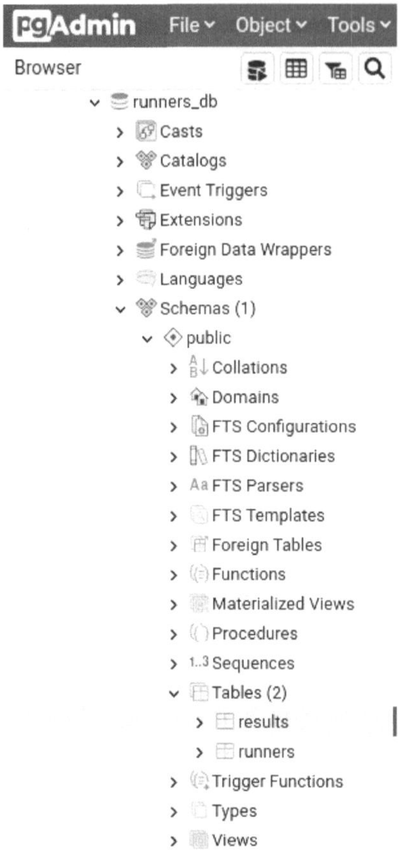

***Figure 7.11**: Database tables*

Our database is ready, so now we can continue with the development of our web server application.

Repository layer

Content related to the repository layer is placed inside the repositories package (*Figure 7.12*). Each repository will be placed into a *dedicated* file (**`runnersRepository.go`** and **`resultsRepository.go`**) while the *third* file (**`transactionHandler.go`**) will hold functions for transaction management (starting, roll-backing, and committing):

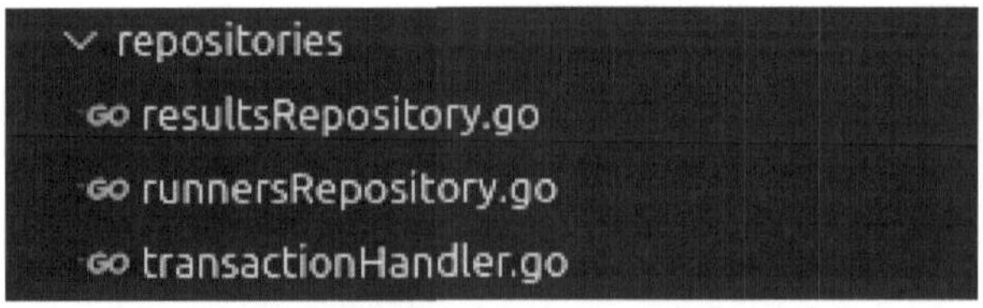

***Figure 7.12**: Repositories packages*

We will start with the **runners** repository. The **struct** that represents the repository has two fields, **dbHandler** which is basically a representation of the database layer and transaction that holds the current transaction. Inside the initialization function, **NewRunnersRepository()** only **dbHandler** will be initialized, and the transaction will be set when needed:

```
package repositories

import (
	"database/sql"
	"net/http"
	"runners-postgresql/models"
)

type RunnersRepository struct {
	dbHandler   *sql.DB
	transaction *sql.Tx
}

func NewRunnersRepository(dbHandler *sql.DB) *RunnersRepository {
	return &RunnersRepository{
		dbHandler: dbHandler,
	}
}

func (rr RunnersRepository) CreateRunner(
	runner *models.Runner) (*models.Runner,
	*models.ResponseError) {
	...
}

func (rr RunnersRepository) UpdateRunner(
	runner *models.Runner) *models.ResponseError {
	...
}

func (rr RunnersRepository) UpdateRunnerResults(
	runner *models.Runner) *models.ResponseError {
	...
```

```
}

func (rr RunnersRepository) DeleteRunner(
        runnerId string) *models.ResponseError {
        ...
}

func (rr RunnersRepository) GetRunner(
        runnerId string) (*models.Runner, *models.ResponseError) {
        ...
}

func (rr RunnersRepository) GetAllRunners()
        ([]*models.Runner, *models.ResponseError) {
        ...
}

func (rr RunnersRepository) GetRunnersByCountry(
        country string) ([]*models.Runner, *models.ResponseError) {
        ...
}

func (rr RunnersRepository) GetRunnersByYear(
        year int) ([]*models.Runner, *models.ResponseError) {
        ...
}
```

Each repository method can be separated into three parts:

- Create SQL query
- Execute query
- Map response

We can see this in the implementation of the **CreateRunner()** method. String variable query will hold SQL query (**INSERT** command in this case). Symbols **$1**, **$2**, **$3**, and **$4** are *query arguments,* and they will be replaced with current values during execution. This **INSERT** command uses **RETURNING** statement to return the *ID* generated in the database layer.

Method **Query()** from the database layer will execute the query and return rows. This method is mainly used for **SELECT** commands and accepts the query and query arguments. The order of passed query arguments is important. The first argument **runner.FirstName** will replace **$1** from the query, second **runner.LastName** will replace **$2** from the query, and so on.

If the query expects, for example, *five* arguments, and we pass only three to **Query()** method, panic will be triggered, and the query will not be executed. If any error occurs during query execution, we will map that error as *Internal Server Error* (*HTTP status 500*) and return it to the service layer.

Rows must be closed when they are not needed anymore. We can call the **Close()** method in defer in order to be sure that it will always be closed:

```
func (rr RunnersRepository) CreateRunner(
        runner *models.Runner) (*models.Runner,
        *models.ResponseError) {

        query := `
                INSERT INTO runners(first_name, last_name, age,
                        country)
                VALUES ($1, $2, $3, $4)
                RETURNING id`

        rows, err := rr.dbHandler.Query(query, runner.FirstName,
                 runner.LastName, runner.Age, runner.Country)
        if err != nil {
                return nil, &models.ResponseError{
                        Message: err.Error(),
                        Status:  http.StatusInternalServerError,
                }
        }

        defer rows.Close()

        var runnerId string
        for rows.Next() {
                err := rows.Scan(&runnerId)
                if err != nil {
                        return nil, &models.ResponseError{
                                Message: err.Error(),
                                Status:  http.
```

```
                                StatusInternalServerError,
                        }
                }
        }

        if rows.Err() != nil {
                return nil, &models.ResponseError{
                        Message: err.Error(),
                        Status:  http.StatusInternalServerError,
                }
        }

        return &models.Runner{
                ID:         runnerId,
                FirstName: runner.FirstName,
                LastName:  runner.LastName,
                Age:        runner.Age,
                IsActive:  true,
                Country:   runner.Country,
        }, nil
}
```

Now we can map responses by reading data from rows. Rows are iterative structures, so in order to get the result we must iterate through it with the **`Next()`** method. When there are no more rows to read, the method will return *false* and the loop will stop.

Method **`Scan()`** copies columns from the current row into values pointed by provided arguments. Our query will return only one column (**`id`**) so we need only one string variable. Again, all errors will be mapped as *Internal Server Errors* and returned to the service layer.

Method **`Err()`** will return any error encountered during iterations. It is a good practice to check it before mapping the response. If the method returns *nil,* everything was completed successfully and we can map the response.

Method **`CreateRunner()`** will return a fully filled runner model, for that we can use values provided as a method input (because they are identical to ones written into the database) and ID returned from the database layer.

Other repository methods are similar, so in the rest of the section, we will just pinpoint differences and interesting details.

Method **`UpdateRunner()`** will have **`UPDATE`** command in the query variable. This time we will use the method **`Exec()`** to execute the query. This method will execute the query without returning any rows. Still, this method will return the **`Result`** that can be used for some checks.

We can use the method **`RowsAffected()`** to check how many rows were affected by the executed query. If this value is equal to *zero,* this means that provided runner ID does not exist, which automatically means that the runner does not exist and we can map that into a *Not Found (HTTP status 404)* error:

```
func (rr RunnersRepository) UpdateRunner(
	runner *models.Runner) *models.ResponseError {

	query := `
		UPDATE runners
		SET
			first_name = $1,
			last_name = $2,
			age = $3,
			country = $4
			WHERE id = $5`

	res, err := rr.dbHandler.Exec(query, runner.FirstName,
		runner.LastName, runner.Age, runner.Country, runner.ID)
	if err != nil {
		return &models.ResponseError{
			Message: err.Error(),
			Status:  http.StatusInternalServerError,
		}
	}

	rowsAffected, err := res.RowsAffected()
	if err != nil {
		return &models.ResponseError{
			Message: err.Error(),
			Status:  http.StatusInternalServerError,
		}
	}

	if rowsAffected == 0 {
```

```
                return &models.ResponseError{
                        Message: "Runner not found",
                        Status:  http.StatusNotFound,
                }
        }

        return nil
}
```

Method **UpdateRunnerResults()** is similar to **UpdateRunner()** with a couple of differences. *First,* different columns will be updated, *second* this query will be executed in the transaction because it is connected with the creation and deletion of results, and *third,* it is possible to execute a query that will not affect any row (there will be no changes in results). We will talk more about this later:

```
func (rr RunnersRepository) UpdateRunnerResults(
        runner *models.Runner) *models.ResponseError {

        query := `
                UPDATE runners
                SET
                        personal_best = $1,
                        season_best = $2
                WHERE id = $3`

        _, err := rr.transaction.Exec(query, runner.PersonalBest,
                runner.SeasonBest, runner.ID)
        if err != nil {
                return &models.ResponseError{
                        Message: err.Error(),
                        Status:  http.StatusInternalServerError,
                }
        }

        return nil
}
```

Method **DeleteRunner()** will not execute **DELETE** command. The runner will never be deleted from the system, it will only become inactive, and so this method will actually execute the **UPDATE** command that will set the value of the **is_active** column to **false**:

```
func (rr RunnersRepository) DeleteRunner(
        runnerId string) *models.ResponseError {

        query := `
                UPDATE runners
                SETis_active = 'false'
                WHERE id = $1`

        res, err := rr.dbHandler.Exec(query, runnerId)
        if err != nil {
                return &models.ResponseError{
                        Message: err.Error(),
                        Status:  http.StatusInternalServerError,
                }
        }
        rowsAffected, err := res.RowsAffected()
        if err != nil {
                return &models.ResponseError{
                        Message: err.Error(),
                        Status:  http.StatusInternalServerError,
                }
        }

        if rowsAffected == 0 {
                return &models.ResponseError{
                        Message: "Runner not found",
                        Status:  http.StatusNotFound,
                }
        }

        return nil
}
```

The next method **GetRunner()** will execute a query that returns all columns from the runners table. This means that we will need more pointers in **Scan()** method, one for each column:

```
func (rr RunnersRepository) GetRunner(
	runnerId string) (*models.Runner, *models.ResponseError) {

	query := `
		SELECT *
		FROM runners
		WHERE id = $1`

	rows, err := rr.dbHandler.Query(query, runnerId)
	if err != nil {
		return nil, &models.ResponseError{
			Message: err.Error(),
			Status:  http.StatusInternalServerError,
		}
	}

	defer rows.Close()

	var id, firstName, lastName, country string
	var personalBest, seasonBest sql.NullString
	var age int
	var isActive bool
	for rows.Next() {
		err := rows.Scan(&id, &firstName, &lastName, &age,
			&isActive, &country, &personalBest, &seasonBest)
		if err != nil {
			return nil, &models.ResponseError{
				Message: err.Error(),
				Status: http.StatusInternalServerError,
			}
		}
	}

	if rows.Err() != nil {
		return nil, &models.ResponseError{
			Message: err.Error(),
			Status:  http.StatusInternalServerError,
```

```
                }
        }

        return &models.Runner{
                ID:           id,
                FirstName:    firstName,
                LastName:     lastName,
                Age:          age,
                IsActive:     isActive,
                Country:      country,
                PersonalBest: personalBest.String,
                SeasonBest:   seasonBest.String,
        }, nil
}
```

In method **`GetAllRunners()`**, in each iteration new model will be initialized, and appended to the result slice. If the runners table has no data, an empty slice will be returned:

```
func (rr RunnersRepository) GetAllRunners() ([]*models.Runner,
        *models.ResponseError) {

        query := `
                SELECT *
                FROM runners`

        rows, err := rr.dbHandler.Query(query)
        if err != nil {
                return nil, &models.ResponseError{
                        Message: err.Error(),
                        Status:  http.StatusInternalServerError,
                }
        }
        defer rows.Close()

        runners := make([]*models.Runner, 0)
        var id, firstName, lastName, country string
        var personalBest, seasonBest sql.NullString
```

```
    var age int
    var isActive bool

    for rows.Next() {
        err := rows.Scan(&id, &firstName, &lastName, &age,
            &isActive, &country, &personalBest,
            &seasonBest)
        if err != nil {
            return nil, &models.ResponseError{
                Message: err.Error(),
                Status:  http.
                    StatusInternalServerError,
            }
        }

        runner := &models.Runner{
            ID:           id,
            FirstName:    firstName,
            LastName:     lastName,
            Age:          age,
            IsActive:     isActive,
            Country:      country,
            PersonalBest: personalBest.String,
            SeasonBest:   seasonBest.String,
        }

        runners = append(runners, runner)
    }

    if rows.Err() != nil {
        return nil, &models.ResponseError{
            Message: err.Error(),
            Status:  http.StatusInternalServerError,
        }
    }

    return runners, nil
}
```

Since we must get the *top ten runners* from the selected *country,* we must sort runners by *personal best* and use the **LIMIT** statement to get the ten best ones. This is implemented in the method **GetRunnersByCountry()**:

```
func (rr RunnersRepository) GetRunnersByCountry(
	country string) ([]*models.Runner, *models.ResponseError) {

	query := `
		SELECT *
		FROM runners
		WHERE country = $1 AND is_active = 'true'
		ORDER BY personal_best
		LIMIT 10`

	rows, err := rr.dbHandler.Query(query, country)
	if err != nil {
		return nil, &models.ResponseError{
			Message: err.Error(),
			Status:  http.StatusInternalServerError,
		}
	}

	defer rows.Close()

	runners := make([]*models.Runner, 0)
	var id, firstName, lastName string
	var personalBest, seasonBest sql.NullString
	var age int

	for rows.Next() {
		err := rows.Scan(&id, &firstName, &lastName, &age,
			&personalBest, &seasonBest)
		if err != nil {
			return nil, &models.ResponseError{
				Message: err.Error(),
				Status:  http.StatusInternalServerError,
			}
		}
```

```
			runner := &models.Runner{
				ID:           id,
				FirstName:    firstName,
				LastName:     lastName,
				Age:          age,
				IsActive:     true,
				Country:      country,
				PersonalBest: personalBest.String,
				SeasonBest:   seasonBest.String,
			}

			runners = append(runners, runner)
		}

		if rows.Err() != nil {
			return nil, &models.ResponseError{
				Message: err.Error(),
				Status:  http.StatusInternalServerError,
			}
		}

		return runners, nil
	}
```

The last method from the runners repository, **GetRunnersByYear()**, should return the *top ten runners* from the specified year. But there is no information about the year in the **runners** table, that information is placed inside the **result** table.

We will need the best runner's result for a specified year, so there is no need to join the **runners** table with the whole results table. Sub-query will be used as another side of the **JOIN** command, which will get only the best result for each runner in a specified year. The aggregation function **MIN()** is used to determine the best result.

Each column should be referenced with the table name in front, to clearly indicate which column belongs to which table and to avoid potential conflicts where both tables contain columns with the same name:

```
	func (rr RunnersRepository) GetRunnersByYear(
		year int) ([]*models.Runner, *models.ResponseError) {

		query := `
```

```
		SELECT runners.id, runners.first_name,
			runners.last_name,runners.age, runners.is_active,
			runners.country,runners.personal_best,
			results.race_result
		FROM runners
		INNER JOIN (
			SELECT runner_id,
				MIN(race_result) as race_result
			FROM results
			WHERE year = $1
			GROUP BY runner_id) results
		ON runners.id = results.runner_id
		ORDER BY results.race_result
		LIMIT 10`

	rows, err := rr.dbHandler.Query(query, year)
	if err != nil {
		return nil, &models.ResponseError{
			Message: err.Error(),
			Status:  http.StatusInternalServerError,
		}
	}

	defer rows.Close()

	runners := make([]*models.Runner, 0)
	var id, firstName, lastName, country string
	var personalBest, seasonBest sql.NullString
	var age int
	var isActive bool
	for rows.Next() {
		err := rows.Scan(&id, &firstName, &lastName, &age,
			&isActive, &country, &personalBest,
			&seasonBest)
		if err != nil {
			return nil, &models.ResponseError{
```

```
                        Message: err.Error(),
                        Status: http.StatusInternalServerError,
                    }
                }

                runner := &models.Runner{
                    ID:           id,
                    FirstName:    firstName,
                    LastName:     lastName,
                    Age:          age,
                    IsActive:     isActive,
                    Country:      country,
                    PersonalBest: personalBest.String,
                    SeasonBest:   seasonBest.String,
                }

                runners = append(runners, runner)
            }

            if rows.Err() != nil {
                return nil, &models.ResponseError{
                    Message: err.Error(),
                    Status:  http.StatusInternalServerError,
                }
            }

            return runners, nil
        }
```

We will not introduce anything new in the methods of the results repository (except that **`DeleteResult()`** method will actually execute the **`DELETE`** command), so we will just provide complete code from the **`resultsRepository.go`** file (*Figure 7.12*) in order to show the complete solution:

```
package repositories

import (
        "database/sql"
        "net/http"
```

```
        "runners-postgresql/models"
)

type ResultsRepository struct {
        dbHandler   *sql.DB
        transaction *sql.Tx
}

func NewResultsRepository(dbHAndler *sql.DB) *ResultsRepository {
        return &ResultsRepository{
                dbHandler: dbHAndler,
        }
}

func (rr ResultsRepository) CreateResult(
        result *models.Result) (*models.Result, *models.ResponseError) {

        query := `
                INSERT INTO results(runner_id, race_result, location,
                position, year)
                VALUES ($1, $2, $3, $4, $5)
                RETURNING id`

        rows, err := rr.transaction.Query(query, result.RunnerID,
                result.RaceResult, result.Location, result.Position,
                result.Year)
        if err != nil {
                return nil, &models.ResponseError{
                        Message: err.Error(),
                        Status:  http.StatusInternalServerError,
                }
        }

        defer rows.Close()

        var resultId string
        for rows.Next() {
```

```
			err := rows.Scan(&resultId)
			if err != nil {
				return nil, &models.ResponseError{
					Message: err.Error(),
					Status: http.StatusInternalServerError,
				}
			}
		}

		if rows.Err() != nil {
			return nil, &models.ResponseError{
				Message: err.Error(),
				Status:  http.StatusInternalServerError,
			}
		}

		return &models.Result{
			ID:         resultId,
			RunnerID:   result.RunnerID,
			RaceResult: result.RaceResult,
			Location:   result.Location,
			Position:   result.Position,
			Year:       result.Year,
		}, nil
	}

	func (rr ResultsRepository) DeleteResult(
		resultId string) (*models.Result, *models.ResponseError) {

		query := `
			DELETE FROM results
			WHERE id = $1
			RETURNING runner_id, race_result, year`

		rows, err := rr.transaction.Query(query, resultId)
		if err != nil {
```

```
            return nil, &models.ResponseError{
                Message: err.Error(),
                Status:  http.StatusInternalServerError,
            }
        }

        defer rows.Close()
        var runnerId, raceResult string
        var year int
        for rows.Next() {
            err := rows.Scan(&runnerId, &raceResult, &year)
            if err != nil {
                return nil, &models.ResponseError{
                    Message: err.Error(),
                    Status:  http.StatusInternalServerError,
                }
            }
        }

        if rows.Err() != nil {
            return nil, &models.ResponseError{
                Message: err.Error(),
                Status:  http.StatusInternalServerError,
            }
        }

        return &models.Result{
            ID:         resultId,
            RunnerID:   runnerId,
            RaceResult: raceResult,
            Year:       year,
        }, nil
}

func (rr ResultsRepository) GetAllRunnersResults(
    runnerId string) ([]*models.Result,
```

```
*models.ResponseError) {

query := `
	SELECT id, race_result, location, position, year
	FROM results
	WHERE runner_id = $1`

rows, err := rr.dbHandler.Query(query, runnerId)
if err != nil {
	return nil, &models.ResponseError{
		Message: err.Error(),
		Status:  http.
			StatusInternalServerError,
	}
}

defer rows.Close()

results := make([]*models.Result, 0)
var id, raceResult, location string
var position, year int

for rows.Next() {
	err := rows.Scan(&id, &raceResult, &location,
		&position, &year)
	if err != nil {
		return nil, &models.ResponseError{
			Message: err.Error(),
			Status:  http.
				StatusInternalServerError,
		}
	}

	result := &models.Result{
		ID:         id,
		RunnerID:   runnerId,
		RaceResult: raceResult,
```

```
                Location:   location,
                Position:   position,
                Year:       year,
            }

            results = append(results, result)
        }

        if rows.Err() != nil {
            return nil, &models.ResponseError{
                Message: err.Error(),
                Status:  http.
                        StatusInternalServerError,
            }
        }

        return results, nil
    }

    func (rr ResultsRepository) GetPersonalBestResults(
        runnerId string) (string, *models.ResponseError) {

        query := `
            SELECT MIN(race_result)
            FROM results
            WHERE runner_id = $1`

        rows, err := rr.dbHandler.Query(query, runnerId)
        if err != nil {
            return "", &models.ResponseError{
                Message: err.Error(),
                Status:  http.
                        StatusInternalServerError,
            }
        }

        defer rows.Close()
```

```
	var raceResult string

	for rows.Next() {
		err := rows.Scan(&raceResult)
		if err != nil {
			return "", &models.ResponseError{
				Message: err.Error(),
				Status:  http.
					StatusInternalServerError,
			}
		}
	}

	if rows.Err() != nil {
		return "", &models.ResponseError{
			Message: err.Error(),
			Status:  http.
				StatusInternalServerError,
		}
	}

	return raceResult, nil
}

func (rr ResultsRepository) GetSeasonBestResults(
	runnerId string, year int) (string,
	*models.ResponseError) {

	query := `
		SELECT MIN(race_result)
		FROM results
		WHERE runner_id = $1 AND year = $2`

	rows, err := rr.dbHandler.Query(query, runnerId, year)
	if err != nil {
		return "", &models.ResponseError{
			Message: err.Error(),
			Status:  http.
```

```
                    StatusInternalServerError,
            }
        }

        defer rows.Close()

        var raceResult string

        for rows.Next() {
            err := rows.Scan(&raceResult)
            if err != nil {
                return "", &models.ResponseError{
                    Message: err.Error(),
                    Status:  http.
                        StatusInternalServerError,
                }
            }
        }

        if rows.Err() != nil {
            return "", &models.ResponseError{
                Message: err.Error(),
                Status:  http.
                    StatusInternalServerError,
            }
        }

        return raceResult, nil
    }
```

The *third* file, **transactionHandler.go**, contains three functions for transaction manipulations (*Figure 7.12*). Each function will receive both repositories and manipulate them with the transaction field.

The *first* function, **BeginTransaction()**, will create a new transaction and assign it to **runners** and **result** repositories. Each transaction must have its own context, which will be created with the **Background()** function from the **context** package. This function will create an empty context.

The transaction may also have some options, but for our usage, default options are enough, so we can pass empty **TxOptions struct**:

```
func BeginTransaction(runnersRepository *RunnersRepository,
      resultsRepository *ResultsRepository) error {

      ctx := context.Background()
      transaction, err := resultsRepository.dbHandler.
            BeginTx(ctx, &sql.TxOptions{})
      if err != nil {
            return err
      }

      runnersRepository.transaction = transaction
      resultsRepository.transaction = transaction

      return nil
}
```

The *second* function, **`RollbackTransaction()`** will be used in the case when some error occurs. It will set transaction fields to **`nil`** (because the transaction will not be used anymore) in both repositories and roll-back transactions:

```
func RollbackTransaction(runnersRepository *RunnersRepository,
      resultsRepository *ResultsRepository) error {

      transaction := runnersRepository.transaction

      runnersRepository.transaction = nil
      resultsRepository.transaction = nil
      return transaction.Rollback()
}
```

And finally, the *third* function, **`CommitTransaction()`** will be used if all SQL queries are executed as expected. It will set transaction fields to **`nil`** in both repositories and execute the **`commit`**:

```
func CommitTransaction(runnersRepository *RunnersRepository,
      resultsRepository *ResultsRepository) error {

      transaction := runnersRepository.transaction

      runnersRepository.transaction = nil
      resultsRepository.transaction = nil
```

```
        return transaction.Commit()
    }
```

Now let us take back to the *service layer*, for a moment. These transaction functions will be used in **CreateResult()** and **DeleteResult()** methods. Before we call any repository method, we should call **BeginTransaction()** function.

In case of any error, we should call **RollbackTransaction()** function, and if everything is successful we will call **CommitTransaction()**, usually at the end of the function, before the *last* return. Read operations from repository layers do not affect the database state, so they can be omitted from the transaction, but if any error occurs during these operations transaction should be roll-backed.

Here is the updated **DeleteResult()** function from the results service that uses these transaction functions:

```
    func (rs ResultsService) DeleteResult(
            resultId string) *models.ResponseError {
            if resultId == "" {
                    return &models.ResponseError{
                            Message: "Invalid result ID",
                            Status:  http.StatusBadRequest,
                    }
            }

            err := repositories.BeginTransaction(
                    rs.runnersRepository, rs.resultsRepository)
            if err != nil {
                    return &models.ResponseError{
                            Message: "Failed to start transaction",
                            Status:  http.StatusBadRequest,
                    }
            }

            result, responseErr := rs.resultsRepository.
                    DeleteResult(resultId)
            if responseErr != nil {
                    return responseErr
            }
```

```
runner, responseErr := rs.runnersRepository.GetRunner(
	result.RunnerID)
if responseErr != nil {
	repositories.RollbackTransaction(
		rs.runnersRepository, rs.resultsRepository)
	return responseErr
}

// Checking if the deleted result is
// personal best for the runner
if runner.PersonalBest == result.RaceResult {
	personalBest, responseErr := rs.resultsRepository.
		GetPersonalBestResults(result.RunnerID)
	if responseErr != nil {
		repositories.RollbackTransaction(
			rs.runnersRepository,
			rs.resultsRepository)
		return responseErr
	}
	runner.PersonalBest = personalBest
}

// Checking if the deleted result is
// season best for the runner
currentYear := time.Now().Year()
if runner.SeasonBest == result.RaceResult &&
	result.Year == currentYear {

	seasonBest, responseErr := rs.resultsRepository.
		GetSeasonBestResults(result.RunnerID,
			result.Year)
	if responseErr != nil {
		repositories.RollbackTransaction(
			rs.runnersRepository, rs.resultsRepository)
		return responseErr
	}
```

```
                runner.SeasonBest = seasonBest
        }

        responseErr = rs.runnersRepository.
                UpdateRunnerResults(runner)
        if responseErr != nil {
                repositories.RollbackTransaction(
                        rs.runnersRepository, rs.resultsRepository)
                return responseErr
        }

        repositories.CommitTransaction(
                rs.runnersRepository, rs.resultsRepository)

        return nil
}
```

This transaction solution is not the best one, and the most optimal. But idea was to show *school* examples of how transactions can be used. In the following section, we will develop the last layer, the database layer, and complete our solution.

Database layer

The database layer will mostly use a database package from the Go standard library, so there would not be much code. First, we must download and install the PostgreSQL driver for the Go programming language, with the following command:

```
go get github.com/lib/pq
```

If we want to use this driver in our code, this line must be added to the **`import`** statement of the file where the **`main()`** function is:

```
_ "github.com/lib/pq"
```

Let's take another look at the database connection string from the configuration file (**`runners.toml`**):

```
connection_string = "host=localhost port=5432 user=postgres
        password=postgres dbname=runners_db sslmode=disable"
```

As we can see, all parameters from the connection string are ones configured during database creation in **pgAdmin** (*host name, port, database name*) or during **installation** (*user* and *password*).

The whole logic for the database layer is placed in **dbServer.go** inside the **server** package (*Figure 7.13*). This file will have only one function, **InitDatabase()**:

Figure 7.13*: Server packages*

At the start of the function, we will use **Viper** to read database-related configuration. If the connection string is *empty*, there is no need to try to establish a connection with the database, that attempt will fail. An empty connection string will terminate the application.

Function **Open()** from the **sql** package will *open* the database. This function may just validate its arguments without creating a connection to a database, to verify that everything is valid we must call **Ping()** function.

Function **Ping()** verifies a connection to the database is *still alive* and establishes a connection if necessary. Between calls of these two functions, values from the configuration will be assigned to **dbHandler**.

If any error occurs, the application will be terminated:

```
func InitDatabase(config *viper.Viper) *sql.DB {
	connectionString := config.GetString(
		"database.connection_string")
	maxIdleConnections := config.GetInt(
		"database.max_idle_connections")
	maxOpenConnections := config.GetInt(
		"database.max_open_connections")
	connectionMaxLifetime := config.GetDuration(
		"database.connection_max_lifetime")
	driverName := config.GetString("database.driver_name")

	if connectionString == "" {
		log.Fatalf("Database connection string is missing")
	}

	dbHandler, err := sql.Open(driverName, connectionString)
	if err != nil {
		log.Fatalf("Error while initializing database: %v",
			err)
```

```
        }

        dbHandler.SetMaxIdleConns(maxIdleConnections)
        dbHandler.SetMaxOpenConns(maxOpenConnections)
        dbHandler.SetConnMaxLifetime(connectionMaxLifetime)

        err = dbHandler.Ping()
        if err != nil {
                dbHandler.Close()
                log.Fatalf("Error while validating database: %v",
                        err)
        }

        return dbHandler
}
```

Congratulations!!! Our solution is now completed and we can start it with the following command:

```
go run main.go
```

If everything is started properly, this should be the last line displayed in the terminal:

```
[GIN-debug] Listening and serving HTTP on :8080
```

At the end of the chapter, we will see how to use different relational database management systems (MySQL) to implement the repository and database layer.

MySQL

MySQL is an *open-source* relational database management system. It was owned by *MySQL AB,* a *Swedish* software company, and currently is owned by *Oracle Corporation*. It is one of the most popular database management systems.

Setting up a database

MySQL is supported by all modern operating systems. First, we should install MySQL Server. Community distribution is *free,* so we will install that server distribution. Installation files can be found on the official website:

https://dev.mysql.com/downloads/mysql/

Latest supported *MySQL Community Server* version can be installed on Linux with the following commands:

- Red Hat Enterprise Linux (6 and 7):

  ```
  sudo yum install mysql-community-server
  ```

- Red Hat Enterprise Linux 8 and Fedora:

  ```
  sudo dnf install mysql-community-server
  ```

- Debian and Ubuntu:

  ```
  sudo apt install mysql-server
  ```

After MySQL server installation, security installation should be started, where *username* and *password* can be set:

```
sudo mysql_secure_installation
```

MySQL will not be started automatically after installation, so it must be started with one of the following commands:

- Red Hat Enterprise Linux (6 and 7):

  ```
  sudo service mysqld start
  ```

- Red Hat Enterprise Linux 8 and Fedora:

  ```
  sudo systemctl start mysqld
  ```

- Debian and Ubuntu:

  ```
  sudo service start mysql
  ```

For Windows, we should only download the installation file and follow the installation instructions. Again, we should set up a *username* and *password* during installation.

MySQL is included in some versions of Mac. If that is not the case, we should download the installation file and follow the instructions.

MySQL Workbench is popular administration and development platform for MySQL. We will also use *Community distribution*. Installation files can be found on the official website:

https://dev.mysql.com/downloads/workbench/

On the *Download* page, we can select our operating system and download the installation file. When a file is downloaded, we should just follow installation instructions.

During MySQL Server installation on Windows or Mac, it is possible that MySQL Workbench will be installed, so we should check that before we download installation files.

When the installation is complete, we can start MySQL Workbench and create a new MySQL Connection by clicking on the plus (**+**) icon (*Figure 7.14*):

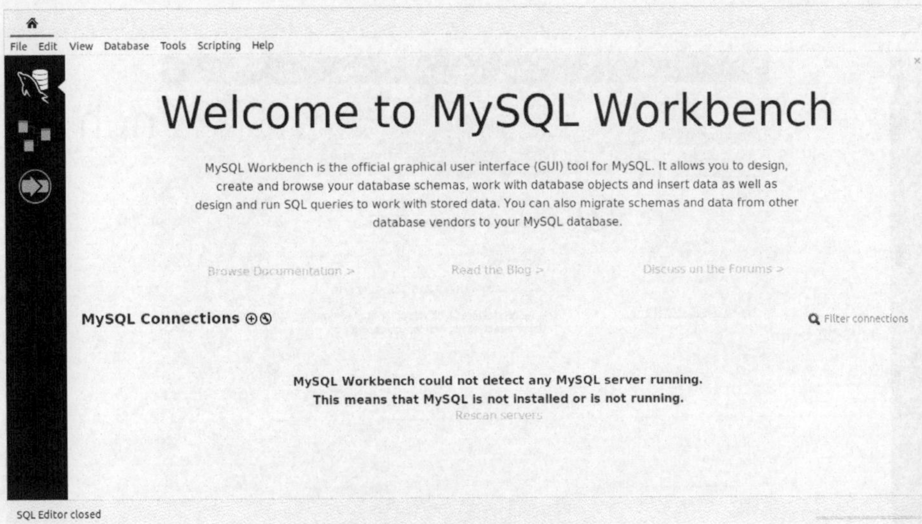

***Figure 7.14**: MySQL Workbench*

In the newly opened panel, we should enter **`localhost`** for **Connection Name** and leave the **Hostname** and **Port** setting to designated values (port **`3306`** is the standard port used for MySQL databases). Here we can use a *username* and *password* set up during installation. We can also use our **`root`** user for this case (*Figure 7.15*):

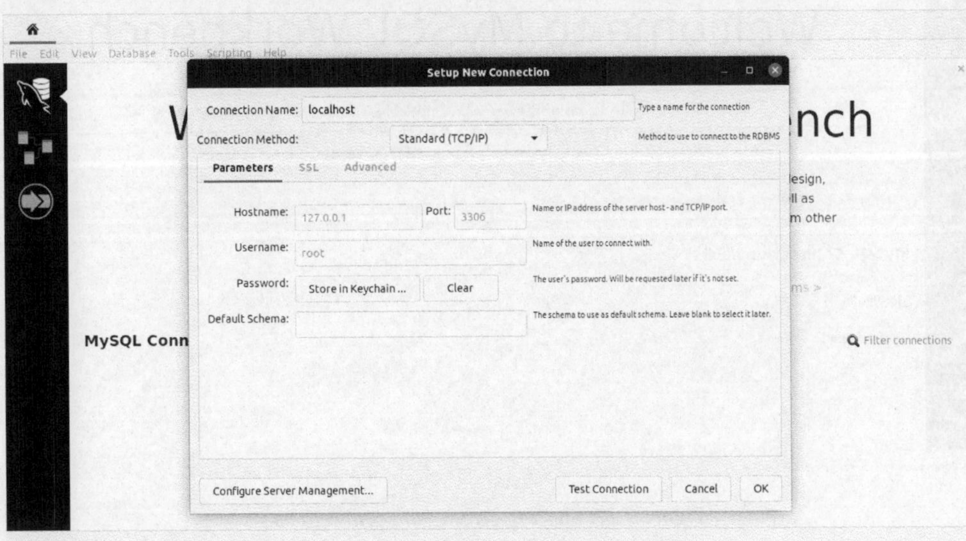

***Figure 7.15**: Create a new connection*

We can use the **Test Connection** button to check if our connection works. If everything works as expected successful message will be displayed (*Figure 7.16*). If everything is fine, we can click on the **OK** button:

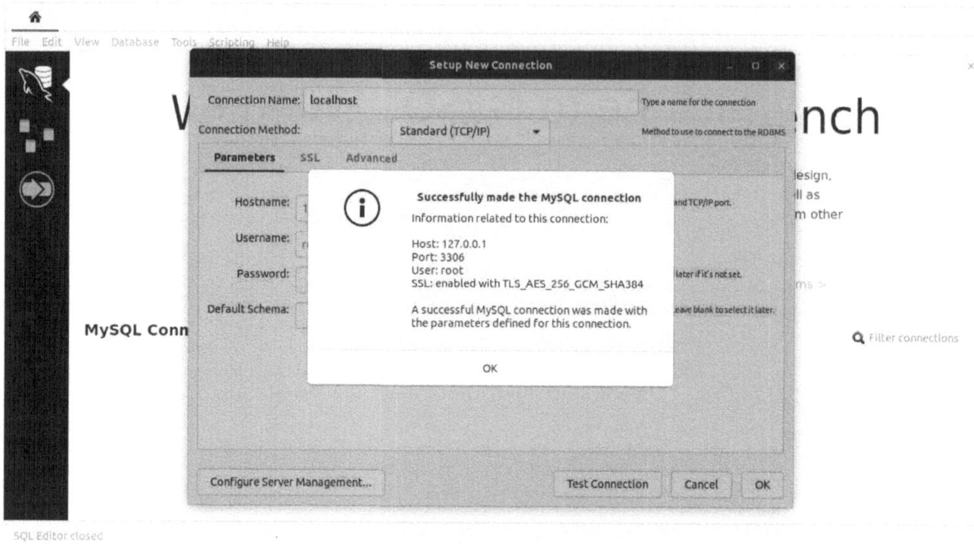

Figure 7.16: Test connection

Now we can see our connection on starting screen (*Figure 7.17*):

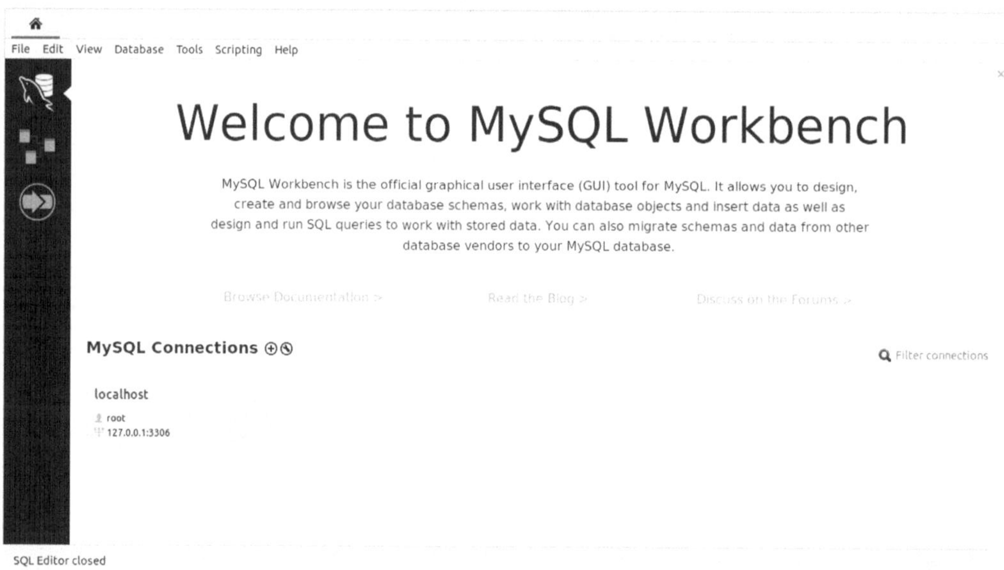

Figure 7.17: Starting screen with connections

Now we can create our database. First, we must *double-click* on our connection. Then, we must click on the *Create a new schema in the connected server* icon (*Figure 7.18*):

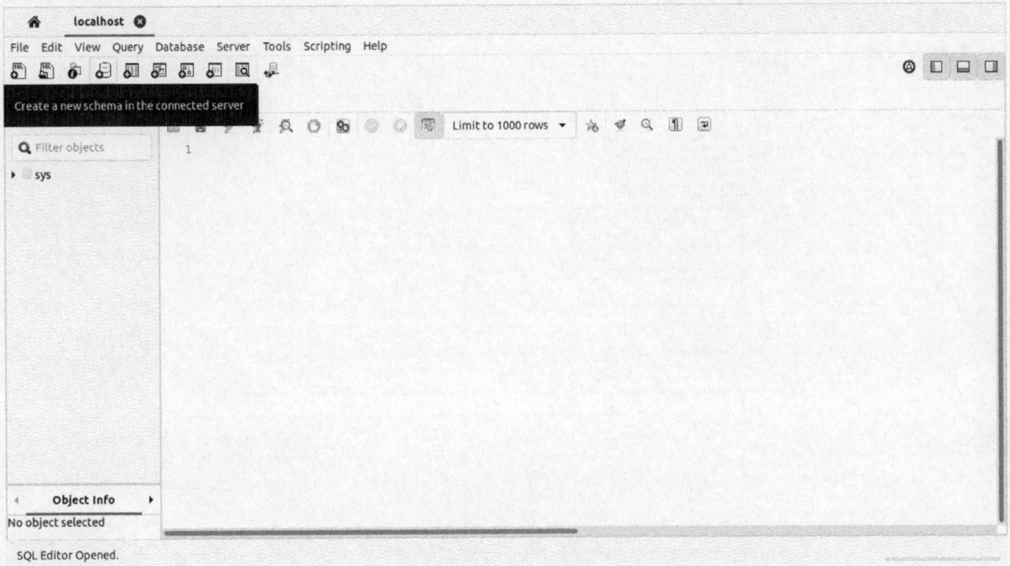

Figure 7.18: Create a new schema in the connected server

In the **Schema Editor** panel, we will enter `runners_db` for **Schema Name**, and set the **Character set** to **utf8** (*Figure 7.19*):

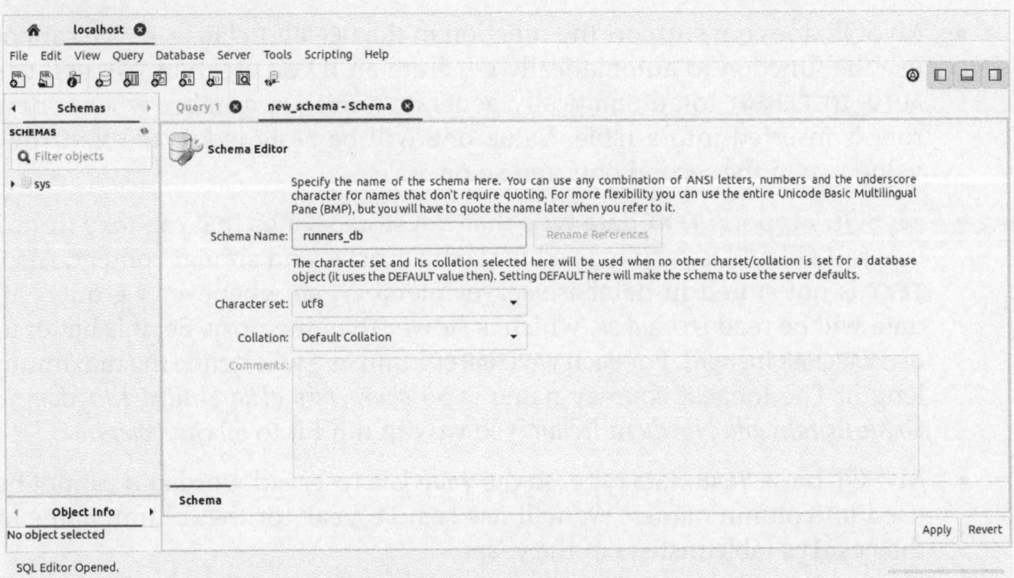

Figure 7.19: Schema editor panel

We will use a query editor to create our tables (*Figure 7.20*). Again, we will use the `public_schema.sql` file from the `dbscripts` directory:

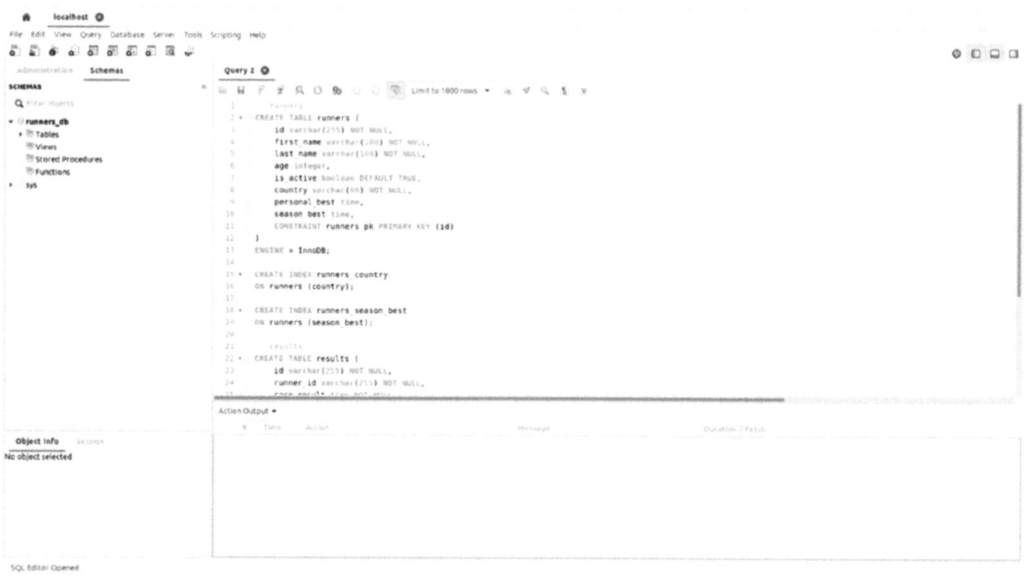

Figure 7.20: Query editor

We will comment on the differences between this script, and one used for PostgreSQL:

- MySQL does not support the function in the **DEFAULT** clause, so we cannot use the function to automatically generate an ID on creation. We will use **AUTO_INCREMENT** to automatically generate a unique number when a new row is inserted into a table. Value one will be assigned to the first row, value two to the second one, and so on.
- MySQL supports **TEXT** data type that can store strings that can take from *1 byte* to *4 GB* and is mainly used for some articles and similar content. Also, **TEXT** is not stored in database server memory, so whenever we query it, data will be read from *disk*, which is slower than memory. So, it is better to use **VARCHAR** instead. For each **VARCHAR** column, we will define the maximum length. The longest country name is *56 characters* (*The United Kingdom of Great Britain and Northern Ireland*) so we can limit it to *60 characters*.
- MySQL has a **YEAR** data type, so the **year** is a reserved word and cannot be used for column names. We will use **result_year** for the column name in the **results** table instead of the **year**.

Here is the content of the **public_schema.sql** file:

```
-- runners
CREATE TABLE runners (
    id int NOT NULL AUTO_INCREMENT,
```

```
        first_name varchar(100) NOT NULL,
        last_name varchar(100) NOT NULL,
        age integer,
        is_active boolean DEFAULT TRUE,
        country varchar(60) NOT NULL,
        personal_best time,
        season_best time,
        CONSTRAINT runners_pk PRIMARY KEY (id)
    )
    ENGINE = InnoDB;

    CREATE INDEX runners_country
    ON runners (country);

    CREATE INDEX runners_season_best
    ON runners (season_best);

    -- results
    CREATE TABLE results (
        id int NOT NULL AUTO_INCREMENT,
        runner_id int NOT NULL,
        race_result time NOT NULL,
        location varchar(100) NOT NULL,
        position integer,
        result_year integer NOT NULL,
        CONSTRAINT results_pk PRIMARY KEY (id),
        CONSTRAINT fk_results_runner_id FOREIGN KEY (runner_id)
            REFERENCES runners (id)
            ON UPDATE NO ACTION
            ON DELETE NO ACTION
    )
    ENGINE = InnoDB;
```

For each table, we should define the *storage engine*. If tables use different engines, we cannot create foreign keys. A **storage engine** can be defined as a software module that a database management system uses to create, read, and update database data.

There are two types of storage engines in MySQL:

- Transactional
- Non-Transactional

InnoDB is the most popular engine with transaction support, and it is the default engine since MySQL 5.5.

Now, we can copy the content of the `public_schema.sql` file into the query editor and click on the *lightning* icon to execute the script. If everything is successfully executed, a success message will be displayed and tables can be seen in the **SCHEMAS** tab (*Figure 7.21*):

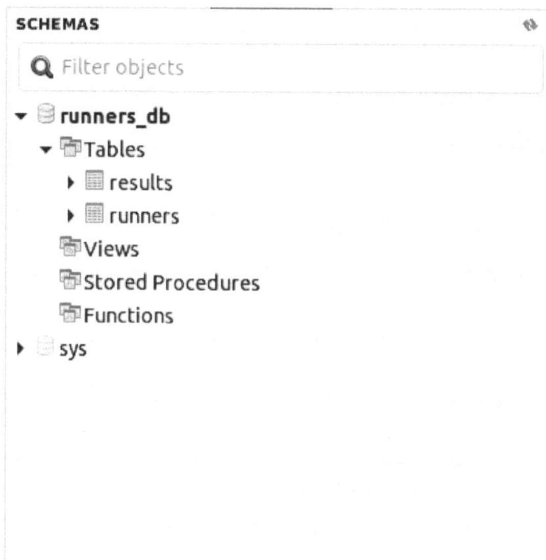

***Figure 7.21**: Schemas tab*

Now we can see differences between repository layers implemented with MySQL and PostgreSQL.

Repository layer

MySQL and PostgreSQL support similar syntax, so changes will be *minimal*, but there are a couple of important differences:

- Query arguments are passed with a *dollar sign* (**$**) and numbers for PostgreSQL, but MySQL expects *question mark* (**?**) without numbers. So, the following PostgreSQL query:

```
query := `
        UPDATE runners
        SET
```

```
                first_name = $1,
                last_name = $2,
                age = $3,
                country = $4
        WHERE id = $5`
```

Must be converted to:

```
query := `
        UPDATE runners
        SET
                first_name = ?,
                last_name = ?,
                age = ?,
                country = ?
        WHERE id = ?`
```

- For Boolean data type in PostgreSQL, we can use **TRUE**, **FALSE**, or string representations (**true** and **false**). In MySQL, we must use **TRUE** or **FALSE**.
- There is no **RETURNING** statement in MySQL, but we can use **LastInsertId()** method to get an ID generated during the **INSERT** command. The method will return an *integer value,* so we must convert it to a string in order to avoid changes in the model and other application layers.

Here is **CreateRunner()** method updated to follow MySQL restrictions:

```
func (rr RunnersRepository) CreateRunner(
        runner *models.Runner) (*models.Runner,
        *models.ResponseError) {

        query := `
                INSERT INTO runners(first_name, last_name,
                        age, country)
                VALUES (?, ?, ?, ?)`

        res, err := rr.dbHandler.Exec(query, runner.FirstName,
                runner.LastName, runner.Age, runner.Country)
        if err != nil {
                return nil, &models.ResponseError{
                        Message: err.Error(),
                        Status:  http.StatusInternalServerError,
```

```
            }
        }

        runnerId, err := res.LastInsertId()
        if err != nil {
            return nil, &models.ResponseError{
                Message: err.Error(),
                Status:  http.StatusInternalServerError,
            }
        }

        return &models.Runner{
            ID:        strconv.FormatInt(runnerId, 10),
            FirstName: runner.FirstName,
            LastName:  runner.LastName,
            Age:       runner.Age,
            IsActive:  true,
            Country:   runner.Country,
        }, nil
    }
```

We used **RETURNING** statement in **DeleteResult()** method to get the runner ID, race result, and year. But method **LastInsertId()** will not return these values. So, we must create a new repository layer method to **GetResult()** and call it in the service layer before **DeleteResult()** method in order to keep the existing business logic.

Here is a code for **GetResult()** method from the repository layer:

```
    func (rr ResultsRepository) GetResult(
        resultId string) (*models.Result, *models.ResponseError) {

        query := `
            SELECT *
            FROM results
            WHERE id = ?;`

        rows, err := rr.dbHandler.Query(query, resultId)
        if err != nil {
            return nil, &models.ResponseError{
```

```
                Message: err.Error(),
                Status:  http.StatusInternalServerError,
            }
        }

        defer rows.Close()

        var id, runnerId, raceResult, location string
        var position, year int
        for rows.Next() {
            err := rows.Scan(&id, &runnerId, &raceResult,
                &location, &position, &year)
            if err != nil {
                return nil, &models.ResponseError{
                    Message: err.Error(),
                    Status:  http.
                        StatusInternalServerError,
                }
            }
        }

        if rows.Err() != nil {
            return nil, &models.ResponseError{
                Message: err.Error(),
                Status:  http.
                    StatusInternalServerError,
            }
        }

        return &models.Result{
            ID:         id,
            RunnerID:   runnerId,
            RaceResult: raceResult,
            Location:   location,
            Position:   position,
            Year:       year,
```

```
        }, nil
}
```

And here is an updated **DeleteResult()** method from the service layer:

```
func (rs ResultsService) DeleteResult(
        resultId string) *models.ResponseError {

        if resultId == "" {
                return &models.ResponseError{
                        Message: "Invalid result ID",
                        Status:  http.StatusBadRequest,
                }
        }

        err := repositories.BeginTransaction(
                rs.runnersRepository, rs.resultsRepository)
        if err != nil {
                return &models.ResponseError{
                        Message: "Failed to start transaction",
                        Status:  http.StatusBadRequest,
                }
        }

        result, responseErr := rs.resultsRepository.
                GetResult(resultId)
        if responseErr != nil {
                return responseErr
        }

        responseErr = rs.resultsRepository.DeleteResult(resultId)
        if responseErr != nil {
                return responseErr
        }

        runner, responseErr := rs.runnersRepository.
                GetRunner(result.RunnerID)
        if responseErr != nil {
```

```
            repositories.RollbackTransaction(
                rs.runnersRepository,
                rs.resultsRepository)
            return responseErr
        }

        // Checking if the deleted result is
        // personal best for the runner
        if runner.PersonalBest == result.RaceResult {
            personalBest, responseErr := rs.resultsRepository.
                GetPersonalBestResults(result.RunnerID)
            if responseErr != nil {
                repositories.RollbackTransaction(
                    rs.runnersRepository,
                    rs.resultsRepository)
                return responseErr
            }
            runner.PersonalBest = personalBest
        }

        // Checking if the deleted result is
        // season best for the runner
        currentYear := time.Now().Year()
        if runner.SeasonBest == result.RaceResult &&
            result.Year == currentYear {

            seasonBest, responseErr := rs.resultsRepository.
                GetSeasonBestResults(result.RunnerID,
                result.Year)
            if responseErr != nil {
                repositories.RollbackTransaction(
                    rs.runnersRepository,
                    rs.resultsRepository)
                return responseErr
            }
            runner.SeasonBest = seasonBest
```

```
        }

        responseErr = rs.runnersRepository.
                UpdateRunnerResults(runner)
        if responseErr != nil {
                repositories.RollbackTransaction(
                        rs.runnersRepository,
                        rs.resultsRepository)
                return responseErr
        }

        repositories.CommitTransaction(rs.runnersRepository,
                rs.resultsRepository)

        return nil
}
```

When all required changes are applied, we can move to the database layer.

Database layer

The database layer will undergo the least changes. A new driver for MySQL must be installed and used. The following command will download and install the driver:

```
go get github.com/go-sql-driver/mysql
```

Now we will put this line to the import statement of the file where the **main()** function is placed:

```
_ "github.com/go-sql-driver/mysql"
```

Only two lines from the configuration file must be changed, the connection string (because MySQL uses a different format), and the driver name. Again, all parameters from the connection string are ones configured during database creation in MySQL Workbench (*host name, port, database name*). Additional *usernames* and *passwords* configured during the installation of MySQL or during security configuration will also be used in the connection string:

```
connection_string = "root:root123@tcp(localhost:3306)/runners_db"
driver_name = "mysql"
```

Congratulations!!! We completed the application with a different database management system. We can start it and check if everything will run as expected.

Improvements

In *Chapter 6, Application Layers,* we mentioned that each time we delete or create a result, season best, and personal best results for the specified runners must be updated. Basically, we duplicated that data, the same information is stored in both tables and that is not a good practice.

The solution for this problem is quite simple; we can remove **personal_best** and **season_best** columns from the **runners** table, and get this information with a sub-query. Here is an example of a PostgreSQL query that will get runner information from the **runners** table, while personal best and season best results will be retrieved from the **results** table:

```
SELECT *, pb.personal_best, sb.season_best
FROM runners,
        (
                SELECT MIN(race_result) AS personal_best
                FROM results
                WHERE runner_id = $1
        ) pb,
        (
                SELECT MIN(race_result) AS season_best
                FROM results
                WHERE runner_id = $1 AND year = $2
        ) sb
WHERE id = $1;
```

The *first* solution (where data is duplicated) is efficient for reading, especially, for queries where multiple runners are read from the database, but it can cause inconsistency if the data is not properly updated. The *second* solution with sub-queries is more consistent, but it can be less efficient when reading a lot of data.

If we have much more reading than writing, the first solution is a better option. In other cases, the second consistent solution is the one we need.

Conclusion

In this chapter, we finally completed our server applications. We introduced basic concepts of relational databases and designed a repository layer to utilize them. Two different types of database management systems (PostgreSQL and MySQL) are shown and compared in this chapter, each with its own advantages and disadvantages.

In the next chapter, we will introduce concepts of NoSQL databases and see some different implementations of the repository layer.

References

- https://www.postgresql.org
- https://www.pgadmin.org
- https://github.com/lib/pq
- https://dev.mysql.com/downloads/mysql/
- https://dev.mysql.com/downloads/workbench/
- https://github.com/go-sql-driver/mysql

Points to remember

- Indices are a mechanism for improving performance on a database table, but for systems where data will be often created than read, indices are not efficient.
- SQL queries can be executed in the terminal, but it is much easier to use some tools.
- Data type **INTERVAL** (PostgreSQL) and **TIME** (MySQL) should be used to represent **duration** data.
- Read operations can be omitted from the transaction, but if any error occurs during these operations transaction should be roll-backed.
- Data type **TEXT** (MySQL) will not be stored in database server memory, data will be stored on disk, which makes read operations slower. It is better to use the **VARCHAR** data type.
- We should try to avoid storing the same data in multiple database tables.

Multiple choice questions

1. Which of these cardinalities is non-existent?
    a. One-to-More
    b. One-to-One
    c. One-to-Many
    d. One-to-Optional-One

2. Which aggregation function does not ignore the NULL value?

    b. `MAX()`

    c. `MIN()`

    d. `SUB()`

    e. `COUNT()`

3. What is not a type of JOIN?

    c. INNER JOIN

    d. RIGHT JOIN

    e. EMPTY JOIN

    f. LEFT JOIN

Answers

1. a
2. d
3. c

Questions

1. What NULL value represents?
2. Differences between primary and foreign keys?
3. What are transactions?
4. When index can be created automatically?
5. Which are the basic modifications of SQL commands?

Key terms

- **Relational databases**: Databases based on a relational model, where data is organized in tuples grouped into relations.
- **SQL (Structured Query Language)**: Language designed for manipulation of data from relational databases.
- **PostgreSQL**: Open source object-relational database management system.
- **MySQL**: Open source relational database management system.

CHAPTER 8

NoSQL Databases and Repository Layer

Introduction

In this chapter, we will introduce the basic concepts of NoSQL databases. After that, we will learn more about the **MongoDB** database and how to implement the repository layer with it. After that, we will use another technology (**DynamoDB**) to implement a repository layer. At the end of the chapter, we will have a light comparison of these solutions and solutions that used a relational database and propose some potential improvements.

Structure

In this chapter, we will discuss the following topics:

- NoSQL databases
- MongoDB
    - Database design
    - Read operations
    - Write operations
    - Aggregation pipeline
    - Setting up a database
    - Repository layer
    - Database layer
- DynamoDB
    - Database design

    - Read operation
    - Write operations
    - Setting up a database
    - Repository layer
    - Database layer
- Improvements

NoSQL databases

NoSQL databases are databases used for the storage and manipulation of data modeled in a different way than tabular relations. They become popular in the early *twenty-first century* with the increased development of real-time web applications.

There is no exact classification of NoSQL databases, but we can define the following categories based on the data model:

- **Key-value databases**, where data is represented as a collection of *key-value pairs* (DynamoDB).
- **Document-oriented databases**, where data is represented in a form of a *document*. The document can be defined as data encapsulated and encoded in some standard format, like **XML**, **YAML**, or **JSON** (MongoDB).
- **Graph databases**, where data is represented in a form of a *graph*.

MongoDB

MongoDB is a *document-oriented NoSQL database* that uses **BSON (Binary JSON)** documents. Here are some main MongoDB concepts:

- **Database**: Group of collections. One database can have multiple collections.
- **Collection**: Group of documents. It is equivalent to a table in *a relational database*. There is no strict schema in NoSQL databases, each document can contain different fields.
- **Document**: Record in a collection and basic data unit. It is equivalent to a row in a relational database.
- **Field**: The basic unit of which the document is composed. It is equivalent to a column in a relational database.
- **BSON**: Binary representation of JSON documents, but with more types.
- **Index**: Data structure for query optimization. For the `_id` field index is automatically created. The following indices can be defined in MongoDB:

  - **Single field index**: Index on a single field of a document
  - **Compound index**: Index on two or more fields of a document
  - **Text index**: Index on a textual field of a document that supports search for string content
- **Transaction**: Sequence of read or write operations to multiple documents treated as a single (atomic) operation. If the transaction is aborted all changes will be discarded. Changes will be applied and visible after the commit.
- **Batch**: Set of documents that are processed together.
- **Cursor**: Set of documents returned by a read operation.
- **Sharding**: The method for distributing data across multiple *machines*, mainly used for systems with large data sets that can overload a single database server. MongoDB shards data on the collection level (*Figure 8.1*), distributing data across the shards by *shard key* (single field index or compound index).
- **Sharded cluster**: Data from the same collection is distributed across multiple servers:

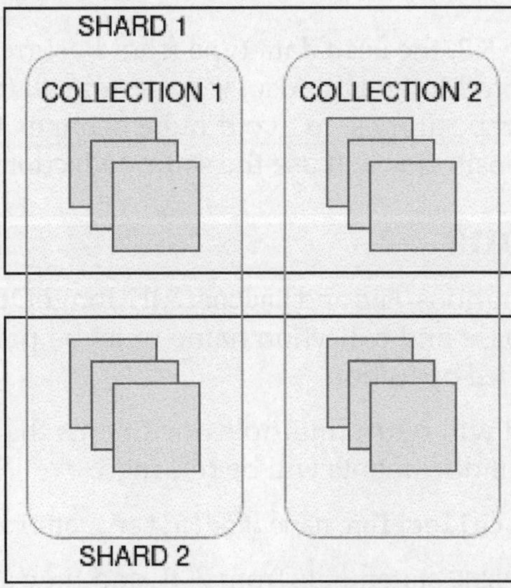

***Figure 8.1**: MongoDB sharding*

Now that we are familiar with basic MongoDB concepts, we can *redesign* the database from *Chapter 5, Design of Web Application*, to utilize and follow these concepts.

Database design

In our *old* database design, we had two tables, one for each resource. MongoDB documents are different than rows from a relational database, so *we can use that fact to merge these tables into one collection!* All results will be stored in arrays as part of runner documents (*Figure 8.2*):

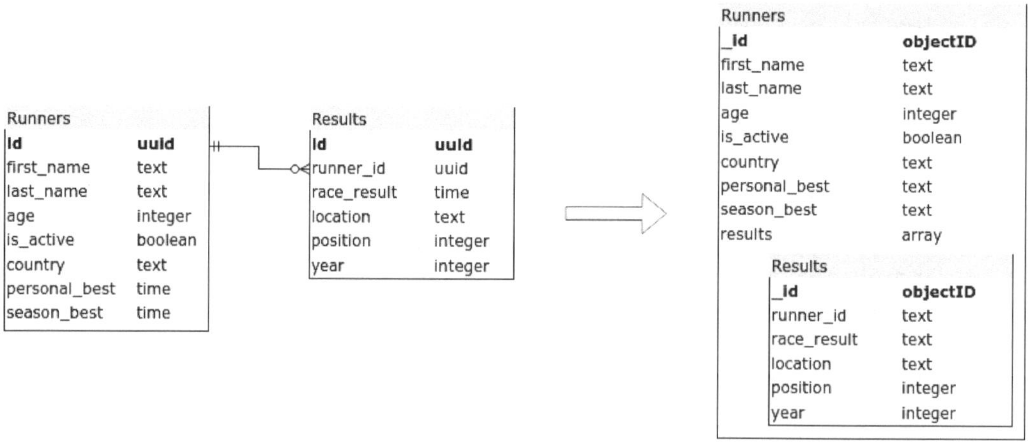

***Figure 8.2**: Database redesign*

As we can see in *Figure 8.2*, the **uuid** data type from PostgreSQL must be changed to the **objectID** type from MongoDB. Also, we can store all *time-related fields* as text. We can still have two repositories, to avoid huge changes to the original layered design, where both repositories will use the same collection.

Read operations

There are two read operations, **find** and **findOne**. All MongoDB operations follow the same syntax, the database and collection name must be provided (in that order), after which we use *desired* operation.

The first operation find will return multiple documents that fulfill the filter. If the filter is not provided, all documents will be returned:

```
database_name.collection_name.find(filter, options)
```

The filter is similar to **WHERE** statements from SQL and they are used to extract only documents that fulfill conditions defined in the filter. Filter follows this form:

```
{ field_name: condition }
```

The condition can be a simple value, for example, if we have a *collection of cars*, and the color is defined for each car, the following filter will extract only *blue* cars:

```
{ "color": "blue" }
```

There are multiple ways to define a simple condition on an array field:

- The entire array must match:

```
{ array_field: [ element1, element2, …, elementN ]}
```

- The array must contain the specified element:

```
{ array_field: element }
```

- The array must contain the specified element in the specified position:

```
{ array_field.position: element }
```

Conditions can contain expressions, usually in one of the following two forms (the second form is used for arrays):

```
{ field_name: { operator: value }}
{ field_name: { operator: [ value1, value2, …, valueN ]}}
```

There are several groups of operators used in expressions, and now we will go through each of them.

Comparison operators are used to compare two values. In MongoDB we can use these comparison operators:

- **`$eq`**: Checks if the field value is *equal* to the specified value.
- **`$gt`**: Checks if the field value is *greater than* the specified value.
- **`$gte`**: Checks if the field value is *greater or equal* to the specified value.
- **`$lt`**: Checks if the field value is *less than* the specified value.
- **`$lte`**: Checks if the field value is *less or equal* to the specified value.
- **`$ne`**: Checks if the field value is *not equal* to the specified value.
- **`$in`**: Checks if the field value *is in* the specified array.
- **`$nin`**: Checks if the field value *is not in* the specified array.

Let us go back to the previous example with cars. This filter will extract only cars produced in *2005*:

```
{ "produced": { $eq: 2005 }}
```

Element operators are used to extract data based on the existence of a certain field or data type. Two operators are available:

- **`$exists`**: Checks if a field *exists* in the document.
- **`$type`**: Checks if the field is of the *specified data type*.

Array operators will extract data based on array conditions. The following operators can be used:

- **`$all`**: Extracts documents with an array field that contain *all* specified elements.
- **`$size`**: Extracts documents with an array field of *specified size*.
- **`$elemMatch`**: Extracts documents with array field, where all elements fulfill *all specified conditions*.

Evaluation operators are used for the extraction of documents based on some sort of evaluation. Two operators are most widely used:

- **`$regex`**: Extracts documents where field value matches *specified regular expression* (can be used only on textual fields).
- **`$text`**: Extracts documents based on *text search* performed on the field indexed with a text index.

Logical operators can be used to combine multiple conditions in the following form:

```
{ operator: [
        { condition1 }, { condition2 }, …, { conditionN }
]}
```

We can use logical operators to combine our two previous examples, in order to extract all *blue* cars produced in *2005*:

```
{ $and: [
        { "color": "blue" },
        { "produced": { $eq: 2005 }}
]}
```

The following logical operators are supported by MongoDB:

- **`$or`**: Logical AND
- **`$and`**: Logical OR
- **`$not`**: Negation
- **`$nor`**: Logical NOR

Now that we are familiar with filters and know how to define them, we can continue with MongoDB operations.

The second operation **`findOne`** will return a document that fulfills the filter. If multiple documents satisfy the filter, the first one (according to the *order* of the documents on a disk) will be returned:

```
database_name.collection_name.findOne(filter, options)
```

The following options are available for *read* operations:

- **AllowDiskUse**: If is set to *true*, the MongoDB server can write temporary data to disk during the execution of find operations. The default value is *false*.
- **AllowPartialResult**: If is set to *true*, the *find* operation executed on a sharded cluster will return partial results if some shards are down. The default value is *false*.
- **Batch size**: This represents the maximum number of documents that will be included in each batch.
- **Collation**: Specifies a collation that will be used for string comparison during operation.
- **CursorType**: Specifies cursor type. *Non-tailable cursor* (cursor that will be closed when the last batch is received) is the default one.
- **Hint**: Specifies an index that will be used for operation, by default only the index created for the `_id` field will be used.
- **Limit**: Specifies the maximum number of documents that will be returned. The default value is *0*, which means *no limit*, all documents will be returned.
- **Max**: Document that specifies the upper bound for a specific index. The default value is *0*, which means *no maximum value* is defined.
- **MaxAwaitTime**: Specifies the maximum amount of time that the MongoDB server should *wait* for documents to satisfy a tailable cursor query. This option can be used only with tailable cursors, for other cursors, it will be ignored.
- **MaxTime**: Defines the maximum amount of time for which a query can be executed on the MongoDB server.
- **Min**: Document that specifies *lower bound* for a specific index. The default value is *0*, which means no minimum value is defined.
- **NoCursorTimeout**: Defines if the cursor created by the operation will timeout after a certain amount of inactivity. The default value is *false*.
- **Projection**: Specifies which fields will be included in the returned document, by default all fields will be included. **Projection** can be defined as a set of *key-value pairs*, where the *key* is a field name and the *value* is an integer number. Integer value *1* means that the field is *included*, while integer value *0* means that the field is *excluded*. Field `_id` is included by default unless it is explicitly excluded with `{_id: 0}`.
- **ReturnKey**: Specifies if returned documents will only include fields related

to the used index. The default value is *false*.

- **ShowRecordId**: If is set to *true*, **`$recordId`** field will be included in the returned document. Field **`$recordId`** represents the internal key that uniquely identifies a document in a collection. The default value is *false*.
- **Skip**: Defines how many documents will be skipped. The default value is *0*.
- **Sort**: Defines the order in which documents will be returned.
- **Let**: Specifies parameters for the *find* operation.

Write operations

MongoDB has a couple of basic operations for *inserting, updating,* and *deleting* documents. These operations are collectively called **write operations**.

The **`insertOne`** operation is used to create a new document. In the command, we specify the document and insert options. Options are not required, without them, the default setting will be used:

```
database_name.collection_name.insertOne(document, options)
```

The **`insertMany`** operation is used to create multiple documents:

```
database_name.collection_name.insertMany(
        [document1, doucment2, …, documentN], options)
```

The following options are available for insert operations:

- **BypassDocumentValidation**: For document-level validation, the default value is *false*.
- **Ordered (insertMany only)**: If is set to *true*, when one write fails, none after it will be executed. The default value is *true*.

There are three update operations in MongoDB: **`updateOne`**, **`updateMany`** and **`replaceOne`**. First operation **`updateOne`** will update one document. If the filter is satisfied by multiple documents, one of them will be selected from the matching set. In case there are no documents that satisfy the filter, the operation will be executed as *successful*, with returning result that indicates that *zero* documents have been updated.

```
database_name.collection_name.updateOne(filter, updates, options)
```

Updates represent a set of statements that defines what and how something should be updated. Each update statement consists of an *update* operator and modification specification, usually in the following form:

```
update_operator: { field_name: value }
```

Here is a list of some of the most used update operators:

- **`$set`**: Sets or adds a new value to a field.
- **`$unset`**: Removes field from a document.
- **`$min`**: Field will be updated only if the specified value is *less* than the current field value.
- **`$max`**: Field will be updated only if the specified value is *greater* than the current field value.
- **`$inc`**: Increments field value for a specified amount.
- **`$addToSet`**: Adds an element to the array, only if the element is *not* already present in the array.
- **`$pop`**: Removes the *first* or *last* element of an array.
- **`$pullAll`**: Removes all *matching* elements from an array.
- **`$push`**: Adds a *new* element into an array.

Next operation **`updateMany`** will update all documents that satisfy the filter. If there are no documents that satisfy the filter, the operation will be *successful with zero* updated documents:

```
database_name.collection_name.updateMany(filter, updates, options)
```

Last update operation, **`replaceOne`** will replace one document that satisfies the filter with provided replacement document. If multiple documents satisfy the filter, one will be selected from the matching set and replaced with a provided document. Same as for all *update* operations if there are no documents that satisfy the filter, the operation will be considered as *successful*:

```
database_name.collection_name.replaceOne(
        filter, replacement, options)
```

Update and *replace* operations can use the following options:

- **ArrayFilters**: Set of filters used to specify to which array element an update should apply. This option will have an effect only on documents that contain arrays. Here is a simple use case where this can be useful: *update only array elements that are higher than a certain value.*
- **BypassDocumentValidation**: For document-level validation, the default value is *false*.
- **Collation**: Specifies a collation that will be used for string comparison during operation.
- **Hint**: Specifies an index that will be used for update/replace operation.
- **Upsert**: If is set to *true,* when the filter does not match any document, a new

one will be created. The default value is *false*.

- **Let**: Specifies parameters for the update/replace operation.

Operation **deleteOne** will remove a document that fulfills the filter. If multiple documents satisfy the filter, one will be selected from the matching set. If there are no documents that match the filter, the operation will be considered *successful* and returned result will indicate that *zero* documents were deleted:

```
database_name.collection_name.deleteOne(filter, options)
```

Operation **deleteMany** will remove all documents that fulfill the filter. Again, if there are no documents that satisfy the filter, the operation will be *successful* with *zero deleted* documents:

```
database_name.collection_name.deleteMany(filter, options)
```

These options can be used for *delete* operations:

- **Collation**: Specifies a collation that will be used for string comparison during operation.
- **Hint**: Specifies an index that will be used for the delete operation.
- **Let**: Specifies parameters for the delete operation.

Aggregation pipeline

The MongoDB aggregation pipeline has multiple stages. Each stage performs a specified operation on input documents and passes it to the next stage as output (*Figure 8.3*):

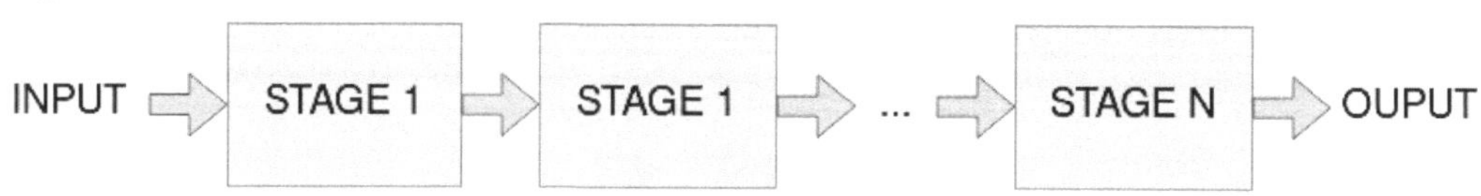

***Figure 8.3**: Aggregation pipeline*

The aggregation pipeline can be defined with the following syntax:

```
database_name.collection_name.aggregate(pipeline, options)
```

Where pipeline is defined as an array of stages:

```
[{ stage1 }, { stage2 }, … { stageN }]
```

Some of the most popular and mostly used stages are:

- **`$match`**: Filter input documents and pass only ones that match specified criteria. Should be placed in the pipeline as early as possible.
- **`$project`**: *Edit* input documents, by *including*, *excluding*, or *adding* new

fields.

- **`$group`**: Group input documents by specified group key (*field* or *set of fields*), similar to **`GROUP BY`** statement from SQL. Group can also apply accumulation expressions, like:
    - o **`$sum`**: Calculates the sum of numerical values. Non-numerical values will be ignored.
    - o **`$avg`**: Calculates average value. Can be used only on numerical values, non-numerical values will be ignored.
    - o **`$max`**: Finds the highest value.
    - o **`$min`**: Finds the lowest value.
- **`$count`**: Counts documents.
- **`$skip`**: Skips a specified number of documents.
- **`$limit`**: Passes only a specified number of elements as an output. Limit sets to *0* means *no limit*.
- **`$sort`**: Sorts documents by specified sort key (*field* or *set of fields*) in defined sort order (*1 ascending, -1 descending*).
- **`$unwind`**: *Unwinds* specified array from the document. Here is a simple example, a document that contains **`product`** name and **`colors`**:

```
{ "product": "T-Shirt", "colors": [ "red", "blue", "green" ]}
```

After unwind stage, the following documents will be passed to the next stage:

```
{ "product": "T-Shirt", "colors": "red" }
{ "product": "T-Shirt", "colors": "blue" }
{ "product": "T-Shirt", "colors": "green" }
```

- **`$lookup`**: Combines data from different collections (similar to **`LEFT JOIN`** from SQL). Lookup can be defined in the following way:

```
$lookup: {
        from: collection_to_join,
        localField: field_from_input_documents,
        foreignField: field_from_joined_documents,
        as: output_array_field
}
```

Options available for aggregation are similar to ones available to *find* operation:

- **AllowDiskUse**: Specifies if *temporary* data can be written to disk.

- **BatchSize**: Is the maximum number of documents that can be included in *each* batch.
- **BypassDocumentValidation**: Specifies if *document-level validation* will be performed.
- **Collation**: Specifies a collation that will be used for *string* comparison.
- **MaxTime**: Is the maximum allowed amount of time for *query execution* on MongoDB server.
- **MaxAwaitTime**: Is the maximum allowed amount of time that the server will *wait* for the document to satisfy the tailable cursor.
- **Hint**: Specifies an *index* that will be used for aggregation.
- **Let**: Specifies parameters for aggregate expressions.
- **Custom**: Custom options that can be defined and added. Options must be in *BSON format*.

Now that we are familiar with all the basic concepts of MongoDB, we can start with database setup and implementation.

Setting up a database

MongoDB is available for all popular platforms. Installation files are available on the official web (**https://www.mongodb.com/try/download/community**), again like with MySQL we will use the *community version*.

To install the latest supported version on **Debian** and **Ubuntu**, the following steps should be executed:

1. Import MongoDB public GPG key:

   ```
   wget -qO - https://www.mongodb.org/static/pgp/
   server-6.0.asc | sudo apt-key add -
   ```

   This command should respond with *OK*, if that is *not* the case `gnupg` should be installed:

   ```
   sudo apt-get install gnupg
   ```

2. Create a list file for MongoDB:

   ```
   echo "deb [ arch=amd64,arm64 ] https://repo.mongodb.org/
   apt/ubuntu
   focal/mongodb-org/6.0 multiverse" |
   sudo tee /etc/apt/sources.list.d/mongodb-org-6.0.list
   ```

3. Install:

   ```
   sudo apt-get install mongodb-org
   ```

4. If installation *fails*, the following command should be executed and after that, the command from *Step 3* should be repeated:

```
sudo apt --fix-broken install
```

For Red Hat Enterprise Linux and Fedora, different steps should be executed:

1. Configure the package management system (`yum`):

```
[mongodb-org-6.0]
name=MongoDB Repository
baseurl=https://repo.mongodb.org/yum/redhat/$releasever/
mongodb-org/6.0/x86_64/
gpgcheck=1
enabled=1
gpgkey=https://www.mongodb.org/static/pgp/server-6.0.asc
```

2. Install:

```
sudo yum install mongodb-org
```

After installation is completed, we can start the MongoDB server with one of the following commands:

- Red Hat Enterprise Linux and Fedora:

```
sudo systemctl start mongod
```

- Debian and Ubuntu:

```
sudo service mongod start
```

Windows installation is simpler. The *MSI installer* should be downloaded from the official web page and executed. After that, we just need to follow installation instructions in order to properly install the MongoDB server.

Before we can install the MongoDB server on macOS, our system must meet some prerequisites:

- **Xcode command-line tool** must be installed. If that is *not* the case, it can be installed with the following command:

```
xcode-select --install
```

- If Homebrew is *not* included with macOS, it should be installed with this command:

```
/bin/bash -c "$(curl -fsSL https://raw.githubusercontent.com/
Homebrew/install/HEAD/install.sh)"
```

Now we can use Homebrew to install MongoDB server with the following commands:

```
brew tap mongodb/brew
brew install mongodb-community@6.0
```

In the end, we can start the MongoDB server (again with Homebrew):

```
brew services start mongodb-community@6.0
```

MongoDB Compass is a tool for querying, optimizing, and analyzing MongoDB data. Of course, it is available for all popular operating systems. Installation files can be found on the official website:

https://www.mongodb.com/try/download/compass

MongoDB Compass can be downloaded and installed on Linux with the following commands:

- Red Hat Enterprise Linux and Fedora:

```
wget https://downloads.mongodb.com/compass/
mongodb-compass_1.33.1_amd64.deb
sudo dpkg -i mongodb-compass_1.33.1_amd64.deb
```

- Debian and Ubuntu:

```
wget https://downloads.mongodb.com/compass/
mongodb-compass-1.33.1.x86_64.rpm
sudo yum install mongodb-compass-1.33.1.x86_64.rpm
```

The first command will download the *installation file*, while the second one will install *Compass*.

In order to install MongoDB Compass on Windows, M*icrosoft .NET Framework version 4.5 or later* is required. If .NET Framework is *not* installed, the Compass installer will prompt us to install the minimum required version.

Installation files are available as an `.exe` file, `.msi` package, or `.zip` archive. When the installer is downloaded and executed, we should just follow installation instructions to successfully install MongoDB Compass. When the installation is complete, Compass can prompt us to *privacy settings configuration*.

For macOS, the `dmg` file should be downloaded and we only need to follow installation instructions. For operating systems prior to **Big Sur**, **Rosetta** must be installed.

When the installation is completed, we can start **MongoDB Compass**. On the home screen, a panel with the option to create a new connection will be present (*Figure 8.4*):

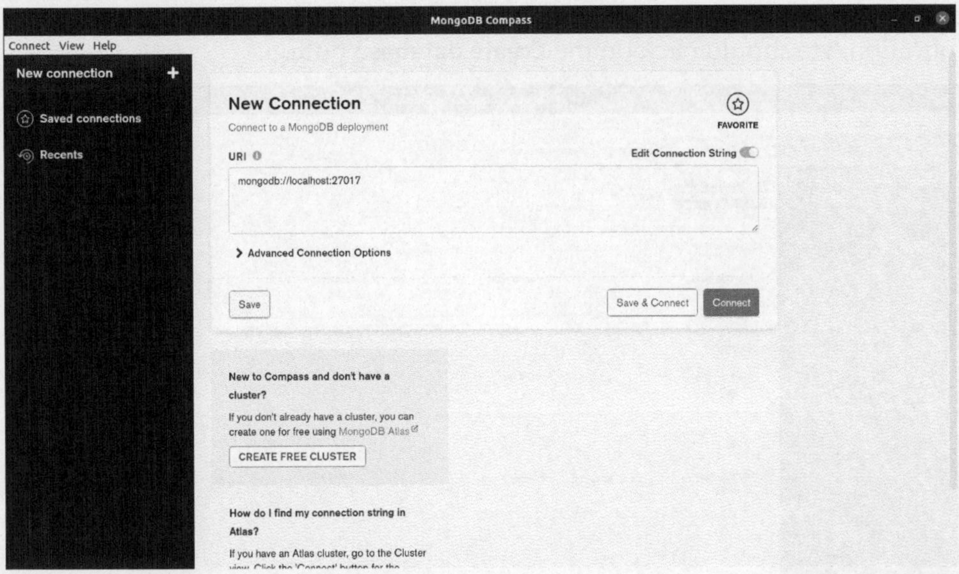

Figure 8.4: MongoDB Compass home screen

If we click on the **Save & Connect** button, a new dialog will be prompted (*Figure 8.5*). Here we can choose the *name* (and *color*) for our connection. Again, we should click on the **Save & Connect** button, to establish a connection and save it into *favorites*. Next time, when we open MongoDB Compass, the connection will be found under **Saved connections** on the left side of the screen:

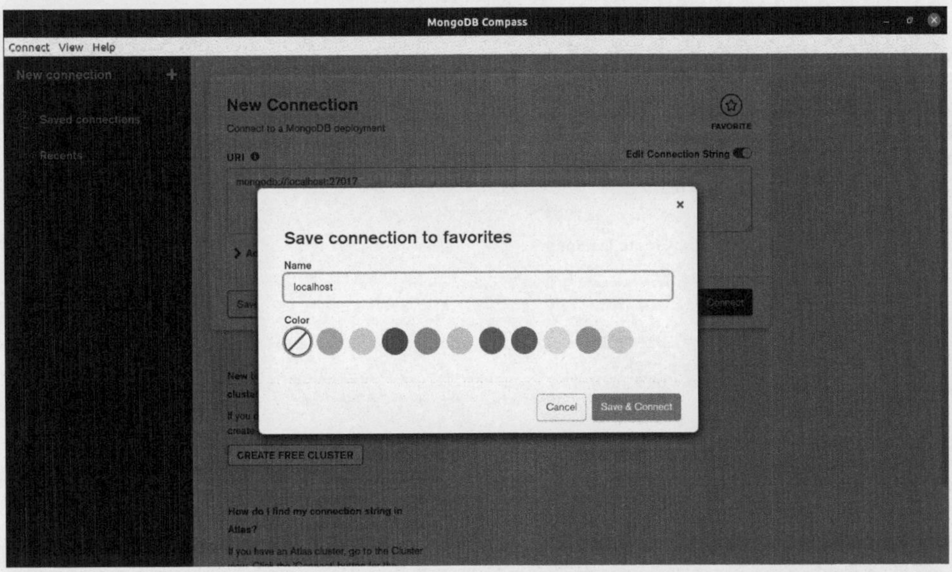

Figure 8.5: Save connection

When the connection is *opened*, we can move to the **Databases** tab (*Figure 8.6*) where we should find some default databases. In order to create a database for our application, we should click on the **Create database** button:

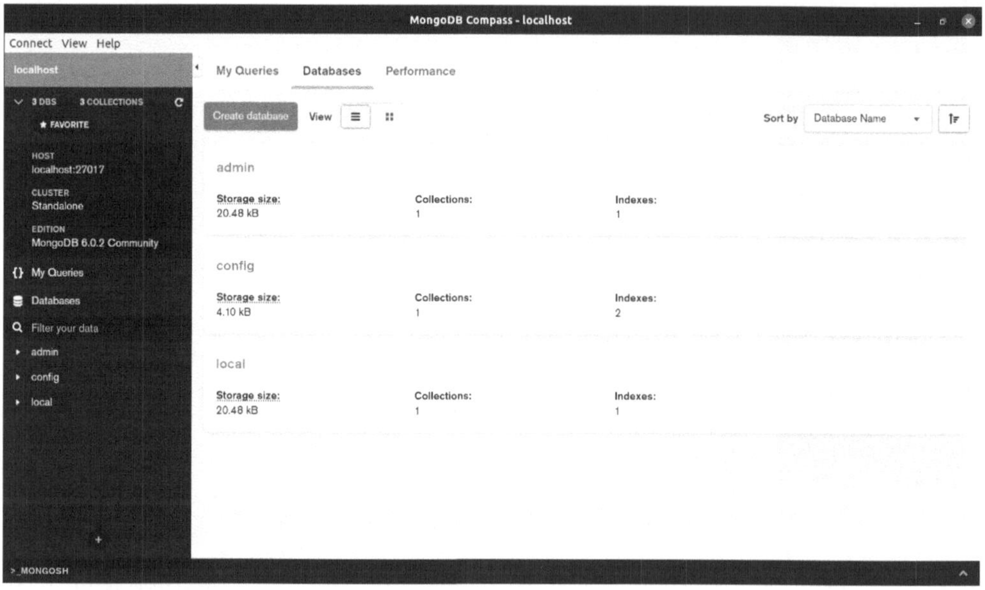

Figure 8.6: Databases tab

On the *prompted* dialog, we can enter **Database Name**, and **Collection Name** (**runners_db** and **runners** respectively), and click on the **Create Database** button (*Figure 8.7*). This will create a new database with one collection:

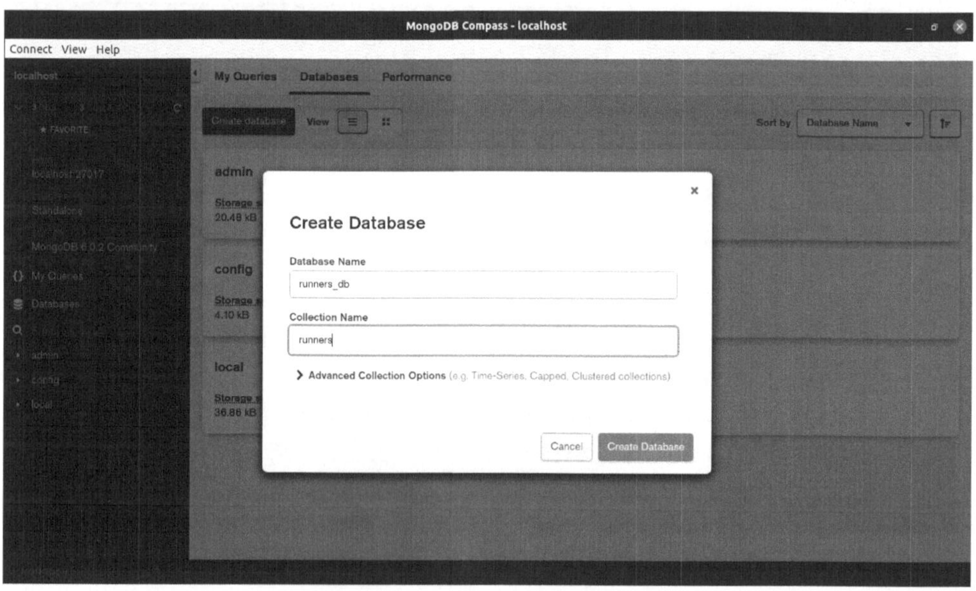

Figure 8.7: Create database dialog

Now our *database* (and *collection*) should be visible in the **Databases** tab. Because there is no strict schema in MongoDB, there is no need for database scripts. The only thing left is to create **indices**. We can create two indices, one on the *country* field and the second on the *year* field from *results* because these fields will be used in *find* operations.

In order to create an index, first we must select our database (**runners_db**), select the **Indexes** tab, and click on the **Create Index** button (*Figure 8.8*):

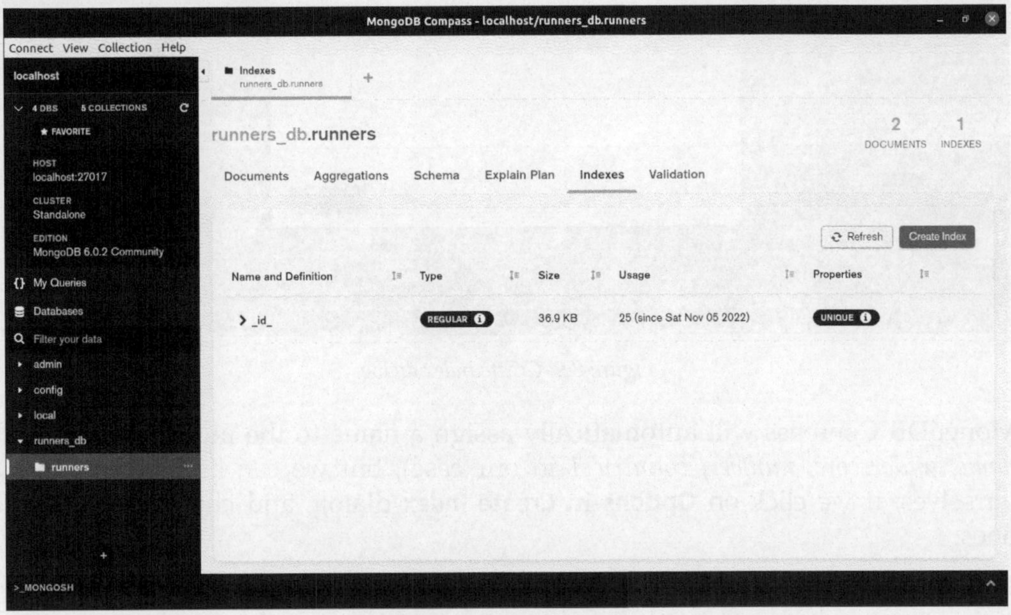

Figure 8.8: Indexes tab

In the *prompted* dialog (*Figure 8.9*), we will enter the field name on which the index will be created, and the index type. We will never use the **country** for a partial match, so there is no need for a text index, we can use a simple one. In that case, we should choose between *ascending* on *descending*. In our case, we can choose *ascending* and click on the **Create Index** button:

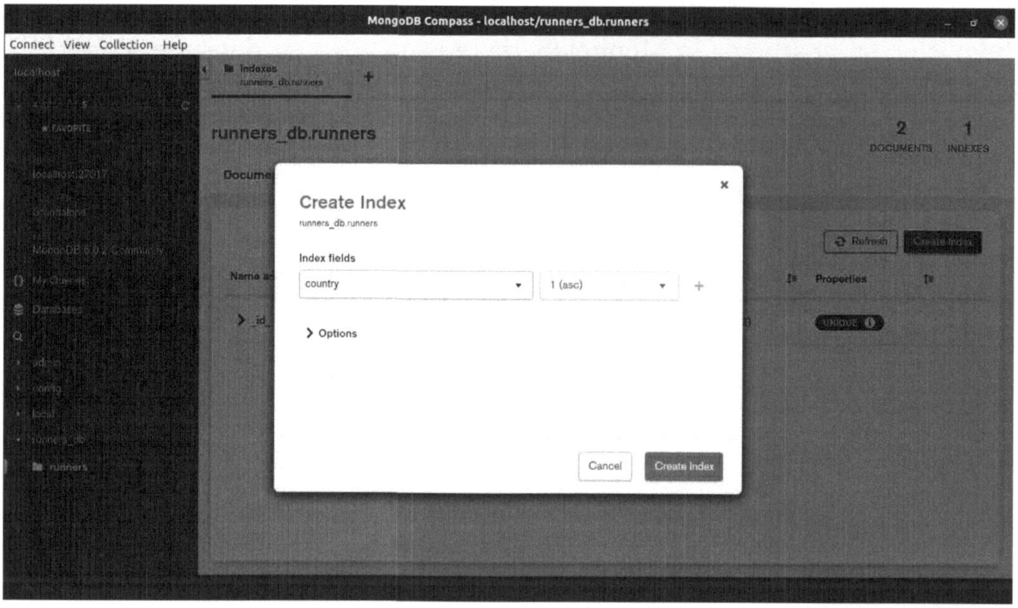

Figure 8.9: Create index dialog

MongoDB Compass will automatically assign a name to the index (usually *field name, underscore, number, country_1* in our case), but we can assign a name by ourselves, if we click on **Options** in **Create Index** dialog, and change the default ones.

In the same way, we can create an *index* on the *year* field from the *results* array. To create an index on the proper field, we should type **`results.year`** for the field name in the **Create Index** dialog.

Indices can be created later when the application is developed and some data is already stored in a database. It is *not* a problem. Our database is now ready and we can proceed to implementation.

Repository layer

Before we take a deeper look into the implementation of the repository layer, we must discuss a couple of issues. Unique identifiers in MongoDB are stored as **`ObjectID`** type. We can observe this type as a wrapper around the textual representation of the index. The problem is, **`ObjectID`** will not be converted into a string when data is read from the database and mapped into any **`struct`** from the models package.

We have two potential *solutions*. We can create separate models for database data and DTO for requests/responses, or we can *duplicate* fields in a model **`struct`** that are problematic. Since we have a problem with only *one* field, we can duplicate the field:

```
type Runner struct {
        ID           string             `json:"id" bson:"-"`
        ObjectID     primitive.ObjectID `json:"-" bson:"_id"`
        FirstName    string             `json:"first_name"`
        LastName     string             `json:"last_name"`
        Age          int                `json:"age,omitempty"
                                            bson:"age,omitempty"`
        IsActive     bool               `json:"is_active"`
        Country      string             `json:"country"`
        PersonalBest string             `json:"personal_best,
                                            omitempty"
                                            bson:"personalbest,
                                            omitempty"`
        SeasonBest   string             `json:"season_best,
                                            omitempty"
                                            bson:"seasonbest,
                                            omitempty"`
        Results      []*Result          `json:"results,
                                            omitempty"
                                            bson:"results,
                                            omitempty"`
}
```

Now, **ObjectID** field will be used for *database-related operations,* while **ID** will be used in all other cases. We will see how to convert unique identifiers from one form to another later in this section.

As we can see in the previous code example, we can combine json and bson tags to properly define how certain fields will be handled in each case. For example, database-related content should ignore the **ID** field, while in all other cases, **ObjectID** should be ignored. Also, we can *omit* empty fields from documents in the collection.

Now when results are stored together with corresponding runners, there is no need for the method **GetAllRunnersResults()** from the **results** repository, which was used in **GetRunner()** method from the **runners** service. Results will now be included when we get the specified runner. But there are some situations where *results* should be excluded from the *response* (in all, *get batch operations*), so we will also see later how to exclude a certain field from the *response*.

First, let us take a look at the **runners** repository. Code will be placed into **runnersRepository.go** file inside the **repositories** package:

```
import (
	"context"
	"net/http"
	"runners-mongodb/models"

	"go.mongodb.org/mongo-driver/bson"
	"go.mongodb.org/mongo-driver/bson/primitive"
	"go.mongodb.org/mongo-driver/mongo"
	"go.mongodb.org/mongo-driver/mongo/options"
)

type RunnersRepository struct {
	client *mongo.Client
}

func NewRunnersRepository(
	client *mongo.Client) *RunnersRepository {

	return &RunnersRepository{
		client: client,
	}
}

func (rr RunnersRepository) CreateRunner(
	runner *models.Runner) (*models.Runner,
	*models.ResponseError) {
	...
}

func (rr RunnersRepository) UpdateRunner(
	runner *models.Runner) *models.ResponseError {
	...
}

func (rr RunnersRepository) DeleteRunner(
	runnerId string) *models.ResponseError {
```

```
    ...
}

func (rr RunnersRepository) GetRunner(
        runnerId string) (*models.Runner, *models.ResponseError) {
        ...
}

func (rr RunnersRepository) GetAllRunners() ([]*models.Runner,
        *models.ResponseError) {
        ...
}

func (rr RunnersRepository) GetRunnersByCountry(
        country string) ([]*models.Runner,
        *models.ResponseError) {
        ...
}

func (rr RunnersRepository) GetRunnersByYear(
        year int) ([]*models.Runner, *models.ResponseError) {
        ...
}
```

If we compare this solution with previous solutions, we can notice couple of differences:

- Transaction-related field are removed from the **`struct`** that represents the **`runners`** repository. Due to the new data organization, now we can update data in a single MongoDB operation so there is no need for transactions.
- The **`UpdateRunnerResults()`** method is absent from repository. Actually, this method is *not* removed from the solution, it is just moved to the **`results`** repository because now it makes more sense to place it there (we will soon see why).

All repository methods will follow this form:

- Create and prepare MongoDB operation
- Execute operation
- Map response

The first method in the **runners** repository is **CreateRunner()**. At the start of this method, we will select a collection from the database, in our case **runners**. Collection selection will be executed in all **repository** methods.

In a solution with relational databases, the value *true* will be assigned to the **is_active** column during the SQL creation command. As we already know, MongoDB does not have default values, and the runner must be active after the *creation* operation, so we must assign a value *true* to a **struct** field before the *insert* operation.

Method **InsertOne()** will insert a *new* document and return the *result*. Potential errors will be handled in a *standard* way, as with the previous solutions. Returned results will contain generated unique identifiers assigned to a newly created document in form of **objectID** type. We will place a string representation of this identifier in response.

This is a good place to discuss one important thing. There are two methods that can be used to convert **ObjectID** to *string*, **String()** and **Hex()**. If we assume that the following **ObjectID** is assigned to the document:

```
"_id": {
        "$oid": "635c206f14950bc3d5fd459a"
}
```

Method **String()** will return this string:

```
"ObjectID('635c206f14950bc3d5fd459a')"
```

While method **Hex()** will return this string:

```
"635c206f14950bc3d5fd459a"
```

Since method **Hex()** returns a more natural and expected format, we will use it for **ObjectID** to *string* conversion:

```
func (rr RunnersRepository) CreateRunner(
        runner *models.Runner) (*models.Runner,
        *models.ResponseError) {

        collection := rr.client.Database("runners_db").
                Collection("runners")

        runner.IsActive = true

        result, err := collection.InsertOne(context.TODO(), runner)
        if err != nil {
                return nil, &models.ResponseError{
```

```
                Message: err.Error(),
                Status:  http.StatusInternalServerError,
            }
        }

        id := result.InsertedID.(primitive.ObjectID)

        return &models.Runner{
            ID:         id.Hex(),
            FirstName: runner.FirstName,
            LastName:  runner.LastName,
            Age:       runner.Age,
            IsActive:  runner.IsActive,
            Country:   runner.Country,
        }, nil
    }
```

At the start of the **UpdateRunner()** method, we will execute the *reverse* operation. A unique identifier for the runner will be received as a string in HTTP requests, so it must be converted into **ObjectID** so that we can use it to filter documents.

All data passed to methods from the collection package must be in BSON format that follows a simple *key-value convention*. The filter will exclude all documents where the value of **_id** filed is *not* the one received through an HTTP request. It is expected that only one document will be selected.

In the **update** variable, we will define which fields will be updated and how. In our case, we will set new values for fields that represent the *first name*, *last name*, *age*, and *country*. The result returned from **UpdateOne()** method can be ignored, it contains how many documents are affected by the *update* operation, which is not important to us at this moment. On the other hand, errors will be handled:

```
func (rr RunnersRepository) UpdateRunner(
        runner *models.Runner) *models.ResponseError {

        objectId, err := primitive.ObjectIDFromHex(runner.ID)
        if err != nil {
                return &models.ResponseError{
                        Message: "Invalid runner ID",
                        Status:  http.StatusBadRequest,
                }
```

```
        }

        collection := rr.client.Database("runners_db").
              Collection("runners")
        filter := bson.D{{Key: "_id", Value: objectId}}
        update := bson.D{{Key: "$set", Value: bson.D{
              {Key: "firstname", Value: runner.FirstName},
              {Key: "lastname", Value: runner.LastName},
              {Key: "age", Value: runner.Age},
              {Key: "country", Value: runner.Country},
        }}}

        _, err = collection.UpdateOne(context.TODO(), filter,
              update)
        if err != nil {
              return &models.ResponseError{
                    Message: err.Error(),
                    Status:  http.StatusInternalServerError,
              }
        }

        return nil
  }
```

Method **`DeleteRunner()`** is almost identical to **`UpdateRunner()`**. The only difference is that only one field (**`isactive`**) will be updated:

```
  func (rr RunnersRepository) DeleteRunner(
        runnerId string) *models.ResponseError {

        objectId, err := primitive.ObjectIDFromHex(runnerId)
        if err != nil {
              return &models.ResponseError{
                    Message: "Invalid runner ID",
                    Status:  http.StatusBadRequest,
              }
        }

        collection := rr.client.Database("runners_db").
```

```
            Collection("runners")
        filter := bson.D{{Key: "_id", Value: objectId}}
        update := bson.D{{Key: "$set", Value: bson.D{
            {Key: "isactive", Value: false}}}}}

        _, err = collection.UpdateOne(context.TODO(), filter,
            update)
        if err != nil {
            return &models.ResponseError{
                Message: err.Error(),
                Status:  http.StatusInternalServerError,
            }
        }

        return nil
    }
```

The next method, **GetRunner()** will return one runner based on the provided **ID** of the runner. This can be archived with **FindOne()** method from the **collection** package.

Method **Decode()** will map the result of the **FindOne()** method, but it cannot convert the **ObjectID** value into a *string* as we need. That is the reason why our new **Runner** model contains two identifier-related fields. Method **Decode()** will assign an **ObjectID** value to the corresponding field, and we will convert it to a *string*. The same thing should be done for all **result** identifiers:

```
    func (rr RunnersRepository) GetRunner(
        runnerId string) (*models.Runner, *models.ResponseError) {

        objectId, err := primitive.ObjectIDFromHex(runnerId)
        if err != nil {
            return nil, &models.ResponseError{
                Message: "Invalid runner ID",
                Status:  http.StatusBadRequest,
            }
        }

        collection := rr.client.Database("runners_db").
            Collection("runners")
```

```
        filter := bson.D{{Key: "_id", Value: objectId}}

        var runner *models.Runner
        err = collection.FindOne(context.TODO(), filter).
              Decode(&runner)
        if err != nil {
              return nil, &models.ResponseError{
                    Message: err.Error(),
                    Status:  http.StatusInternalServerError,
              }
        }

        runner.ID = runner.ObjectID.Hex()
        for _, result := range runner.Results {
              result.ID = result.ObjectID.Hex()
        }

        return runner, nil
}
```

In **GetAllRunners()** method, we can see that we can exclude the field from a returned document by marking it with the value **0** in the **projection** option.

Operation **Find()** will return a cursor that we can use to iterate through all returned documents and map them into a response. If any error occurs during iteration, it can be fetched with **Err()** method and properly handled:

```
func (rr RunnersRepository) GetAllRunners() ([]*models.Runner,
        *models.ResponseError) {

        collection := rr.client.Database("runners_db").
              Collection("runners")
        filter := bson.D{}
        options := options.Find().SetProjection(
              bson.D{{Key: "results", Value: 0}})

        cursor, err := collection.Find(context.TODO(), filter,
              options)
        if err != nil {
              return nil, &models.ResponseError{
```

```
                Message: err.Error(),
                Status:  http.StatusInternalServerError,
            }
        }

        var runners []*models.Runner
        for cursor.Next(context.TODO()) {
            var runner *models.Runner
            err = cursor.Decode(&runner)
            if err != nil {
                return nil, &models.ResponseError{
                    Message: err.Error(),
                    Status:  http.
                              StatusInternalServerError,
                }
            }
            runner.ID = runner.ObjectID.Hex()
            runners = append(runners, runner)
        }

        if err := cursor.Err(); err != nil {
            return nil, &models.ResponseError{
                Message: err.Error(),
                Status:  http.StatusInternalServerError,
            }
        }

        return runners, nil
    }
```

Method **GetRunnersByCountry()** is similar to the previous method but will introduce something new. First, we will filter documents based on two field values, **country** and **isactive**, in order to retrieve the *best active runners* from a specified country.

Some new options will be introduced. Besides the option to exclude **results** through **projection**, we will use *sort* options to sort **runners** by *personal best results* in *ascending* order and **limit** option to return only the *ten best runners*:

```
func (rr RunnersRepository) GetRunnersByCountry(
	country string) ([]*models.Runner,
	*models.ResponseError) {

	collection := rr.client.Database("runners_db").
		Collection("runners")
	filter := bson.D{{Key: "country", Value: country},
		{Key: "isactive", Value: true}}
	options := options.Find().
		SetProjection(bson.D{{Key: "results", Value: 0}}).
		SetSort(bson.D{{Key: "personalbest", Value: 1}}).
		SetLimit(10)

	cursor, err := collection.Find(context.TODO(), filter,
		options)
	if err != nil {
		return nil, &models.ResponseError{
			Message: err.Error(),
			Status:  http.StatusInternalServerError,
		}
	}

	var runners []*models.Runner
	for cursor.Next(context.TODO()) {
		var runner *models.Runner
		err = cursor.Decode(&runner)
		if err != nil {
			return nil, &models.ResponseError{
				Message: err.Error(),
				Status:  http.
					StatusInternalServerError,
			}
		}
		runner.ID = runner.ObjectID.Hex()
		runners = append(runners, runner)
	}
```

```
        if err := cursor.Err(); err != nil {
                return nil, &models.ResponseError{
                        Message: err.Error(),
                        Status:  http.StatusInternalServerError,
                }
        }

        return runners, nil
}
```

The last method from the **runners** repository is the *most interesting one!* Here we will use the pipeline to get the *ten best runners* from a specified year. Our pipeline will have the following stages:

- **Unwind stage** will unwind the results array so we easily select the ten best ones.
- **Match stage** where only documents that contain results set in the specified year will pass in the next stage.
- **Sort stage** will sort all results in ascending order.
- **Limit stage** where only the ten best results will be selected.

In **options**, we can set **Hint** to aggregate operation to use the index created on the **year** field from the **result**. When the index is *created* on some sub-fields or array elements, it is a good practice to set a *hint,* because often MongoDB will not properly recognize and use these indices:

```
func (rr RunnersRepository) GetRunnersByYear(
        year int) ([]*models.Runner, *models.ResponseError) {

        collection := rr.client.Database("runners_db").
                Collection("runners")
        unwindStage := bson.D{{Key: "$unwind",
                Value: bson.D{{Key: "path", Value: "$results"}}}}
        matchStage := bson.D{{Key: "$match",
                Value: bson.D{{Key: "results.year", Value: year}}}}
        sortStage := bson.D{{Key: "$sort",
                Value: bson.D{{Key: "results.raceresult",
                Value: 1}}}}
        limitStage := bson.D{{Key: "$limit", Value: 10}}
```

```
options := options.Aggregate().SetHint("results.year_1")
pipeline := mongo.Pipeline{unwindStage, matchStage,
      sortStage,limitStage}

cursor, err := collection.Aggregate(context.TODO(),
      pipeline, options)
if err != nil {
      return nil, &models.ResponseError{
            Message: err.Error(),
            Status:  http.StatusInternalServerError,
      }
}

var unwindRunners []unwindRunner
err = cursor.All(context.TODO(), &unwindRunners)
if err != nil {
      return nil, &models.ResponseError{
            Message: err.Error(),
            Status:  http.StatusInternalServerError,
      }
}

runners := make([]*models.Runner, 0)
for _, ur := range unwindRunners {

      runner := &models.Runner{
            ID:           ur.ID.Hex(),
            FirstName:    ur.FirstName,
            LastName:     ur.LastName,
            Age:          ur.Age,
            IsActive:     ur.IsActive,
            Country:      ur.Country,
            PersonalBest: ur.PersonalBest,
            SeasonBest:   ur.Results.RaceResult,
      }

      runners = append(runners, runner)
```

```
        }

        return runners, nil
}
```

At the end of the function, we will iterate through *returned documents* and *map responses*. But here we have one small problem. In our original **Runner** model, field **Results** is a slice of pointers, but when we *unwind* that slice, **Results** will become a pointer. This will cause that returned documents to *not* be properly decoded and mapped to the response.

We can easily fix this issue by introducing a private **struct** where the **Results** field is a pointer instead of an array. This **struct** will be used just in this method, so there is no need to export it from the **repository** package:

```
type unwindRunner struct {
        ID           primitive.ObjectID `json:"-" bson:"_id"`
        FirstName    string
        LastName     string
        Age          int
        IsActive     bool
        Country      string
        PersonalBest string
        SeasonBest   string
        Results      *models.Result
}
```

Now we can take a look at the **results** repository. In this solution, this repository will be simpler than the previous ones and contains fewer methods. Code will be placed into **resultsRepository.go** file inside the **repositories** package:

```
package repositories

import (
        "context"
        "net/http"
        "runners-mongodb/models"

        "go.mongodb.org/mongo-driver/bson"
        "go.mongodb.org/mongo-driver/bson/primitive"
        "go.mongodb.org/mongo-driver/mongo"
)
```

```
type ResultsRepository struct {
      client *mongo.Client
}

func NewResultsRepository(
      client *mongo.Client) *ResultsRepository {

      return &ResultsRepository{
            client: client,
      }
}

func (rr ResultsRepository) CreateResult(result *models.Result,
      currentYear int) (*models.Result, *models.ResponseError) {
      ...
}

func (rr ResultsRepository) UpdateRunnerResults(
      runner *models.Runner,
      resultId string) *models.ResponseError {
      ...
}

func (rr ResultsRepository) GetRunnerByResultId(
      resultId string) (*models.Runner, *models.ResponseError) {
      ..
}
```

If we carefully analyze the content of the repository, something seems to be missing. *There is no* **`DeleteResult()`** *method!*

`Results` is now part of **`Runners`**, so when we need to delete some result we should just remove it from the corresponding array. Besides that, we should update *personal best* and *season best results* if they are equal to deleted one. This will be archived in **`UpdateRunnerResult()`** method, so it made sense to move it here from the **`Runners`** repository.

In this method, we will set new values for *personal best* and *season best results,* and use the *pull* operator to remove a specified field from the **`results`** array:

```
func (rr ResultsRepository) UpdateRunnerResults(
	runner *models.Runner,
	resultId string) *models.ResponseError {

	runnerObjectId, err := primitive.ObjectIDFromHex(
		runner.ID)
	if err != nil {
		return &models.ResponseError{
			Message: "Invalid runner ID",
			Status:  http.StatusBadRequest,
		}
	}

	resultObjectId, err := primitive.ObjectIDFromHex(resultId)
	if err != nil {
		return &models.ResponseError{
			Message: "Invalid result ID",
			Status:  http.StatusBadRequest,
		}
	}

	collection := rr.client.Database("runners_db").
		Collection("runners")
	filter := bson.D{{Key: "_id", Value: runnerObjectId}}
	update := bson.D{
		{Key: "$set", Value: bson.D{
			{Key: "personalbest",
				Value: runner.PersonalBest},
			{Key: "seasonbest",
				Value: runner.SeasonBest}}},
		{Key: "$pull", Value: bson.D{
			{Key: "results",
			Value: bson.D{{Key: "_id", Value: resultObjectId}}},
		}},
	}

	_, err = collection.UpdateOne(context.TODO(), filter,
```

```
            update)
        if err != nil {
            return &models.ResponseError{
                Message: err.Error(),
                Status:  http.StatusInternalServerError,
            }
        }

        return nil
    }
```

If we remember our API calls, the *delete result* method will send only the results ID. In order to find out which runner holds, these results we will need a new method **`GetRunnerByResultId()`**.

To successfully perform this operation, we will use the **`$elemMatch`** operator. This operator will check if the **`results`** array contains a result that matches the specified result ID. If there are no errors, we proper *response* will be returned:

```
    func (rr ResultsRepository) GetRunnerByResultId(
        resultId string) (*models.Runner, *models.ResponseError) {

        objectId, err := primitive.ObjectIDFromHex(resultId)
        if err != nil {
            return nil, &models.ResponseError{
                Message: "Invalid result ID",
                Status:  http.StatusBadRequest,
            }
        }

        collection := rr.client.Database("runners_db").
            Collection("runners")
        filter := bson.D{{Key: "results", Value: bson.D{{
            Key: "$elemMatch",
            Value: bson.D{{Key: "_id", Value: objectId}}},
        }}}

        var runner *models.Runner
        err = collection.FindOne(context.TODO(), filter).
            Decode(&runner)
```

```
        if err != nil {
                return nil, &models.ResponseError{
                        Message: err.Error(),
                        Status:  http.StatusInternalServerError,
                }
        }

        runner.ID = runner.ObjectID.Hex()
        for _, result := range runner.Results {
                result.ID = result.ObjectID.Hex()
        }

        return runner, nil
}
```

We can conclude that methods **UpdateRunnerResult()** and **GetRunnerByResultId()** are the substitutions for **DeleteResult()** method from previous solutions.

Third and the *last* method from the results repository, **CreateResult()** will create a new result and add (push) it to the results array of the specified runner. If the new result is *better* than the *current personal best* or *season best result,* these fields will be also updated. We will use the **$min** operator to perform these checks. The *season-best result* should be updated only if the new result is set in the current year:

```
func (rr ResultsRepository) CreateResult(result *models.Result,
        currentYear int) (*models.Result, *models.ResponseError) {

        objectId, err := primitive.ObjectIDFromHex(result.RunnerID)
        if err != nil {
                return nil, &models.ResponseError{
                        Message: "Invalid runner ID",
                        Status:  http.StatusBadRequest,
                }
        }

        result.ObjectID = primitive.NewObjectID()

        collection := rr.client.Database("runners_db").
                Collection("runners")
        filter := bson.D{{Key: "_id", Value: objectId}}
```

```
update := bson.D{
      {Key: "$push", Value: bson.D{
            {Key: "results", Value: result}}},
      {Key: "$min", Value: bson.D{
            {Key: "personalbest",
            Value: result.RaceResult}}},
}

if result.Year == currentYear {
      update = bson.D{
            {Key: "$push", Value: bson.D{
                  {Key: "results", Value: result}}},
            {Key: "$min", Value: bson.D{
                  {Key: "personalbest",
                  Value: result.RaceResult}}},
            {Key: "$min", Value: bson.D{
                  {Key: "seasonbest",
                  Value: result.RaceResult}}},
      }
}

_, err = collection.UpdateOne(context.TODO(), filter,
      update)
if err != nil {
      return nil, &models.ResponseError{
            Message: err.Error(),
            Status:  http.StatusInternalServerError,
      }
}

return &models.Result{
      ID:         result.ObjectID.Hex(),
      RunnerID:   result.RunnerID,
      RaceResult: result.RaceResult,
      Location:   result.Location,
      Position:   result.Position,
      Year:       result.Year,
```

```
        }, nil
    }
```

The method from the **results** service will be different than the ones in the previous solution. Method **CreateResult()** will now have only *field validations* and call to the repository method:

```
    func (rs ResultsService) CreateResult(
            result *models.Result) (*models.Result,
            *models.ResponseError) {

            if result.RunnerID == "" {
                    return nil, &models.ResponseError{
                            Message: "Invalid runner ID",
                            Status:  http.StatusBadRequest,
                    }
            }

            if result.RaceResult == "" {
                    return nil, &models.ResponseError{
                            Message: "Invalid race result",
                            Status:  http.StatusBadRequest,
                    }
            }

            if result.Location == "" {
                    return nil, &models.ResponseError{
                            Message: "Invalid location",
                            Status:  http.StatusBadRequest,
                    }
            }

            if result.Position < 0 {
                    return nil, &models.ResponseError{
                            Message: "Invalid position",
                            Status:  http.StatusBadRequest,
                    }
            }
```

```
        currentYear := time.Now().Year()
        if result.Year < 0 || result.Year > currentYear {
                return nil, &models.ResponseError{
                        Message: "Invalid year",
                        Status:  http.StatusBadRequest,
                }
        }

        response, responseErr := rs.resultsRepository.CreateResult(
                result, currentYear)
        if responseErr != nil {
                return nil, responseErr
        }

        return response, nil
}
```

Service method **DeleteResult()** will validate provided result ID and find the runner that holds that result. We will use three private functions in this method. The *first* one, **findResult()** will find the *result* that should be *deleted*, the *second* one will find the *new personal best result*, and the *third* one will find the *new season-best result*. The *second* and *third* functions will be called only if the condition is not fulfilled (deleted result is not personal or season best):

```
func (rs ResultsService) DeleteResult(
        resultId string) *models.ResponseError {

        if resultId == "" {
                return &models.ResponseError{
                        Message: "Invalid result ID",
                        Status:  http.StatusBadRequest,
                }
        }

        runner, responseErr := rs.resultsRepository.
                GetRunnerByResultId(resultId)
        if responseErr != nil {
                return responseErr
        }
```

```
        result := findResult(runner.Results, resultId)

        // Checking if the deleted result is
        // personal best for the runner
        if runner.PersonalBest == result.RaceResult {
                runner.PersonalBest = getPersonalBestResult(
                        runner.Results, resultId)
        }

        // Checking if the deleted result is
        // season best for the runner
        currentYear := time.Now().Year()
        if runner.SeasonBest == result.RaceResult &&
                result.Year == currentYear {

                runner.SeasonBest = getSeasonBestResult(
                        runner.Results, result.Year, resultId)
        }

        responseErr = rs.resultsRepository.UpdateRunnerResults(
                runner, resultId)
        if responseErr != nil {
                return responseErr
        }

        return nil
}
```

Three private methods are quite simple, they only iterate through the array, and try to find a match (**findResult()**), or minimum value (**getPersonalBestResult()** and **getSeasonBestResult()**):

```
func findResult(results []*models.Result,
        resultId string) *models.Result {

        for _, result := range results {
                if result.ID == resultId {
                        return result
                }
```

```
        }

        return nil
}

func getPersonalBestResult(results []*models.Result,
        resultId string) string {

        personalBest := results[0].RaceResult
        for _, result := range results {
                if result.ID != resultId &&
                        result.RaceResult < personalBest {

                        personalBest = result.RaceResult
                }
        }

        return personalBest
}

func getSeasonBestResult(results []*models.Result, year int,
        resultId string) string {

        var seasonBest string
        for _, result := range results {
                if result.Year == year {
                        if result.ID != resultId &&
                                result.RaceResult < seasonBest {

                                        seasonBest = result.RaceResult
                        }
                }
        }

        return seasonBest
}
```

Now we can develop a database layer and complete solution that will use MongoDB.

Database layer

Since we will use different technology, the database layer will undergo a few changes relative to a solution that uses relational databases. First, the MongoDB driver must be installed with **go get** command:

```
go get go.mongodb.org/mongo-driver/mongo
```

In the configuration file, we need only one line, the connection string (in the format expected by MongoDB). All other lines, that are used for relational databases will not be used here, because some of these parameters are not available as options for MongoDB. After these changes, the database section of the configuration file will now look like this:

```
####################################################################

# Database configuration

# Connection string is in Go mongodb driver format:
# mongodb://host:port

[database]

connection_string = "mongodb://localhost:27017"
####################################################################
```

As we mentioned before, different technology will be used, so the whole content of **dbServer.go** file from the **server** package (**InitDatabase()** function) must be rewritten.

Traditionally, at the start of the function, we will read the database configuration with **Viper**. If the connection string is *empty*, we will terminate our application because of an invalid configuration. The *read* configuration will be used for the creation of **Client** options.

The **client** is a handler that represents a connection pool to the MongoDB database. It opens and closes *connections* automatically, and maintains a *pool of idle connections*. **Client** options will be passed to **Connect()** function from the **mongo** package. This function will create a new **Client** that will be used for the execution of MongoDB operations.

Function **Connect()** receives one more argument, **context**. Here we can use **TODO()**

function, which will return an *empty non-nil context*. We can use **TODO()** in all cases when is *not* clear which **context** should be used. We will use it for all MongoDB-related content that requires **context**.

At the end of the **InitDatabase()** function, we can use **Ping()** to verify that **Client** can connect to the MongoDB server. Here is a function with all related imports:

```
package server

import (
	"context"
	"log"

	"github.com/spf13/viper"
	"go.mongodb.org/mongo-driver/mongo"
	"go.mongodb.org/mongo-driver/mongo/options"
)

func InitDatabase(config *viper.Viper) *mongo.Client {
	connectionString := config.GetString(
		"database.connection_string")

	if connectionString == "" {
		log.Fatalf("Database connection string is missing")
	}

	clientOptions := options.Client().
		ApplyURI(connectionString)

	client, err := mongo.Connect(context.TODO(), clientOptions)
	if err != nil {
		log.Fatalf("Error while initializing database: %v",
			err)
	}

	err = client.Ping(context.TODO(), nil)
	if err != nil {
		client.Disconnect(context.TODO())
		log.Fatalf("Error while validating database: %v",
			err)
```

```
        }

        return client
    }
```

In the solution with relational databases, **`InitDatabase()`** function was returning **`dbHandler`**. The only other difference between that and MongoDB solution (besides the ones that we already described) is that **`client`** should be used instead **`dbHandler`** in all places in the code. For example, in the **`struct`** that represents the **`runners`** repository:

```
    type RunnersRepository struct {
            client *mongo.Client
    }
```

Our first NoSQL solution is completed! Now with much more confidence, we can develop another similar solution with a different database system.

DynamoDB

DynamoDB is a *key-value* fully managed NoSQL database service developed by **Amazon.com**. It is often provided as a part of **Amazon Web Service** (**AWS**). Dynamo is designed with elasticity in mind and offers highly redundant storage.

Some of the basic concepts of DynamoDB are:

- **Database**: Group of tables.
- **Table**: Group of items. It is equivalent to a table in a relational database or a collection in MongoDB.
- **Item**: Record in a table, equivalent to a row in a relational database, and document in MongoDB.
- **Attribute**: The item is composed of attributes, equivalent to a column in a relational database, and a field in MongoDB.
- **Primary key**: A key that uniquely identifies the item. DynamoDB is a *key-value database* service, in such a constellation *primary key* is the key, and everything else is considered a *value*.
- **Partition key**: Simple primary key composed of a single attribute, previously known as **Hash key**. It is a good practice to use known information for this key because querying can be difficult with randomly generated values (we will see how later).
- **Sort key**: Single attribute that determines the order of items in the database, previously known as **Range key**. It is good practice to use data that can be queried with comparison operators. This is the only way to sort DynamoDB

data, there is no *sort* operator or *function* like we had in previous database systems.

- **Composite primary key**: A key consisting of a combination of partition and sort keys.
- **Local Secondary Index**: Index that has the same partition key as the table but a different sort key. This key is scoped to base table partitions. Maximum *five Local Secondary Indices* can be created per table.
- **Global Secondary Index**: Index that can have different partition and sort key than the table. This key is spawned across all partitions and has its own throughput settings and pricing. A maximum of *twenty Global Secondary Indices* can be created per table.
- **Transaction**: Sequence of operations treated as a single operation.
- **Table Throughput Capacity**: Amount of *read* and *write* activity that the table can support.

We will talk about *Table Throughput Capacity* in more detail because this concept is important for DynamoDB. **Write Throughput Capacity** is measured in **Write Capacity Units** (**WCU**). **One WCU** represents one **write operation per second of 1 KB**.

Read Throughput Capacity is represented by **Read Capacity Units** (**RCU**) where **one RCU** represents **one or two read operations per second of 4 KB**. The number of operations (one or two) depends on *read consistency*.

In DynamoDB we have two types of consistent reads:

- **Eventually Consistent Read** where the application does not immediately query updated items. In this case, we will use *two read operations* in the *Read Throughput Capacity* calculation.
- **Strongly Consistent Reads** where the application will immediately query updated items. Here we will use *one read operation* in the calculation.

In order to calculate the expected throughput we should know the following:

- Approximate size of items
- Amount of items that will be read every second
- Read consistency

Let's start with *Read Throughput Capacity*. Let's assume that our application will read *20 items of around 5 KB per second* and *Strong Consistent Reads* will be used. First, we must round up item size to the nearest *4 KB* increment, in our case *8 KB*. Number of necessary read units is calculated by this formula:

$$\frac{\frac{\text{Rounded Item Size}}{4KB}\times\text{Item Reads per Second}}{ReadsConsistency}$$

In our case, the rounded item size is *8 KB*, we will have *20 item reads per second* and because we use *Strong Consistent Reads*, the *Reads Consistency* is *1*. Now we can substitute these values in the formula:

$$\frac{\frac{8KB}{4KB}\times 20}{1} = 40RCU$$

Read Throughput Capacity for our use case is *40 Read Capacity Units*.

For *Write Throughput Capacity*, let us assume that the application will *write 5 items*, of around *9 KB per second*. The formula is simpler than the previous one:

$$\text{Item Size} \times \text{Item Writes per SecondItem Size} \times \text{Item Writes per Second}$$

Mirrored to our case, *item size is 9 KB*, and *Item Writes per Second is 5*, so the *Write Throughput Capacity* is:

$$9KB \times 5 = 45WCU$$

The maximum size for an item supported by DynamoDB is *400 KB*. Now we can proceed with *read* and *write* operations.

Database design

Because DynamoDB is a *key-value-oriented* database, rather than a document oriented, we will use a similar database design, as we used in our solution with relational databases (*Figure 8.10*). Data types will be aligned with data types supported by DynamoDB.

Also, the **year** is a reserved word in DynamoDB so we will use **race_year** for the attribute name:

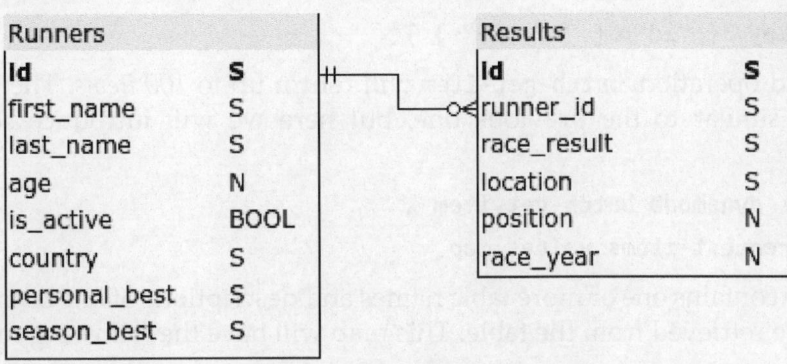

***Figure 8.10**: Database design*

Now we learn more about operations supported by DynamoDB.

Read operations

In DynamoDB we have *four* read operations:

- **Get Item**, which reads one item from a specified table.
- **Batch Get Item**, which reads up to *100 items* from one or more tables.
- **Scan**, which reads all items from a specified table.
- **Query**, which gets multiple items.

All operations will be presented in a form used in AWS **CLI (Command Line Interface**) tool.

The first operation, `get-item` will return one item from the specified table, that matches provided value for the key. Partition is often used in those cases:

```
aws dynamodb get-item \
--table-name ‘table_name’
--key ‘{ “key_name”: { “key_type”: “key_value” } }’
```

Before we continue to the next operation, we should discuss data types that can be used for attributes. The following types are supported:

- **S**: string
- **N**: number
- **B**: binary

Some additional special types (like **BOOL**) can be also used. So in the previous operation, if we wanted to return `item` from table `cars`, where the `key`, named `id` has a numerical value of `5`, the operation will look like this:

```
aws dynamodb get-item \
--table-name ‘cars’
--key ‘{ “id”: { “N”: “5” } }’
```

The second operation, `batch-get-item` will return up to *100 items*. The operation format is similar to the previous one, but here we will introduce some new concepts:

```
aws dynamodb batch-get-item \
--request-items values_map
```

Values map contains one or more table names and descriptions of one or more items that will be retrieved from the table. This map will have the following form:

```
{
        "table_name": {
                "keys": [
                        {
                                "key_name": {
                                        "key_type": "key_value_1"
                                }
                        }
                ]
        }
}
```

If we have *five* descriptions in the **keys** map, *batch- get-item* will basically execute *five get-item* operations.

The *third* read operation, **scan**, will read and return all items from the table:

```
aws dynamodb scan
--table-name 'table_name'
```

Scan is a very expensive operation that consumes a huge amount of read capacity. It should be *avoided*, if possible. *Filter expression* can be assigned to the command, but this will not reduce operation costs. The operation will read all items and then perform *filter expression* on returned item set:

```
--filter-expression filter
```

Inside the filter we can use:

- **Comparison operators**: = (equal), <> (not equal), < (less than), > (greater than), <= (less or equal to), >= (greater or equal to), **BETWEEN** (check if the value is between specified values) and **IN** (check if the specified value is in the set).
- **Logical operators**: AND, OR, and NOT.
- **Condition functions**:
    - **attribute_exists(attribute_name)**: Returns *true* if an attribute with the specified name *exists* in the item.
    - **attribute_not_exists(attribute_name)**: Returns *true* if the attribute with the specified name *does not exist* in the item.
    - **attribute_type(attribute_name, type)**: Returns *true* if the attribute with the specified name is of the *specified* type.

In order to reduce costs, we can set a limit on returned items. Scan operation will stop and return items when the **limit** is reached:

```
--limit numerical_value
```

The last read operation is **query**. This operation, at the first glance, is identical to a **scan**, but that is *not* the case. Yes, it will return multiple items, but not all of them, and it will use the primary key to find them, so it will *not* read all items:

```
aws dynamodb query
--table-name 'table_name'
--key-condition-expression key_condition
--expression-attribute-values attribute_values
```

The *key condition expression* is used to specify match criteria for a query operation. As the name suggests, only key attributes can be used in key condition expression in combination with one of the *comparison* operators: = (equal), <> (not equal), < (less than), > (greater than), <= (less than or equal to), >= (greater than or equal to), BETWEEN (check if the value is greater than lower bound and less than or equal upper bound).

On special function is also supported in condition expressions, **begins_with(s, substring)**. This function will return *true* if string **s** begins with a specified substring. Also, conditions can be combined with *logical* operators.

Condition expression can have one of two following forms:

```
attribute_name comparison_operator :comparison_value
begins_with(attribute_name, substring)
```

Comparison values and substrings are defined in *expression attribute values* in the following form:

```
{
        "attribute_value_1": {
                "attribute_type_1": "attribute_value_1"
        }
},
…,
{
        "attribute_value_N": {
                "attribute_type_N": "attribute_value_N"
        }
}
```

We can also define *filter expression* for *query operation* similar to *scan operation* with one important difference, we can use only non-key attributes. For **scan** and **query** operations we can define projection, in order to return only some specific *attributes*.

Now that we know how to read data from DynamoDB, we will learn how to write it.

Write operations

The following write operations are supported by DynamoDB:

- **Put Item** creates a new item or replaces an old item with a new one in the specified table.
- **Update Item** updates specified item.
- **Delete Item** removes the specified item from the table.
- **Batch Write Item** creates or deletes up to *25 items*.

The first operation, **put-item**, is used when a new item should be created:

```
aws dynamodb put-item \
--table-name 'table_name'
--item 'new_item'
--return-values return_values_option
```

Provided item (**new_item**) in the previous operation must follow the *name-type-value* convention for each attribute:

```
{
        {
                "attribute_name_1": {
                        "attribute_type_1": "attribute_value_1"
                }
        },
        …
        {
                "attribute_name_N": {
                        "attribute_type_N": "attribute_value_N"
                }
        }
}
```

Return values are *optional,* for this operation, two return values options are available:

- **NONE**: Nothing will be returned, this option is the default one.
- **ALL_OLD**: In the case when *Put Item* replaces the item, the content of the *old item* will be returned.

Next operation, **update-item** will update the existing item, or create a new one if it does not exist:

```
aws dynamodb update-item \
--table-name 'table_name'
--key '{ "key_name": { "key_type": "key_value" } }'
--update-expression update_expression
--expression-attribute-values attribute_values
--return-values return_values_option
```

Update expressions represent a set of expressions in the following format:

```
update_operand attribute_name_1 = :attribute_value_1, …,
attribute_name_N = :attribute_value_N
```

These *update* operands can be used:

- **SET**: Set a new value to the specified attribute, if the attribute does not exist it will be added to the item.
- **REMOVE**: Removes an attribute from the item.
- **ADD**: Adds an attribute with value to the item, if the *attribute* does not exist. If another case, the behavior will depend on the data type. If **ADD** is used with a *number,* a specified value will be added to the *existing value of the item.* If **ADD** is used with the *set,* a specified value will be added to the *set.*
- **DELETE**: Deletes element from a set.

Attribute values from update expressions will be defined under *expression attribute values* in the following form:

```
{
        "attribute_value_1": {
              "attribute_type_1": "attribute_value_1"
        }
},
…,
{
```

```
            "attribute_value_N": {
                  "attribute_type_N": "attribute_value_N"
            }
      }
```

Return values are also optional. Update Item has the most return value options:

- **NONE**: Default option, nothing will be returned.
- **ALL_OLD**: Content of the item before the update operation, will be returned.
- **UPDATE_OLD**: Returns only updated attributes with old values.
- **ALL_NEW**: Content of the item after the update operation, will be returned.
- **UPDATED_NEW**: Returns only updated attributes with new values.

Operation **delete-item** will remove the item from the table and will have this format:

```
aws dynamodb delete-item \
--table-name 'table_name'
--key '{ "key_name": { "key_type": "key_value" } }'
--return-values return_values_option
```

Return values are *optional*. Delete Item operation has two return value options:

- **NONE**: Nothing will be returned (*default option*).
- **ALL_OLD**: Content of old (deleted) items will be *returned*.

The last write operation, **batch-write-item** will basically execute up to *25 create-item and delete-item operations*. The operation format is similar to the previous one, but here we will introduce some new concepts:

```
aws dynamodb batch-write-item \
--request-items values_map
```

Values map contains one or more table names and descriptions of one or more items that will be retrieved from the table. The values map will have the following form:

```
{
      "table_name": [
            {
                  "PutRequest": {
                        "Item": {
```

```
                                        "key_name": {
                                                "key_type": "key_value"
                                        },
                                        "attribute_name": {
                                                "attribute_type":
                                                "attribute_value"
                                        }
                                }
                        }
                },
                {
                        "DeleteRequest": {
                                "Key": {
                                        "key_name": {
                                                "key_type": "key_value"
                                        },
                                }
                        }
                }
        ]
}
```

By default, all write operations are *unconditional*. But we can add a condition in order to control which items will be modified,by addingfollowing *line* in operation:

```
--condition-expression condition
```

Inside the condition, we can use the same comparison operators, logical operators, and functions as *filter expressions* (described with the **scan** operation).

Now that we are familiar with basic DynamoDB concepts and operations, we can start with the database setup.

Setting up a database

DynamoDB can be executed locally on our computer. This *local* distribution is created with the idea to test and develop applications without access to the DynamoDB web service. Usage of the DynamoDB web service is *not* free, so this is the best solution to check everything before the release and to learn, and play with DynamoDB concepts.

Installation is the same for all operating systems. We can download a **.zip** or **.tar.gz** archive from the official web page:

https://docs.aws.amazon.com/amazondynamodb/latest/developerguide/DynamoDBLocal.DownloadingAndRunning.html#DynamoDBLocal.DownloadingAndRunning.title

Now we should extract archive to the desired destination directory.

After installation we can run DynamoDB locally, by opening the console/terminal, navigating to the directory where the file **DynamoDBLocal.jar** is (in the directory where the *archive* is extracted), and executing the following command:

```
java -Djava.library.path=./DynamoDBLocal_lib
-jar DynamoDBLocal.jar -sharedDb
```

If the command is executed *successfully*, the following should be displayed in the console/terminal, without any errors:

```
Initializing DynamoDB Local with the following configuration:
Port: 8000
InMemory:    false
DbPath:      null
SharedDb:    true
shouldDelayTransientStatuses:    false
CorsParams:  null
```

It is important to note, in order to properly run DynamoDB locally, the proper version of Java must be installed.

For DynamoDB, there is no graphical tool like we had for previous database systems. But we can use **AWS CLI** to check the local database and execute operations. Installation files are available on the official web page:

https://aws.amazon.com/cli/

AWS CLI can be installed on Linux (all distributions) by downloading and extracting archives with a Linux installer. After that we can open a terminal, navigate to the directory where the installer is extracted and execute this command:

```
sudo ./aws/install
```

The default installation directory is **/usr/local/bin**, while the default directory where all files will be copied is **/usr/local/aws-cli**. These directories can be changed with **-b** and **-i** flags respectively. The previous command is equivalent to this command:

```
sudo ./aws/install -i /usr/local/aws-cli -b /usr/local/bin
```

To install AWS CLI on Windows, we just need to download, and run the MSI installer, and follow the instructions.

For macOS, the **PKG installer** can be downloaded and run. The default installation directory is `/usr/local/aws-cli` and can be changed during installation.

After these installations, we should set up credentials and other configurations for our DynamoDB with this simple command:

```
aws configure
```

This command will prompt us to enter four options:

- AWS Access Key ID
- AWS Secret Access Key
- Default region name
- Default output name

AWS Access Key ID and **AWS Secret Access Key** are credentials for database access, so you can set whatever suits you the best. We will run a database on our local machine, so for the default region name we can choose whatever we want (*city* or *country* where we live, name of our computer, or simple string *region*). For the default output format, we should enter `json` (*lowercase*).

Now we can create tables and indices. All *scripts* will be placed in JSON files inside the `dbscripts` directory (*Figure 8.11*):

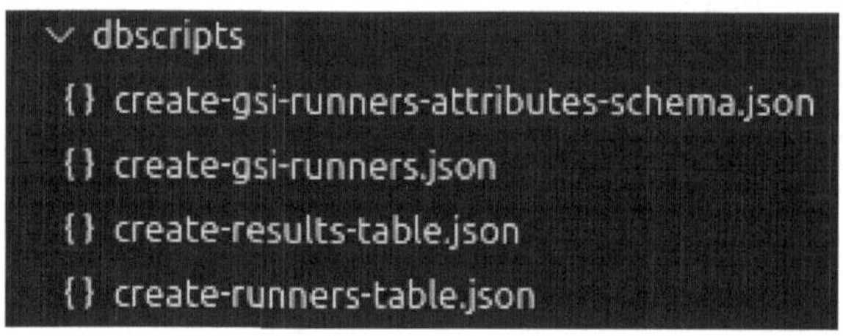

***Figure 8.11**: Database scripts*

Inside `create-runners-table.json` and `create-results-table.json` files are definitions for our tables. Inside each file, we will have declared *table names, partition (hash) keys, sort (range) keys*, and *read and write capacity*.

For the `runners` table, three attributes are important for read operations, *id, country,* and *personal best result*. Only two *attributes* can be set as table keys, but we can create a global secondary index in order to combine these attributes. In case, when we should get the *best ten runners* for a specified country, the returned array should be sorted by personal best results.

We will combine *country* and *personal best* in the global secondary index and use id as the *partition key*. It is not a good practice to use this kind of data for any key, but all resource operations defined with HTTP requests are related to ID, so we must use this attribute as the partition key:

```
{
    "TableName": "Runners",
    "KeySchema": [
        { "AttributeName": "id", "KeyType": "HASH" }
    ],
    "AttributeDefinitions": [
        { "AttributeName": "id", "AttributeType": "S" }
    ],
    "ProvisionedThroughput": {
        "ReadCapacityUnits": 5,
        "WriteCapacityUnits": 5
    }
}
```

We can assume that the approximate item size (in both tables) will be around *1 KB* and that we will have *5 item reads/writes per second*, we can calculate *Read* and *Write Throughput Capacity* with formulas previously introduced in this chapter. *Read Throughput Capacity* will be **5 RCU**, while *Write Throughput Capacity* will be **5 WCU**. These values will be used for all tables and indices.

This AWS CLI command will create a `runners` table:

```
aws dynamodb create-table \
--cli-input-json file://create-runners-table.json \
--endpoint-url http://localhost:8000
```

All DynamoDB operations executed locally must have an endpoint URL set to `http://localhost:8000`, where `8000` is the standard port used for DynamoDB.

The `results` table will use *runner ID* as the *partition key* and *race result* as the *sort key*. This decision is made based on data usage. When we get a certain runner, we should get all his results, so it is suitable to use this attribute as the partition key. Results should be sorted by *race results* (from *best ones* to *worst ones*) so it makes sense to use the `race_result` attribute as the *sort key*:

```
{
    "TableName": "Results",
    "KeySchema": [
        { "AttributeName": "runner_id", "KeyType": "HASH" },
        { "AttributeName": "race_result", "KeyType": "RANGE" }
```

```
        ],
        "AttributeDefinitions": [
            { "AttributeName": "runner_id", "AttributeType": "S" },
            { "AttributeName": "race_result", "AttributeType": "S" }
        ],
        "ProvisionedThroughput": {
            "ReadCapacityUnits": 5,
            "WriteCapacityUnits": 5
        }
    }
```

The following operation will create a **results** table:

```
aws dynamodb create-table \
--cli-input-json file://create-results-table.json \
--endpoint-url http://localhost:8000
```

File **create-gsi-runners.json** will contain a definition of the global secondary index. Here we will declare the *index name, partition (hash) keys, sort (range) keys, projection,* and *read and write capacity*. **Projection** defines which table attributes will be copied (projected) into the index. DynamoDB supports these projection types:

- **ALL**: All table attributes will be projected into the index.
- **KEYS_ONLY**: Only index and primary keys will be projected.
- **INCLUDE**: All attributes covered by **KEYS_ONLY** and additional specified attributes will be projected.

```
[{
    "Create": {
        "IndexName": "runners_global_index",
        "KeySchema": [
            { "AttributeName": "country", "KeyType": "HASH" },
            { "AttributeName": "personal_best",
                    "KeyType": "RANGE" }
        ],
        "Projection": {
            "ProjectionType": "ALL"
        },
        "ProvisionedThroughput": {
            "ReadCapacityUnits": 5,
```

```
            "WriteCapacityUnits": 5
        }
    }
}]
```

The last file, **create-gsi-runners-attributes-schema.json**, will contain a definition of attributes used in the index:

```
[
    { "AttributeName": "country", "AttributeType": "S" },
    { "AttributeName": "personal_best", "AttributeType": "S" }
]
```

This operation will create an index:

```
aws dynamodb update-table --table-name Runners \
--attribute-definitions file://create-gsi-runner-attributes-schema.
json \
--global-secondary-index-updates file://create-gsi-runner.json \
--endpoint-url http://localhost:8000
```

Now when our database is set up and ready, we can continue with implementation.

Repository layer

For the implementation of the *repository layer* with DynamoDB, we will return to the standard version of models (used in solutions with relational databases). This implementation will have the same amount of methods as the MongoDB solution, with one difference, the method **GetRunnersByYear()** will be replaced with **GetRunnersByIdMap()**, we will see why later in this section:

```
package repositories

import (
        "net/http"
        "runners-dynamodb/models"
        "strconv"

        "github.com/aws/aws-sdk-go/aws"
        "github.com/aws/aws-sdk-go/service/dynamodb"
        "github.com/aws/aws-sdk-go/service/dynamodb/
                dynamodbattribute"
```

```
	"github.com/google/uuid"
)

type RunnersRepository struct {
	db *dynamodb.DynamoDB
}

func NewRunnersRepository(
	db *dynamodb.DynamoDB) *RunnersRepository {

	return &RunnersRepository{
		db: db,
	}
}

func (rr RunnersRepository) CreateRunner(
	runner *models.Runner) (*models.Runner,
	*models.ResponseError) {
	...
}

func (rr RunnersRepository) UpdateRunner(
	runner *models.Runner) *models.ResponseError {
	...
}

func (rr RunnersRepository) DeleteRunner(
	runnerId string) *models.ResponseError {
	…
}

func (rr RunnersRepository) GetRunner(
	runnerId string) (*models.Runner, *models.ResponseError) {
	...
}

func (rr RunnersRepository) GetAllRunners() ([]*models.Runner,
	*models.ResponseError) {
```

```
        ...
}

func (rr RunnersRepository) GetRunnersByCountry(
        country string) ([]*models.Runner,
        *models.ResponseError) {
        ...
}

func (rr RunnersRepository) GetRunnersByIdMap(
        runnerIds map[string]struct{}) (map[string]models.Runner,
         *models.ResponseError) {
        ...
}
```

Our first method will be used to create a new runner. DynamoDB does not have any integrated or supported method for generating unique identifiers. It is up to the one who writes the item to generate the *identifier*. For this we can use **uuid**, the official *Google* solution, which can be downloaded with **go get** command:

```
go get github.com/google/uuid
```

Also, there are no default values for *non-key attributes*, so we must set **isActive** to **true**. In order to use data placed in the **Runner** model, we must convert it to a map of attribute values (format supported by DynamoDB, which we introduced in previous sections).

For each DynamoDB operation, **aws-go-sdk** will provide a method that receives *operation-specific input* and returns the *operation-specific output*. All fields in input **structs** are equivalent to options used in AWS CLI operations (everything with a *double hyphen*). For put item input, we will use table name and attribute value map representation of **runner**.

All errors will be handled and the **Runner** model will be returned to the service layer:

```
func (rr RunnersRepository) CreateRunner(
        runner *models.Runner) (*models.Runner,
        *models.ResponseError) {

        runner.ID = uuid.New().String()
        runner.IsActive = true

        runnerAttrMap, err := dynamodbattribute.MarshalMap(runner)
```

```
        if err != nil {
                return nil, &models.ResponseError{
                        Message: "Failed to marshal runner into " + "
                                attribute-value map",
                        Status:  http.StatusBadRequest,
                }
        }

        input := &dynamodb.PutItemInput{
                TableName: aws.String("Runners"),
                Item:      runnerAttrMap,
        }

        _, err = rr.db.PutItem(input)
        if err != nil {
                return nil, &models.ResponseError{
                        Message: err.Error(),
                        Status:  http.StatusInternalServerError,
                }
        }

        return runner, nil
}
```

For the *Update Item operation,* input will have a *table name,* the *key* that specifies which item will be defined, a *map of attribute values* that will be updated, and an *update expression* where is defined how attribute values will be modified:

```
func (rr RunnersRepository) UpdateRunner(
        runner *models.Runner) *models.ResponseError {

        input := &dynamodb.UpdateItemInput{
                TableName: aws.String("Runners"),
                Key: map[string]*dynamodb.AttributeValue{
                        "id": {
                                S: aws.String(runner.ID),
                        },
                },
                ExpressionAttributeValues: map[string]*dynamodb.
```

```
                AttributeValue{
                    ":fn": {
                        S: aws.String(runner.FirstName),
                    },
                    ":ln": {
                        S: aws.String(runner.LastName),
                    },
                    ":a": {
                        N: aws.String(strconv.Itoa(
                            runner.Age)),
                    },
                    ":c": {
                        S: aws.String(runner.Country),
                    },
            },
            UpdateExpression: aws.String(
                "SET first_name = :fn, last_name = :ln," +
                "age = :a, country = :c"),
        }

        _, err := rr.db.UpdateItem(input)
        if err != nil {
            return &models.ResponseError{
                Message: err.Error(),
                Status:  http.StatusInternalServerError,
            }
        }

        return nil
    }
```

Method, **`DeleteRunner()`** is similar to the previous one, the only difference is that only the **`is_active`** attribute will be changed:

```
    func (rr RunnersRepository) DeleteRunner(
        runnerId string) *models.ResponseError {

        input := &dynamodb.UpdateItemInput{
```

```
            TableName: aws.String("Runners"),
            Key: map[string]*dynamodb.AttributeValue{
                  "id": {
                        S: aws.String(runnerId),
                  },
            },
            ExpressionAttributeValues: map[string]*dynamodb.
                  AttributeValue{
                  ":a": {
                        BOOL: aws.Bool(false),
                  },
            },
            UpdateExpression: aws.String("SET is_active = :a"),
      }

      _, err := rr.db.UpdateItem(input)
      if err != nil {
            return &models.ResponseError{
                  Message: err.Error(),
                  Status:  http.StatusInternalServerError,
            }
      }

      return nil
}
```

Method **getRunner()** will get one item from the **Runners** table that matches with partition key (**id**) from the input. Received output must be converted (*unmarshaled*) from the *attribute value map* into the **Runner** model before it can be returned to the service layer:

```
func (rr RunnersRepository) GetRunner(
      runnerId string) (*models.Runner, *models.ResponseError) {

      input := &dynamodb.GetItemInput{
            TableName: aws.String("Runners"),
            Key: map[string]*dynamodb.AttributeValue{
                  "id": {
```

```
                    S: aws.String(runnerId),
                },
            },
        }
        output, err := rr.db.GetItem(input)
        if err != nil {
            return nil, &models.ResponseError{
                Message: err.Error(),
                Status:  http.StatusInternalServerError,
            }
        }
        var runner *models.Runner
        err = dynamodbattribute.UnmarshalMap(output.Item, &runner)
        if err != nil {
            return nil, &models.ResponseError{
                Message: "Failed to unmarshal " +
                    "attribute-value map into runner",
                Status:  http.StatusInternalServerError,
            }
        }
        return runner, nil
    }
```

The next method is a *controversial* one. It will execute a **scan** operation in order to return all runners from the table. Generally, this will work, but the **scan** operation can retrieve a maximum of *1 MB* of data. This can cause some data to be *cut* from the response if more than *1 MB* of data is stored. We can use some *pagination* in order to prevent this problem, but generally, **scan** is not an *optimal* and *performant* operation, but we will show her usage here, just for an example:

```
    func (rr RunnersRepository) GetAllRunners() ([]*models.Runner,
        *models.ResponseError) {
        input := &dynamodb.ScanInput{
            TableName: aws.String("Runners"),
        }
```

```
        output, err := rr.db.Scan(input)
        if err != nil {
              return nil, &models.ResponseError{
                    Message: err.Error(),
                    Status:  http.StatusInternalServerError,
              }
        }

        var runners []*models.Runner
        err = dynamodbattribute.UnmarshalListOfMaps(output.Items,
              &runners)
        if err != nil {
              return nil, &models.ResponseError{
                    Message: "Failed to unmarshal " +
                          "attribute-value map into runners",
                    Status:  http.StatusInternalServerError,
              }
        }

        return runners, nil
}
```

The first complex method, **GetRunnersByCountry()** will return the *top ten active runners* from a specified country. We will use a **query** operation to retrieve this data. Here, we will use the secondary index to get all *runners* from the *specified country* and to make sure that runners will be ordered by the *personal best result* in *ascending* order. The *sorting* order can be set with **Scan Index Forward**, the default value is *ascending (true).*

Since the **is_active** attribute is not a part of any key it can be used only in filter expressions. But the filter will be applied after the **query** option is executed, and that can cause a potential problem. We only need *ten best runners,* and the logic is to use a limit to get only *ten items* from the database. As the filter is applied after the **query** returns items, if we use a **limit**, some *retired runners* can be returned and the **runners** array can have *less than ten runners* after the filter is applied.

This problem can be solved by returning *sub-slice* using Go concepts. We should check if returned array's length is *greater than ten* (some countries can have a smaller amount of runners), in order to prevent index *out-of-range error*:

```
func (rr RunnersRepository) GetRunnersByCountry(
        country string) ([]*models.Runner, *models.ResponseError) {

        input := &dynamodb.QueryInput{
                TableName:                 aws.String("Runners"),
                IndexName:                 aws.String(
                                                   "runners_global_index"),
                KeyConditionExpression: aws.String("country = :c"),
                FilterExpression:       aws.String(
                                                   "is_active = :a"),
                ExpressionAttributeValues: map[string]*dynamodb.
                        AttributeValue{
                        ":c": {
                                S: aws.String(country),
                        },
                        ":a": {
                                BOOL: aws.Bool(true),
                        },
                },
                ScanIndexForward: aws.Bool(true),
        }

        output, err := rr.db.Query(input)
        if err != nil {
                return nil, &models.ResponseError{
                        Message: err.Error(),
                        Status:  http.StatusInternalServerError,
                }
        }

        var runners []*models.Runner
        err = dynamodbattribute.UnmarshalListOfMaps(
                output.Items, &runners)
        if err != nil {
                return nil, &models.ResponseError{
                        Message: "Failed to unmarshal " +
                                "attribute-value map into runners",
```

```
                    Status:  http.StatusInternalServerError,
                }
            }

            if len(runners) > 10 {
                return runners[:10], nil
            }

            return runners, nil
        }
```

There is no concept of **JOIN** in DynamoDB, so it is *impossible* to merge data from different tables through any operation. So, we must merge it in the service layer by combining data returned from runners and the results repository.

The last method in the repository layer will return the *map of runners,* where runner ID will be used as the *key* while the **Runner** model will be used as value (we will later see why we use the *map* and not a *slice*). We will use the *Batch Get Item operation* to get all necessary runners by putting **runner** IDs inside the *key map.*

The *key map* must not contain duplicates, in case when some key is duplicated, *Batch Get Items* will return an *error*. Since we will iterate through the data structure received from the service layer, and arrays and slices can have duplicate elements, iteration will create an *invalid key value map*. On the other hand, a map *cannot* have duplicate keys, so it is better to pack **runner** IDs in the map.

Runner ID will be used for the *map key,* while **value** is not important. In these cases, we should use an empty **struct** in order to reduce memory usage. *Why struct?* For example, a **bool** variable will take one byte, *while an empty struct will take zero bytes!*

Inside returned output, items will be received as a map of maps that represents items per table. We should iterate through table map, and inside that iteration, we should iterate through item map so we can properly convert and map data:

```
func (rr RunnersRepository) GetRunnersByIdMap(
        runnerIds map[string]struct{}) (map[string]models.Runner,
        *models.ResponseError) {

        var keys []map[string]*dynamodb.AttributeValue
        for runnerId := range runnerIds {
                key := map[string]*dynamodb.AttributeValue{
                        "id": {
```

```
                    S: aws.String(runnerId),
                },
            }

            keys = append(keys, key)
        }

        input := &dynamodb.BatchGetItemInput{
            RequestItems: map[string]*dynamodb.
                KeysAndAttributes{

                "Runners": {
                    Keys: keys,
                },
            },
        }

        output, err := rr.db.BatchGetItem(input)
        if err != nil {
            return nil, &models.ResponseError{
                Message: err.Error(),
                Status: http.StatusInternalServerError,
            }
        }

        runnersMap := make(map[string]models.Runner)
        for _, table := range output.Responses {
            for _, item := range table {
                var runner models.Runner
                err = dynamodbattribute.UnmarshalMap(
                    item, &runner)
                if err != nil {
                    return nil, &models.ResponseError{
                        Message: "Failed to unmarshal " +
                            "attribute-value map" +
                            "into runner",
                        Status: http.
```

```
                                        StatusInternalServerError,
                                }
                        }

                        runnersMap[runner.ID] = runner
                }
        }

        return runnersMap, nil
}
```

The **results** repository will have a few more get methods than the one that uses MongoDB:

```
package repositories

import (
        "net/http"
        "runners-dynamodb/models"
        "strconv"

        "github.com/aws/aws-sdk-go/aws"
        "github.com/aws/aws-sdk-go/service/dynamodb"
        "github.com/aws/aws-sdk-go/service/dynamodb/
                dynamodbattribute"
        "github.com/google/uuid"
)

type ResultsRepository struct {
        db *dynamodb.DynamoDB
}

func NewResultsRepository(
        db *dynamodb.DynamoDB) *ResultsRepository {

        return &ResultsRepository{
                db: db,
        }
}
```

```
func (rr ResultsRepository) CreateResult(result *models.Result,
	runner *models.Runner) (*models.Result,
	*models.ResponseError) {
	...
}

func (rr ResultsRepository) DeleteResult(result *models.Result,
	runner *models.Runner) *models.ResponseError {
	...
}

func (rr ResultsRepository) GetResult(
	resultId string) (*models.Result, *models.ResponseError) {
	...
}

func (rr ResultsRepository) GetAllRunnersResults(
	runnerId string) ([]*models.Result, *models.ResponseError) {
	...
}

func (rr ResultsRepository) GetTenBestResultsFromYear(
	year int) ([]*models.Result, *models.ResponseError) {
	...
}
```

The first method, **`CreateResult()`** will use a transaction to execute operations that will create *new result items,* and *update personal best,* and *season best results* for the specified **`runner`**:

```
func (rr ResultsRepository) CreateResult(result *models.Result,
	runner *models.Runner) (*models.Result,
	*models.ResponseError) {

	result.ID = uuid.New().String()

	resultAttrMap, err := dynamodbattribute.MarshalMap(result)
	if err != nil {
		return nil, &models.ResponseError{
```

```
                Message: “Failed to marshal result “ +
                      “into attribute-value map”,
                Status:  http.StatusBadRequest,
          }
    }

    input := &dynamodb.TransactWriteItemsInput{
          TransactItems: []*dynamodb.TransactWriteItem{
                {
                      Put: &dynamodb.Put{
                            TableName: aws.
                                  String(“Results”),
                            Item:      resultAttrMap,
                      },
                },
                {
                      Update: &dynamodb.Update{
                            TableName: aws.
                                  String(“Runners”),
                            Key: map[string]*dynamodb.
                                  AttributeValue{

                                  “id”: {
                                        S: aws.
                                              String(runner.ID),
                                  },
                            },
                            ExpressionAttributeValues:
                                  map[string]*dynamodb.
                                        AttributeValue{
                                  “:pb”: {
                                        S: aws.String(
                                              runner.
                                              PersonalBest),
                                  },
                                  “:sb”: {
```

```
                                        S: aws.String(
                                            runner.
                                            SeasonBest),
                                    },
                                },
                                UpdateExpression: aws.String(
                                    "SET personal_best " +
                                        "= :pb, " +
                                        "season_best " +
                                        "= :sb"),
                            },
                        },
                    },
                }

                _, err = rr.db.TransactWriteItems(input)
                if err != nil {
                    return nil, &models.ResponseError{
                        Message: err.Error(),
                        Status:  http.StatusInternalServerError,
                    }
                }

                return result, nil
            }
```

In the second method, **DeleteResult()** we will again use transaction, which will execute delete operations that will *remove the result item,* and *update the personal best,* and *season best results* for the specified **runner**:

```
func (rr ResultsRepository) DeleteResult(result *models.Result,
    runner *models.Runner) *models.ResponseError {

    input := &dynamodb.TransactWriteItemsInput{
        TransactItems: []*dynamodb.TransactWriteItem{
            {
                Delete: &dynamodb.Delete{
                    TableName: aws.
```

```
                    String("Results"),
                Key: map[string]*dynamodb.
                    AttributeValue{
                    "runner_id": {
                        S: aws.String(
                            result.
                            RunnerID
                        ),
                    },
                    "race_result": {
                        S: aws.String(
                            result.
                            RaceResult
                        ),
                    },
                },
            },
        },
        {
            Update: &dynamodb.Update{
                TableName: aws.String(
                    "Runners"),
                Key: map[string]*dynamodb.
                    AttributeValue{
                    "id": {
                        S: aws.String(
                            runner.ID),
                    },
                },
                ExpressionAttributeValues:
                    map[string]*dynamodb.
                        AttributeValue{
                    ":pb": {
                        S: aws.String(
```

```
                                                            runner.
                                                            PersonalBest
                                                      ),
                                                },
                                                ":sb": {
                                                      S: aws.String(
                                                            runner.
                                                            SeasonBest),
                                                },
                                          },
                                          UpdateExpression: aws.String(
                                                "SET personal_best " +
                                                      "= :pb, " +
                                                      "season_best " +
                                                      "= :sb"),
                                    },
                              },
                        },
            }

            _, err := rr.db.TransactWriteItems(input)
            if err != nil {
                  return &models.ResponseError{
                        Message: err.Error(),
                        Status:  http.StatusInternalServerError,
                  }
            }

            return nil
      }
```

Following the method, **`GetResult()`** is provided here as a *bad example*. Result ID is not a part of any key, so we cannot use *Get Item* or *Query* operation. The only other solution is to scan all items and filter one that matches the specified ID:

```
      func (rr ResultsRepository) GetResult(
            resultId string) (*models.Result, *models.ResponseError) {
```

```
	input := &dynamodb.ScanInput{
		TableName:        aws.String("Results"),
		FilterExpression: aws.String("id = :i"),
		ExpressionAttributeValues: map[string]*dynamodb.
			AttributeValue{
			":i": {
				S: aws.String(resultId),
			},
		},
	}

	output, err := rr.db.Scan(input)
	if err != nil {
		return nil, &models.ResponseError{
			Message: err.Error(),
			Status:  http.StatusInternalServerError,
		}
	}

	var results []*models.Result
	err = dynamodbattribute.UnmarshalListOfMaps(
		output.Items, &results)

	if err != nil {
		return nil, &models.ResponseError{
			Message: "Failed to unmarshal " +
				"attribute-value map " +
				"into result",
			Status:  http.StatusInternalServerError,
		}
	}

	return results[0], nil
}
```

On the other hand, the following method **`GetAllRunnersResults()`** is an example of a well-designed key strategy. This method will return all results for the specified runner. **`Runner`** ID is a *partition key* so querying will be *fast* and *efficient*, and results will be sorted by *race results (sort key)*:

```
func (rr ResultsRepository) GetAllRunnersResults(
    runnerId string) ([]*models.Result, *models.ResponseError) {

    input := &dynamodb.QueryInput{
        TableName:               aws.String("Results"),
        KeyConditionExpression: aws.String(
                                    "runner_id = :rid"),
        ExpressionAttributeValues: map[string]*dynamodb.
            AttributeValue{
            ":rid": {
                S: aws.String(runnerId),
            },
        },
    }

    output, err := rr.db.Query(input)
    if err != nil {
        return nil, &models.ResponseError{
            Message: err.Error(),
            Status:  http.StatusInternalServerError,
        }
    }

    var results []*models.Result
    err = dynamodbattribute.UnmarshalListOfMaps(
        output.Items, &results)
    if err != nil {
        return nil, &models.ResponseError{
            Message: "Failed to unmarshal " +
                "attribute-value map " +
                "into results",
            Status:  http.StatusInternalServerError,
        }
```

```
        }

        return results, nil
}
```

Again one *bad* example is where all items are *scanned, filtered,* and *limited* with *sub-slice.* This method will return the *top ten race results* from the specified year:

```
func (rr ResultsRepository) GetTenBestResultsFromYear(
        year int) ([]*models.Result, *models.ResponseError) {

        input := &dynamodb.ScanInput{
                TableName:         aws.String("Results"),
                FilterExpression: aws.String("race_year = :ry"),
                ExpressionAttributeValues: map[string]*dynamodb.
                        AttributeValue{
                        ":ry": {
                                N: aws.String(strconv.Itoa(year)),
                        },
                },
        }

        output, err := rr.db.Scan(input)
        if err != nil {
                return nil, &models.ResponseError{
                        Message: err.Error(),
                        Status:  http.StatusInternalServerError,
                }
        }

        var results []*models.Result
        err = dynamodbattribute.UnmarshalListOfMaps(
                output.Items, &results)
        if err != nil {
                return nil, &models.ResponseError{
                        Message: "Failed to unmarshal " +
                                "attribute-value map " +
                                "into results",
```

```
                    Status:  http.StatusInternalServerError,
                }
            }

            if len(results) > 10 {
                return results[:10], nil
            }

            return results, nil
        }
```

As we can see, we have two *bad* functions. They both use attributes for filtering that are not key attributes. *Can this be improved?* Actually, it can. The global secondary index can have two keys (*partition* and *sort*). As an exercise, you can try to create a secondary index and use it in these *problematic* functions. Global Secondary Index created for `runners` table can be used as a reference.

Database layer

The database layer must be adjusted to support DynamoDB. The proper driver will be installed with the following command:

```
go get github.com/aws/aws-sdk-go
```

The configuration file will be more complex than the one used with the MongoDB solution. Besides the connection string, configuration set up with *aws configure* operation (**AWS region**, **AWS Access Key**, and **AWS Secret Access Key**) will be used in the `database` section. The configuration file will now contain this section:

```
##############################################################

# Database configuration

# Connection string is in Go dynamodb driver format:
# http://host:port

[database]

connection_string = "http://localhost:8000"
aws_region = "region"
aws_access_key_id = "dusan"
aws_secret_access_key = "dusan"
##############################################################
```

Function **`InitDatabase()`** must be rewritten to follow changes in *database* technology. First, **Viper** will be used to read *database-related configuration,* after that connection string will be checked. If it is *empty,* application execution will be terminated.

The configuration will be used for **session creation**. The session is shared across service clients and it is safe for concurrency usage. Function **`Must()`** is a helper function that checks if the session is *valid* (we used **`Ping()`** in *previous solutions* for this check). In case of any *error,* panic will be triggered.

At the end of the function, the session will be used for the creation of a new instance of the DynamoDB client. Here is the complete content of **`InitDatabase()`** function with all related imports:

```
package server

import (
	"log"

	"github.com/aws/aws-sdk-go/aws"
	"github.com/aws/aws-sdk-go/aws/credentials"
	"github.com/aws/aws-sdk-go/aws/session"
	"github.com/aws/aws-sdk-go/service/dynamodb"
	"github.com/spf13/viper"
)

func InitDatabase(config *viper.Viper) *dynamodb.DynamoDB {
	connectionString := config.GetString(
		"database.connection_string")
	awsRegion := config.GetString("database.aws_region")
	awsAccessKeyID := config.GetString(
		"database.aws_access_key_id")
	awsSecretAccessKey := config.GetString(
		"database.aws_secret_access_key")

	if connectionString == "" {
		log.Fatalf("Database connection string is missing")
	}

	session := session.Must(session.NewSession(
		&aws.Config{
```

```
                    Region:      aws.String(awsRegion),
                    Credentials: credentials.NewStaticCredentials(
                         awsAccessKeyID, awsSecretAccessKey,
                         ""),
                    Endpoint:    aws.String(connectionString),
               },
          ))

          return dynamodb.New(session)
     }
```

The repository layer should now use the client returned by **`InitDatabase()`** to execute DynamoDB operations.

Our second NoSQL solution is almost completed! As we can see, business requirements for our application stopped us to use the advantages of DynamoDB. So, maybe this database system is not the best match for our needs, as some of the previous ones are.

It is a good practice to test multiple database solutions (when possible) in order to find the one that best suits application demands. Let us not be afraid to *investigate* and explore multiple database solutions in order to avoid situations where we, after some development time, find out that the wrong database system was chosen.

Let us take a look at the changes in the service layer. In **`GetRunnersBatch()`** part that returns the *top ten results* for a specified *year* will be changed. *First,* we will get the *top ten results* from the **`results`** repository, *second,* we will get a *map of runners* related to these results from the **`runners`** repository, and *third,* we will iterate through the **`results`** slice and combine **`results`** with **`runners`** in order to return proper data to controller layer:

```
     results, responseErr := rs.resultsRepository.
          GetTenBestResultsFromYear(intYear)
     if responseErr != nil {
          return nil, responseErr
     }

     runnerIdMap := make(map[string]struct{})
     for _, result := range results {
          runnerIdMap[result.RunnerID] = struct{}{}
     }
```

```
runnersMap, responseErr := rs.runnersRepository.
      GetRunnersByIdMap(runnerIdMap)
if responseErr != nil {
      return nil, responseErr
}

var runners []*models.Runner
for _, result := range results {
      runner := runnersMap[result.RunnerID]
      runner.SeasonBest = result.RaceResult
      runners = append(runners, &runner)
}

return runners, nil
```

In **CreateResult()** and **DeleteResult()** from the **results** service, we will (after validation) get all necessary data from **runners**, and **results** repositories, and call methods from the **results** repository that uses transactions:

```
func (rs ResultsService) CreateResult(
      result *models.Result) (*models.Result,
      *models.ResponseError) {

      if result.RunnerID == "" {
            return nil, &models.ResponseError{
                  Message: "Invalid runner ID",
                  Status:  http.StatusBadRequest,
            }
      }

      if result.RaceResult == "" {
            return nil, &models.ResponseError{
                  Message: "Invalid race result",
                  Status:  http.StatusBadRequest,
            }
      }

      if result.Location == "" {
            return nil, &models.ResponseError{
```

```
                Message: "Invalid location",
                Status:  http.StatusBadRequest,
            }
        }

        if result.Position < 0 {
            return nil, &models.ResponseError{
                Message: "Invalid position",
                Status:  http.StatusBadRequest,
            }
        }

        currentYear := time.Now().Year()
        if result.Year < 0 || result.Year > currentYear {
            return nil, &models.ResponseError{
                Message: "Invalid year",
                Status:  http.StatusBadRequest,
            }
        }

        runner, responseErr := rs.runnersRepository.
            GetRunner(result.RunnerID)
        if responseErr != nil {
            return nil, responseErr
        }

        if runner.PersonalBest == "" {
            runner.PersonalBest = result.RaceResult
        } else {
            if result.RaceResult < runner.PersonalBest {
                runner.PersonalBest = result.RaceResult
            }
        }

        if result.Year == currentYear {
            if runner.SeasonBest == "" {
                runner.SeasonBest = result.RaceResult
            } else {
```

```
                if result.RaceResult < runner.SeasonBest {
                        runner.SeasonBest = result.RaceResult
                }
            }
        }

        response, responseErr := rs.resultsRepository.
                CreateResult(result, runner)
        if responseErr != nil {
                return nil, responseErr
        }

        return response, nil
}

func (rs ResultsService) DeleteResult(
        resultId string) *models.ResponseError {

        if resultId == "" {
                return &models.ResponseError{
                        Message: "Invalid result ID",
                        Status:  http.StatusBadRequest,
                }
        }

        result, responseErr := rs.resultsRepository.
                GetResult(resultId)
        if responseErr != nil {
                return responseErr
        }

        results, responseErr := rs.resultsRepository.
                GetAllRunnersResults(result.RunnerID)
        if responseErr != nil {
                return responseErr
        }

        runner, responseErr := rs.runnersRepository.
```

```
            GetRunner(result.RunnerID)
        if responseErr != nil {
            return responseErr
        }

        if runner.PersonalBest == result.RaceResult {
            runner.PersonalBest = getPersonalBestResult(
                results, resultId)
        }

        currentYear := time.Now().Year()
        if runner.SeasonBest == result.RaceResult &&
            result.Year == currentYear {

            runner.SeasonBest = getSeasonBestResult(results,
                result.Year, resultId)
        }

        responseErr = rs.resultsRepository.DeleteResult(
            result, runner)
        if responseErr != nil {
            return responseErr
        }

        return nil
    }
```

At the end of this section, we can show the content of the **getPersonalBestResult()** and **getSeasonBestResult()** functions. In these functions, we will iterate through the slice in order to find the *new personal* or *season-best result,* ignoring deleted results and handling situations when the current result is *empty*:

```
func getPersonalBestResult(results []*models.Result,
        resultId string) string {

        var personalBest string
        for _, result := range results {
            if result.ID != resultId &&
                    (result.RaceResult < personalBest ||
```

```
                personalBest == "") {

                personalBest = result.RaceResult
            }
        }

        return personalBest
}

func getSeasonBestResult(results []*models.Result, year int,
        resultId string) string {

        var seasonBest string
        for _, result := range results {
            if result.Year == year {
                if result.ID != resultId &&
                    (result.RaceResult < seasonBest ||
                    seasonBest == "") {

                    seasonBest = result.RaceResult
                }
            }
        }

        return seasonBest
}
```

Well done! Another solution is completed. Now we can move to some concepts that can improve the quality of our code.

Improvements

In *this* and the *previous* chapters, we developed the same software solution that uses four different database management systems. For each solution, a separate project was created. If we analyze code, *more than 80%* was identical in each solution. *Can we merge them into a single more adaptable project?*

If we define our repositories as interfaces and create **struct** for each database management system that implements that **interface**, we can dynamically load the desired implementation during initialization. Here is an example of the **results** repository defined as **interface**:

```
type ResultsRepositoryInterface interface {
	CreateResult(result *models.Result) (*models.Result,
		*models.ResponseError)
	DeleteResult(resultId string) (*models.Result,
		*models.ResponseError)
	GetAllRunnersResults(runnerId string) ([]*models.Result,
		*models.ResponseError)
	GetPersonalBestResults(runnerId string) (string,
		*models.ResponseError)
	GetSeasonBestResults(runnerId string, year int) (string,
		*models.ResponseError)
	SetTransaction(transaction *sql.Tx)
	GetHandler() *sql.DB
}
```

Since the interface does not have any fields but **structs** that implement the interface will have fields, some **get** and **set** methods will probably be declared (**SetTransaction()** and **GetHandler()**) in this case.

Now in **struct** that represents **results** service and in the *initialization* function, we should use **interface**:

```
type ResultsService struct {
	resultsRepository repositories.ResultsRepositoryInterface
	runnersRepository repositories.RunnersRepositoryInterface
}

func NewResultsService(
	resultsRepository repositories.ResultsRepositoryInterface,
	runnersRepository repositories.RunnersRepositoryInterface)
	*ResultsService {

	return &ResultsService{
		resultsRepository: resultsRepository,
		runnersRepository: runnersRepository,
	}
```

```
}
```

Also in functions that use *repositories* as *parameters*, now we should use an interface, like in the following example:

```
func BeginTransaction(
        runnersRepository RunnersRepositoryInterface,
        resultsRepository ResultsRepositoryInterface) error {

        ctx := context.Background()
        transaction, err := resultsRepository.GetHandler().
                BeginTx(ctx, &sql.TxOptions{})
        if err != nil {
                return err
        }

        runnersRepository.SetTransaction(transaction)
        resultsRepository.SetTransaction(transaction)

        return nil
}
```

We can additionally abstract our solution by defining all layers as *interfaces*.

Conclusion

In this chapter, we introduced the basic concepts of NoSQL databases and implemented a repository layer to utilize these concepts. Two different types of NoSQL databases, **MongoSQL** and **DynamoDB** are studied in this chapter, each with its own advantages and disadvantages.

In the next chapter, we will learn how to test our web server application.

References

- https://www.mongodb.com/try/download/community
- https://www.mongodb.com/try/download/compass
- https://docs.aws.amazon.com/amazondynamodb/latest/developerguide/DynamoDBLocal.DownloadingAndRunning.html#DynamoDBLocal.DownloadingAndRunning.title
- https://aws.amazon.com/cli/

Points to remember

- MongoDB documents are different than classic rows from a relational database, we can use this fact to put data that will be stored in separate tables into one collection.
- We can create separate models for database data and requests/response data, or we can *duplicate fields* in a **`struct`** that are problematic.
- DynamoDB does not have any supported method for generating unique identifiers.
- The use of the DynamoDB scan operation is *not recommended*, it is not an *optimal*, and *performant* operation.

Multiple choice questions

1. MongoDB is?
    a. Key-value database
    b. Document-oriented database
    c. Graph database
    d. Relational database
2. DynamoDB is?
    a. Key-value database
    b. Document-oriented database
    c. Graph database
    d. Relational database
3. What is not an aggregation pipeline stage?
    `a. $match`
    `b. $sort`
    `c. $sum`
    `d. $count`
4. What is the maximum size for the DynamoDB item?
    a. 4 KB
    b. 1 MB
    c. 400 KB
    d. 1 KB

Answers

1. b
2. a
3. c
4. c

Questions

1. What is sharding?
2. What is the MongoDB aggregation pipeline and how to use it?
3. How *Read Throughput Capacity* and *Write Throughput Capacity* for the DynamoDB table are calculated?
4. What are partition and sort keys in DynamoDB?

Key terms

- **NoSQL**: Databases used for storage and manipulation of data modeled in a different way than tabular relations.
- **BSON**: Binary representation of JSON document.
- **Document**: Record in a MongoDB collection.
- **Item**: Record in a DynamoDB table.

CHAPTER 9

Testing

Introduction

In this chapter, we will learn the fundamentals of application testing and discuss the differences between manual and automated testing. After that, we will learn how to manually test our web server application. At the end of the chapter, we will write and run automated tests with the Go programming language.

Structure

In this chapter, we will discuss the following topics:

- Testing fundamentals
- Manual testing
- Testing with Go
  - Unit tests
  - Integration tests
- Testing with Visual Studio Code

Testing fundamentals

Testing can be defined as the process of evaluation and verification of a certain product. In our case, the product is our server-side application or software in general. During the testing phase, developers and testers will check if the application works as expected.

The document in which all important test cases are listed is called the **test plan**. When all cases from the test plan are fulfilled, the application can get the green light to be delivered to users.

We can distinguish two methods of testing:

- **Manual testing**: Software products will be checked manually without any specified tool. The tester will be placed in the role of *application user* and try to *mimic* his behavior. For example, if some mobile phone application is tested, the tester will install it on his phone and use it as a regular application user would.
- **Automated testing**: Specialized tool is used to execute the test suite (group of tests). These tests are often written by developers, and it is a good practice that the test is not written by the developer who developed the tested part of the code (if it is possible). In some cases, if one of the tests fails, the build and deployment of the application can be stopped until the issue is fixed.

Code coverage represents the percentage of source code covered with tests. It is good practice to keep this value *above 80%*. It is very important not to fall into the trap and write tests just to fulfill coverage. These tests can often be illogical and will not improve the functionality and quality of source code.

We can define three testing levels:

- **Unit testing**: Testing functionality of specific parts of code, like function, class in an object-oriented environment or package in our case.
- **Integration testing**: Testing interfaces that will be used in communication between system components. In our case, client applications will use API for communication, so our integration tests will check them.
- **System testing**: Testing the whole software system. This will only be mentioned because we will only develop the *server-side* and without the *client-side* system is not completed.

Mock represents an *object* that mimics the behavior of a real application component that is often used in tests. For example, we want to test an application that has a database. It is not a good practice to mix test and production data and the creation of a test-dedicated database is often expensive. So, we can create a mock that will imitate the database and use it in tests instead of a real database.

Now when we are familiar with testing fundamentals we can actually test our application. We will return back to our **PostgreSQL** solution, for the rest of this book.

Manual testing

Our web server application does not have any graphical interface, but that does not mean that it cannot be manually tested. **Postman** is an application that can be used for that purpose and it is available for all modern operating systems and can be easily installed. Installation files are available on the official website:

https://www.postman.com/downloads/

To install Postman on Linux (all distributions), the **`tar.gz`** archive should be downloaded and unpacked. When the archive is unpacked, double-clicking on the Postman file should start the application.

For Windows, the **`.exe`** file will be downloaded and we should only follow installation instructions.

On macOS, the **`.zip`** archive should be downloaded and unpacked. After that click on the Postman file will start the installation. When the dialog is prompted, we should move the file to the **`Application`** directory, this will provide regular and correct application updates.

We can also use **Homebrew** to install Postman on macOS:

```
brew install --cask postman
```

When the installation is completed, we can start Postman. It is possible that Postman will ask or require an *account* to be created. After that, we can use the application without any problems.

In Postman we can create a new **HTTP Request**, and check the response. We can define the *HTTP method, paths, headers,* and *body* (*Figure 9.1*):

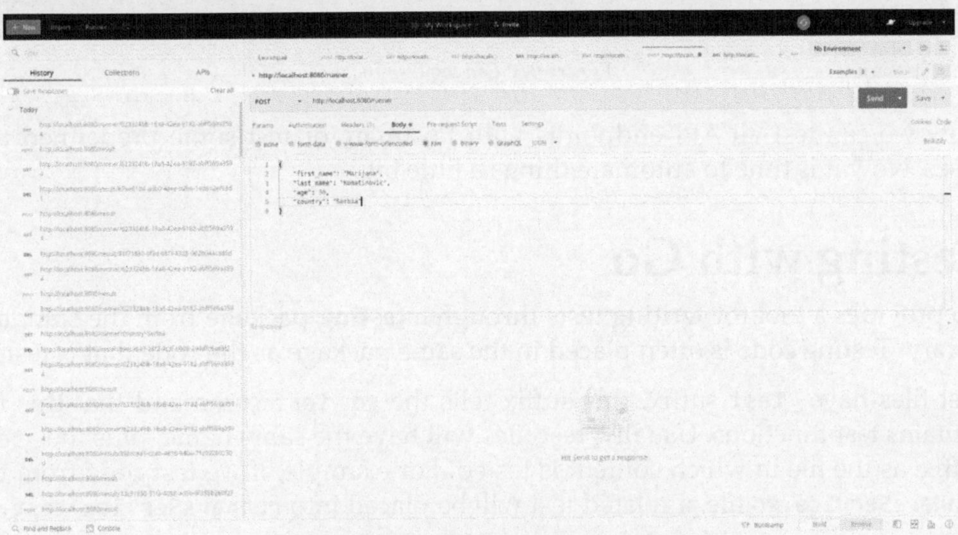

***Figure 9.1:** Postman with prepared request*

If we click on the **Send** button, the HTTP request will be sent to our application. The response will be displayed in the bottom part of the application window (*Figure*

9.2). Here, we can check the response status and body:

***Figure 9.2**: Postman with the received response*

If we check the terminal in Visual Studio Code where the application is run, we should see the response log written by **Gin** (*Figure 9.3*):

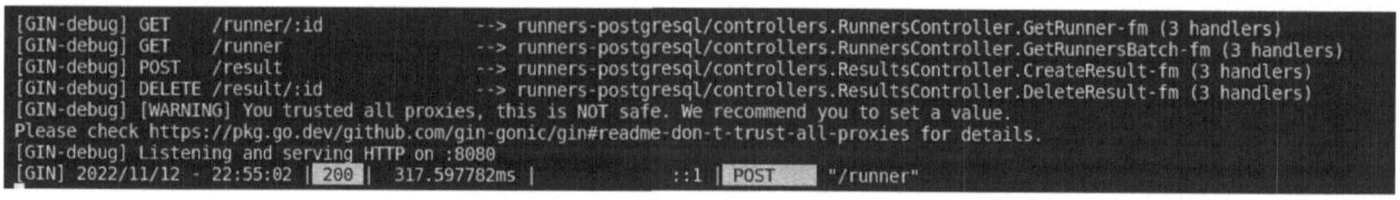

***Figure 9.3**: Gin log terminal*

Now we can test all API endpoints with Postman, or test some predefined test cases. Now it is time to automate things a little bit.

Testing with Go

Go provides a tool for writing tests through a **testing** package from the standard library. Testing code is often placed in the same package as the code that is tested.

Test files have **`_test`** suffix, this suffix tells the **`go test`** command that this file contains test functions. Usually, test files will have the same name, plus the **`_test`** suffix, as the file in which content is tested. For example, if we test code from the **`runnersService.go`** file, a related test will be placed into **`runnersService_test.go`** file.

The **`test`** function must start with `Test`, in order to be executed with the **`go test`** command. Generally speaking, the **`go test`** command will execute all functions from **_test** files that start with **Test**.

Command **go test** will run tests and show execution results. If we want to execute all tests from our project we can run the following command in the projects **root** directory:

```
go test -v ./...
```

In the previous command, **v** stands for **verbose**, verbose will log all tests as they are run, and additionally log everything logged with **Log()** or **Logf()**, even for those tests that were successful. The second part of the command (**./...**) means that the command will be executed *recursively*. In that case, the **test** command will check for **tests** in the **root** directory and all sub-directories.

We can also check code coverage with the **go test** command, by adding the **coverpkg** flag:

```
go test -v -coverpkg=./.. ./...
```

Developers like to use **testify** package because it offers some additional features that allow detailed assertions and mocking. Testify can be downloaded with the following command:

```
go get github.com/stretchr/testify
```

Now we are ready to write our first test.

Unit tests

The private function **validateRunner()** from the **runnersService.go** file is an ideal candidate for our first unit test. Let us remind ourselves, this function will return an error in case that provided runner has an invalid value for one of the following fields: **first name**, **last name**, **age**, or **country**:

First, we will create a **runnersService_test.go** file (*Figure 9.4*). The first case that we can test is what will happen if a runner with an invalid first name is passed to the **validateRunner()** function. We can name a function that will test this **TestValidateRunnerInvalidFirstName()**:

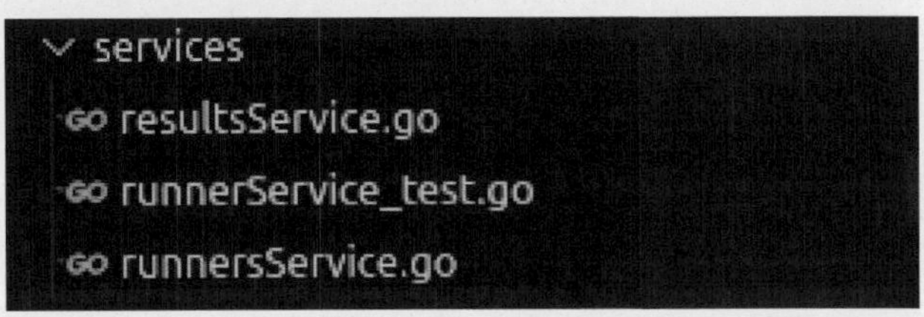

***Figure 9.4**: Test file*

To all **test** functions, we must pass a pointer to the type **T** from the **testing** package. This type is used to manage test state and support formatted test logs.

At the start of the function, we will create an *invalid* runner, without a first name, and pass it to the **validateRunner()** function. At the end of the **test**, we will check if the returned error has the expected message and HTTP status.

Function **NotEmpty()** will check if the specified object is *not* empty. Empty objects are empty strings, slices with zero elements, Booleans with a *false* value, numerical types with a value equal to *0* and *not nil* objects.

Function **Equal** receives expected and actual values in that order. For the actual value, we will always pass the value received from the tested function:

```
func TestValidateRunnerInvalidFirstName(t *testing.T) {
        runner := &models.Runner{
                LastName: "Smith",
                Age:      30,
                Country:  "United States",
        }

        responseErr := validateRunner(runner)

        assert.NotEmpty(t, responseErr)
        assert.Equal(t, "Invalid first name", responseErr.Message)
        assert.Equal(t, http.StatusBadRequest, responseErr.Status)
}
```

Now we can run our **test** with the **go test** command. This should provide output similar to this one:

```
?       runners-postgresql              [no test files]
?       runners-postgresql/config       [no test files]
?       runners-postgresql/controllers  [no test files]
?       runners-postgresql/models       [no test files]
?       runners-postgresql/repositories [no test files]
?       runners-postgresql/server       [no test files]
=== RUN   TestValidateRunnerInvalidFirstName
--- PASS: TestValidateRunnerInvalidFirstName (0.00s)
PASS
ok      runners-postgresql/services     (cached)
```

If we run tests with **coverage**, the output will be similar to the previous one:

```
?       runners-postgresql              [no test files]
```

```
?       runners-postgresql/config       [no test files]
?       runners-postgresql/controllers  [no test files]
?       runners-postgresql/models       [no test files]
?       runners-postgresql/repositories [no test files]
?       runners-postgresql/server       [no test files]
=== RUN   TestValidateRunnerInvalidFirstName
--- PASS: TestValidateRunnerInvalidFirstName (0.00s)
PASS
coverage: 0.4% of statements in ./...
ok      runners-postgresql/services     0.032s  coverage: 0.4% of
statements in ./…
```

As we can see, with this one test we covered *0.4%* of the source code.

Now we can test other cases from the **validateRunner()** function, *invalid last name*, *invalid age*, *invalid country*, and *valid runner*. We can create four smaller **test** functions that will be almost identical to the one that we already write, or we can merge these small test functions into a single one.

We can define a **struct** that will describe each test case. This **struct** will have a test name, runner (*invalid* and *valid*) that will be passed to the **validateRunner()** function and expected (*wanted*) error. For each **test** case, we will define one element in the **struct** array, iterate through them, and check if the actual value returned from the **validateRunner()** function is equal to the expected one:

```
func TestValidateRunner(t *testing.T) {
      tests := []struct {
            name   string
            runner *models.Runner
            want   *models.ResponseError
      }{
            {
                  name: “Invalid_First_Name”,
                  runner: &models.Runner{
                        LastName: “Smith”,
                        Age:      30,
                        Country:  “United States”,
                  },
                  want: &models.ResponseError{
                        Message: “Invalid first name”,
```

```
                        Status:  http.StatusBadRequest,
                },
        },
        {
                name: "Invalid_Last_Name",
                runner: &models.Runner{
                        FirstName: "John",
                        Age:       30,
                        Country:   "United States",
                },
                want: &models.ResponseError{
                        Message: "Invalid last name",
                        Status:  http.StatusBadRequest,
                },
        },
        {
                name: "Invalid_Age",
                runner: &models.Runner{
                        FirstName: "John",
                        LastName:  "Smith",
                        Age:       300,
                        Country:   "United States",
                },
                want: &models.ResponseError{
                        Message: "Invalid age",
                        Status:  http.StatusBadRequest,
                },
        },
        {
                name: "Invalid_Country",
                runner: &models.Runner{
                        FirstName: "John",
                        LastName:  "Smith",
                        Age:       30,
                },
                want: &models.ResponseError{
```

```
                    Message: "Invalid country",
                    Status:  http.StatusBadRequest,
                },
            },
            {
                name: "Valid_Runner",
                runner: &models.Runner{
                    FirstName: "John",
                    LastName:  "Smith",
                    Age:       30,
                    Country:   "United States",
                },
                want: nil,
            },
        }
        for _, test := range tests {
            t.Run(test.name, func(t *testing.T) {
                responseErr := validateRunner(
                    test.runner)
                assert.Equal(t, test.want,
                    responseErr)
            })
        }
}
```

Now if we run our tests again, we will have more test-related outputs in the terminal:

```
?       runners-postgresql      [no test files]
?       runners-postgresql/config       [no test files]
?       runners-postgresql/controllers  [no test files]
?       runners-postgresql/models       [no test files]
?       runners-postgresql/repositories [no test files]
?       runners-postgresql/server       [no test files]
=== RUN   TestValidateRunner
=== RUN   TestValidateRunner/Invalid_First_Name
```

```
=== RUN   TestValidateRunner/Invalid_Last_Name
=== RUN   TestValidateRunner/Invalid_Age
=== RUN   TestValidateRunner/Invalid_Country
=== RUN   TestValidateRunner/Valid_Runner
--- PASS: TestValidateRunner (0.00s)
    --- PASS: TestValidateRunner/Invalid_First_Name (0.00s)
    --- PASS: TestValidateRunner/Invalid_Last_Name (0.00s)
    --- PASS: TestValidateRunner/Invalid_Age (0.00s)
    --- PASS: TestValidateRunner/Invalid_Country (0.00s)
    --- PASS: TestValidateRunner/Valid_Runner (0.00s)
PASS
ok      runners-postgresql/services     0.008s
```

If we check coverage, we will notice that percentage increased from **0.4%** to **1.9%**:

```
?       runners-postgresql      [no test files]
?       runners-postgresql/config       [no test files]
?       runners-postgresql/controllers  [no test files]
?       runners-postgresql/models       [no test files]
?       runners-postgresql/repositories [no test files]
?       runners-postgresql/server       [no test files]
=== RUN   TestValidateRunner
=== RUN   TestValidateRunner/Invalid_First_Name
=== RUN   TestValidateRunner/Invalid_Last_Name
=== RUN   TestValidateRunner/Invalid_Age
=== RUN   TestValidateRunner/Invalid_Country
=== RUN   TestValidateRunner/Valid_Runner
--- PASS: TestValidateRunner (0.01s)
    --- PASS: TestValidateRunner/Invalid_First_Name (0.00s)
    --- PASS: TestValidateRunner/Invalid_Last_Name (0.00s)
    --- PASS: TestValidateRunner/Invalid_Age (0.00s)
    --- PASS: TestValidateRunner/Invalid_Country (0.00s)
    --- PASS: TestValidateRunner/Valid_Runner (0.00s)
PASS
coverage: 1.9% of statements in ./...
ok      runners-postgresql/services     0.045s  coverage: 1.9% of
statements in ./...
```

Now we can move to integration tests.

Integration tests

Integration tests are more complex than unit tests. With integration tests, we will test the entire application flow, from the *controller layer* to the *database layer*, and *back*. For our first integration test, we can choose one API, for example, one that will return a list of all runners.

We will create the **`runnersController_test.go`** file (*Figure 9.5*) and create a **`test`** function that will test get all runners API. We can name this function **`TestGetRunnersResponse()`**:

***Figure 9.5:** Test file*

For testing purposes, we must initialize all layers and routers. Because we will test only certain parts of layers (runner related) we do not need to initialize complete layers. Also, we can define a router that will only handle API that is subject of testing. This initialization is done in the **`initTestRouter()`** private function:

```
func initTestRouter(dbHandler *sql.DB) *gin.Engine {
    runnersRepository := repositories.
        NewRunnersRepository(dbHandler)
    runnersService := services.NewRunnersService(
        runnersRepository, nil)
    runnersController := NewRunnersController(runnersService)

    router := gin.Default()

    router.GET("/runner", runnersController.GetRunnersBatch)

    return router
}
```

We will not use a real database for the test purpose, instead, we will use mock to *mimic* database behavior. It is important to note because some behavior is *mocked*, these tests are not full integration tests. For that, a real database should be used. This is often not possible for some practical reasons (not enough hardware resources, separation of test and production data, and so on), so *mock* is an acceptable solution.

Special mock for SQL driver can be downloaded with:

```
go get github.com/DATA-DOG/go-sqlmock
```

Function **New()** from the **sqlmock** package will create a database connection and mock that will manage expectations. For example, we will use mock in combination with **ExpectQuery()** function to mimic the database response. This function will expect that method **Query()** from **sql** package will be called with the expected SQL query. We do not need to provide the whole SQL query, the starting part is enough.

In **ExpectQuery()**, we will define rows and columns that will be returned. So, *what will actually happen?* When **Query()** method should be called, **mock** will be called instead.

When we handle database **mock**, we can initialize the router and call the request that we are testing. At the end of the **test** function, we can check if the received HTTP response is the expected one and if the response body contains the expected data:

```
func TestGetRunnersResponse(t *testing.T) {
	dbHandler, mock, _ := sqlmock.New()
	defer dbHandler.Close()

	columns := []string{"id", "first_name", "last_name", "age",
		"is_active", "country", "personal_best",
		"season_best"}
	mock.ExpectQuery("SELECT *").WillReturnRows(
		sqlmock.NewRows(columns).
			AddRow("1", "John", "Smith", 30, true,
				"United States", "02:00:41",
				"02:13:13").
			AddRow("2", "Marijana", "Komatinovic", 30,
				true, "Serbia", "01:18:28",
				"01:18:28"))

	router := initTestRouter(dbHandler)
	request, _ := http.NewRequest("GET", "/runner", nil)
	recorder := httptest.NewRecorder()

	router.ServeHTTP(recorder, request)
```

```
        assert.Equal(t, http.StatusOK,
                recorder.Result().StatusCode)

        var runners []*models.Runner
        json.Unmarshal(recorder.Body.Bytes(), &runners)

        assert.NotEmpty(t, runners)
        assert.Equal(t, 2, len(runners))
    }
```

Let us run all tests with coverage. Here is the command output (gin logs are excluded):

```
?       runners-postgresql      [no test files]
?       runners-postgresql/config       [no test files]
=== RUN   TestGetRunnersResponse
--- PASS: TestGetRunnersResponse (0.00s)
PASS
coverage: 6.2% of statements in ./...
ok      runners-postgresql/controllers  0.030s  coverage: 6.2% of
statements in ./...
?       runners-postgresql/models       [no test files]
?       runners-postgresql/repositories [no test files]
?       runners-postgresql/server       [no test files]
=== RUN   TestValidateRunner
=== RUN   TestValidateRunner/Invalid_First_Name
=== RUN   TestValidateRunner/Invalid_Last_Name
=== RUN   TestValidateRunner/Invalid_Age
=== RUN   TestValidateRunner/Invalid_Country
=== RUN   TestValidateRunner/Valid_Runner
--- PASS: TestValidateRunner (0.01s)
    --- PASS: TestValidateRunner/Invalid_First_Name (0.00s)
    --- PASS: TestValidateRunner/Invalid_Last_Name (0.00s)
    --- PASS: TestValidateRunner/Invalid_Age (0.00s)
    --- PASS: TestValidateRunner/Invalid_Country (0.00s)
    --- PASS: TestValidateRunner/Valid_Runner (0.00s)
PASS
coverage: 1.9% of statements in ./...
```

```
ok      runners-postgresql/services     (cached)        coverage: 1.9% of
statements in ./...
```

Coverage for code from the controller is no longer **0%** (it is **6.2%**) as expected. But coverage for code from the service package is still **1.9%**, and now we have one more test that *covers* that code. Actually, the **go test** command will not properly merge coverage if the test is not in the same package as the covered code, which is the case here, the **test** is in the **controllers** package and the covered code is in the **services** package.

If we want to see actual coverage, we should run the **go test** command with the **-coverprofile** flag:

```
go test -v -coverpkg=./... ./... -coverprofile=coverage.out
```

This will create an output file (**coverage.out**) where code **coverage** will be properly calculated and written. We can open that file with the following command:

```
go tool cover -html=coverage.out
```

The **coverage** file will be opened (probably, in a web browser) and here we can check the **coverage** for each file. The *covered* code will be colored *green*, while the *uncovered* code will be colored *red* (*Figure 9.6*). Here, we can see that coverage from all tests is calculated and shown:

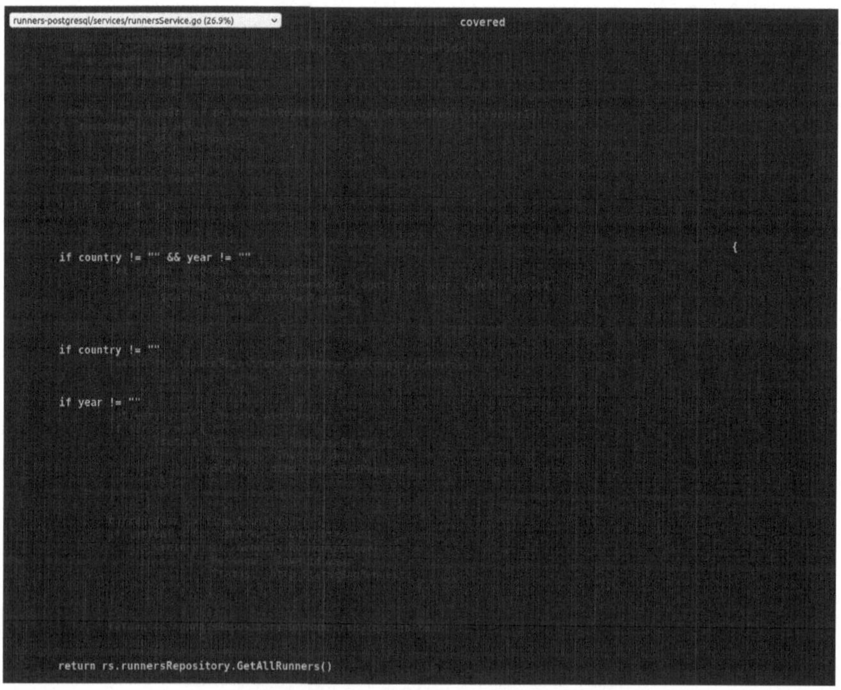

Figure 9.6: *Code coverage*

Quite often, unit and integration tests will cover the same code, good balance should be found here. We do not need to check every scenario with integration tests. For example, the response will be the same for any validation error checked in the unit test from the previous section. So, we can test *one validation error* with an integration test and other validation errors can be checked with more details in unit tests.

We can provide code for more tests here, but nothing radically new will be introduced. You can try, as an exercise, to write more tests and increase code coverage.

Testing with Visual Studio Code

We can use **Visual Studio Code** features for testing. On the left side of the screen, if we click on the *laboratory bottle* icon, we can *run*, or *debug* our test (*Figure 9.7*):

Figure 9.7*: Testing in Visual Studio Code*

We can run individual tests (by clicking on the *play* button on a specific test) or run all tests from the package (by clicking on the *play* button on a specific package). If we use icons on the top of the panel we can run all tests.

Visual Studio Code can also display *coverage*. If we select View from the menu, then **Command Palette** and enter *Coverage*, the **Toggle Test Coverage In Current Package** option should be offered. If we click on it, *coverage* should be displayed in the package that is currently opened (*Figure 9.8*):

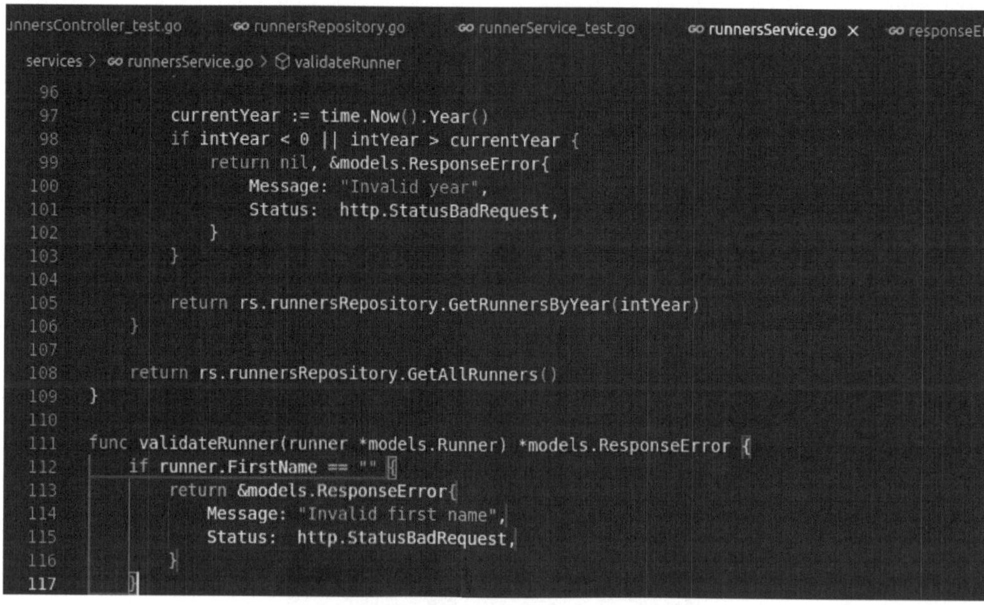

Figure 9.8: *Code coverage in Visual Studio Code*

As we can see in *Figure 9.8*, the *covered* code will be highlighted *green*, while the *uncovered* code will be highlighted *red*.

Conclusion

Testing is one of the most important phases in software development, it helps us to create quality and functional code. Now when we are familiar with testing concepts, we can write, and run tests, and make our code better. In the next chapter, we will learn how to make our application safer.

References

https://www.postman.com/downloads/

Points to remember

- During manual testing, the tester will be placed in the role of *application user* and try to mimic his behavior.
- If it is possible, one developer should develop some part of the code and the other should write tests for that part of the code.
- It is not a good practice to mix test and production data.
- Unit and integration tests will often cover the same code, this should be balanced.

Multiple choice questions

1. What is the name of the application that can be used for manual API testing?
    a. Mailman
    b. Courier
    c. Carrier
    d. Postman
2. What is not a testing level?
    a. Unit testing
    b. Module testing
    c. Integration testing
    d. System testing
3. What is the *object* that mimics the behavior of a real application component called?
    a. fake
    b. imitation
    c. mock
    d. replica

Answers

1. d
2. b
3. c

Questions

1. What are the differences between manual and automated testing?
2. What are the differences between unit and integration testing?

Key terms

- **Testing**: Process of evaluation and verification of a certain product.
- **Code coverage**: Percentage of source code covered with tests.

CHAPTER 10

Security

Introduction

In this chapter, we will learn how to make our application more secure. At the start of the chapter, we will take a deep look at authentication and authorization concepts. After that, we will see how to redesign our initial API design and database design. Then, we will see what should be changed in the implementation of the current layers. At the end of the chapter, we check if our tests are still valid.

Structure

In this chapter, we will discuss the following topics:

- Authentication and authorization
- API design
- Database design
- Models
- HTTP server
- Controller layer
  - Users controller
  - Other controllers
- Service layer
- Setting up a database
- Repository layer
- Testing

Authentication and authorization

Our web server application is completed, but it has one big flaw. Anyone can call any API, so anyone can mess up with data, by adding false results, deleting runners, and so on. *This is not a good practice!* Only authorized users should be able to perform certain actions. Before we can implement these security features, we must introduce some *security-related concepts*.

Two main security concepts related to web server applications are **authentication** and **authorization**.

Authentication can be defined as the concept or process of verification of a user in a software system, or to simplify things, the user is the one who he claims to be. **Verification** is usually provided through some sort of credentials, most commonly username and password.

There are several couple authentication approaches:

- **Basic authentication**: The simplest way to secure REST API, where the client sends *Base 64 encoded credentials* (username and password) through the HTTP header. Based on provided credentials, the *client* will receive an access token that will be used in all future requests for authorization. This is not the safest approach, because sensitive data (in form of credentials) will be shared between system components, recommendation is to use it in combination with secure protocols, like TLS. If data that is protected with basic authentication, is so-called **low-risk data** (does not have any bank accounts, social security numbers, personal ids, card numbers, and so on) this is a perfectly suitable solution.
- **API keys**: This approach represents a modification of the previous one. There are no credentials in classic form, here *machine-generated string* that represents a combination of identifying credentials and the access token is used. The string can be placed in request body HTTP headers or as a query string.
- **HMAC (Hash-based Message Authentication Code)**: Uses *symmetric encryption* (also known as **single key encryption**) to determine which hashing will be used. A unique code will be generated with the *agreed hash* and attached to the relevant message. The *caller* and *receiver* must hold a key in order to know how to interpret the message. This approach is more secure than previous ones, but it is also more complex. *Key management* can be a huge problem, especially, if there are a lot of components in the system, and separated teams are in charge of each of them. Any key changes will require a lot of communication between components and teams.
- **OAuth 2.0**: Short for **open authorization**, is an approach that supports the dynamic collection of users, permissions, and data types. OAuth will

create secured access tokens that are refreshed periodically with a series of procedural verification protocols, known as **grant types**. Grant type can be defined as a mechanism that controls REST API access without exposing credentials or tokens. In modern industry, this approach is the golden standard.

Authorization is a process of verification that the user in a software system is permitted to perform the operation that he is trying to perform. Another definition that can be found in the literature is that authorization is a specification if the user in a software system can access a certain resource. Authorization is performed in the controller layer, or in some special proxy/server in front of the controller layer.

Our application does not handle any sensitive data, so we will use *basic authentication*. This approach is also chosen because it will introduce some concepts during implementation that can be useful for the future career of any software developer (like design updates, database updates, reading HTTP headers, and so on).

A couple more things should be mentioned before we process the design and implementation. Credentials for basic authentication are provided through the Authorization HTTP header:

```
Authorization: Basic <credentials>
```

Credentials are *Base64 encoded* credentials in the following form:

```
username:password
```

We will not deal with user management here, only with *authentication* and *authorization*, but we should mention how this can be handled.

Usually, we will create our own user by filling out some sort of registration form on the web portal or some sort of application. The user can be created with a defined password, and it can receive a *temporary password* through *email*, with instructions on how to set the permanent one.

A new user will have the lowest permissions, but they will probably be some way to increase them by some sort of request, that should be approved or rejected by some users with higher privileges.

It is very important to insert one **superuser** or **superadmin** during the first deployment. This user should be known only to developers and maintainers of the application and can be used to check all kinds of requests until the system is established. For example, in the case of our application, each *country* will have *one admin user* that will manage *runners* and *results*. Without a *superuser*, all new users will have insufficient (lowest) privileges, and the system will be useless.

Now we should describe how our authentication and authorization system will work. In the first step, the *client* will send a login request with credentials. If credentials are *valid*, the client will receive an access token that will be used for authentication in all future HTTP requests. When the *client* finishes the whole work it should send a logout request that will cancel the access token (*Figure 10.1*):

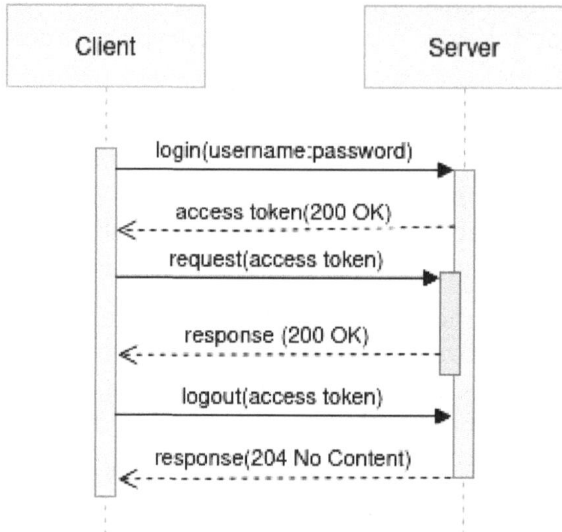

Figure 10.1*: Authentication and authorization flow*

In *Figure 10.1*, inside round brackets, we can see what is used for authentication and authorization (for *requests*) and *response statuses* (for responses). In case of *invalid* credentials, the client will receive a response with status *401 (Unauthorized)*. Now we are ready to proceed to the design phase.

API design

With the introduction of security concepts, our web server will get two more operations:

- Login user
- Logout user

For both of these operations, we can use the `POST` HTTP method. Here, we will not use a system resource (user) in the path, we will use more descriptive paths:

- `/login`
- `/logout`

As we can see, *redesign* is not too complex, and benefits concerning security are invaluable. Now we can redesign our database to support security changes.

Database design

Based on authentication and authorization flow and API design, our user should have the following columns:

- **`id`**: Unique identifier for the user, not necessary for authentication and authorization, but it is a good practice to have identifiers for each row, this column will serve as the *primary key*.
- **`username`**: Username for the user, it is good practice to create a system where usernames are unique, in order to avoid any sort of confusion.
- **`user_password`**: Password for the user, must be stored *encrypted*, never store passwords as plain text.
- **`user_role`**: Role of the user. We will have two roles: **runner** and **admin**. The *runner* will have access only to operations mapped with the HTTP **`GET`** method, while the *admin* will have access to all operations.
- **`access_token`**: A token that will be used for authorization.

Words **`password`** and **`role`** are keywords in PostgreSQL, we added the prefix **`user_`** in order to avoid any confusion. Word **`user`** is also a keyword, but word *users* is not, so there are no obstacles for us to name our table **User**. This table will not be related to any other table, so it can be considered a separate entity (resource).

The new database design is displayed in *Figure 10.2*:

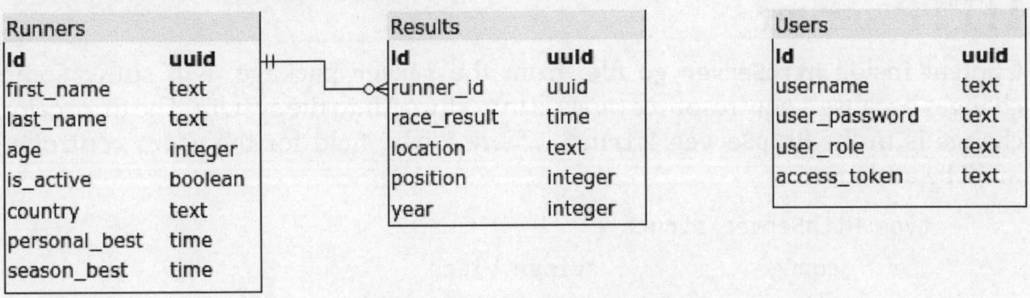

***Figure 10.2**: New database design*

Models

A new **`struct`** that represents the user will be added to the **`models`** package (*Figure 10.3*). Inside file **`user.go`**, we will place the **`User`** model, which will have all columns from the *Users* table mapped to proper **`struct`** fields. JSON tags will correspond with column names:

Figure 10.3: *Models packages*

This is the content of **users.go** file:

```
package models

type User struct {
	ID          string `json:"id"`
	Username    string `json:"username"`
	Password    string `json:"user_password"`
	Role        string `json:"user_role"`
	AccessToken string `json:"access_token"`
}
```

In the next section, we will see how the HTTP server is affected by new resources.

HTTP server

Content inside **httpServer.go** file, from the **server** package, will suffer some changes because a new resource (*user*) is introduced into the system. The first major change is in the **HttpServer struct**, where a new field for the **users** controller must be added:

```
type HttpServer struct {
	config             *viper.Viper
	router             *gin.Engine
	runnersController  *controllers.RunnersController
	resultsController  *controllers.ResultsController
	usersController    *controllers.UsersController
}
```

Inside **InitHttpServer()** function, controller, service, and repository related to *user* resource. Also, all controllers will use **users** service for authorization, so **users** service should be passed to *runners* and *results* controllers.

Two new routes will be added to the *router*, *log in*, and *log out*. Both routes will use the **POST** HTTP method, while proper functions from the **users** controller will handle requests received through these routes.

At the end of the function, the newly created **users** controller should be added to the HTTP server. **InitHttpServer()** function will now look like this:

```
func InitHttpServer(config *viper.Viper, dbHandler *sql.DB) HttpServer {
        runnersRepository := repositories.
                NewRunnersRepository(dbHandler)
        resultRepository := repositories.
                NewResultsRepository(dbHandler)
        usersRepository := repositories.
                NewUsersRepository(dbHandler)
        runnersService := services.NewRunnersService(
                runnersRepository, resultRepository)
        resultsService := services.NewResultsService(
                resultRepository, runnersRepository)
        usersService := services.NewUsersService(usersRepository)
        runnersController := controllers.NewRunnersController(
                runnersService, usersService)
        resultsController := controllers.NewResultsController(
                resultsService, usersService)
        usersController := controllers.NewUsersController(
                usersService)

        router := gin.Default()

        router.POST("/runner", runnersController.CreateRunner)
        router.PUT("/runner", runnersController.UpdateRunner)
        router.DELETE("/runner/:id",
                runnersController.DeleteRunner)
        router.GET("/runner/:id", runnersController.GetRunner)
        router.GET("/runner", runnersController.GetRunnersBatch)
        router.POST("/result", resultsController.CreateResult)
        router.DELETE("/result/:id",
                resultsController.DeleteResult)

        router.POST("/login", usersController.Login)
```

```
        router.POST("/logout", usersController.Logout)

        return HttpServer{
                config:            config,
                router:             router,
                runnersController: runnersController,
                resultsController: resultsController,
                usersController:   usersController,
        }
}
```

Now we can start with the implementation of changes in the first layer, controller layer.

Controller layer

The *controller layer* will probably be the most affected by additional authentication and authorization. Not only a new controller (**users** controller) will be added, other controllers must add an authorization check. First, we will start with the new controller.

Users controller

Code related to the **users** controller will be placed in the **usersController.go** file in the **controllers** package (*Figure 10.4*):

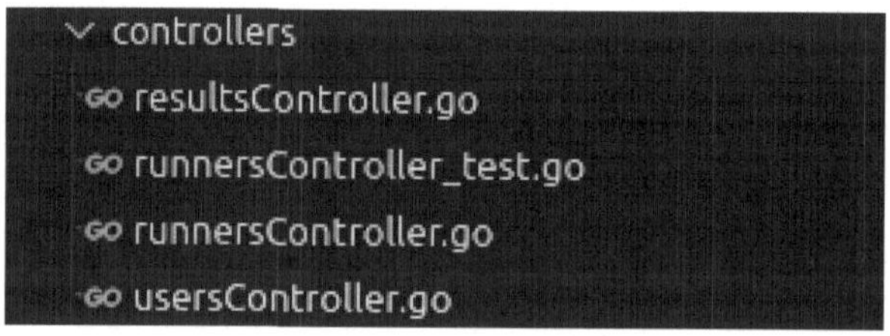

***Figure 10.4**: Controllers package*

The **struct** that represents the **users** controller will have only one field, a representation of the **users** service. Besides **NewUsersControllers()** function, which will initialize the **users** controller, two more methods will be part of it, **Login()** and **Logout()**:

```
package controllers

import (
        "log"
```

```
        "net/http"
        "runners-postgresql/services"

        "github.com/gin-gonic/gin"
)

type UsersController struct {
        usersService *services.UsersService
}

func NewUsersController(
        usersService *services.UsersService) *UsersController {

        return &UsersController{
                usersService: usersService,
        }
}

func (uc UsersController) Login(ctx *gin.Context) {
        ...
}

func (uc UsersController) Logout(ctx *gin.Context) {
        ...
}
```

At the start of the **Login()** method, we will use **Gin** context to read credentials from **request** headers. If an error occurs during the reading of credentials, we will return a response with status *400 (Bad Request).* I there are no reading errors, we will call a function from **users** service, and handle any potential error.

At the end of the function, if everything is passed as expected, we will return the access token received from lower layers to the client. Here, is the complete code for the **Login()** method:

```
func (uc UsersController) Login(ctx *gin.Context) {
        username, password, ok := ctx.Request.BasicAuth()
        if !ok {
                log.Println("Error while reading credentials")
                ctx.AbortWithStatus(http.StatusBadRequest)
```

```
            return
        }

        accessToken, responseErr := uc.usersService.Login(
            username, password)
        if responseErr != nil {
            ctx.AbortWithStatusJSON(responseErr.Status,
                responseErr)
            return
        }

        ctx.JSON(http.StatusOK, accessToken)
    }
```

Method **Logout()** is less complex than the two. At the beginning of the function, we will again use **gin** to read the token HTTP header. After that the service layer will be called, the *potential error* will be handled or a response with status *204 (No Content)* will be returned:

```
    func (uc UsersController) Logout(ctx *gin.Context) {
        accessToken := ctx.Request.Header.Get("Token")

        responseErr := uc.usersService.Logout(accessToken)
        if responseErr != nil {
            ctx.AbortWithStatusJSON(responseErr.Status,
                responseErr)
            return
        }

        ctx.Status(http.StatusNoContent)
    }
```

We have a new controller now, but before we can move to the service layer, we should update other controllers.

Other controllers

Now when authorization is introduced all controllers will be changed a little bit. The first change will be to, anywhere in the **controllers** package (**runnersController.go** or **resultsControllers.go** file), introduce two *string* constants. Each constant will represents one role. The *admin role* will have access to all APIs, while the *runner role* will have access only to APIs that uses the **GET** HTTP method:

```
const ROLE_ADMIN = "admin"
const ROLE_RUNNER = "runner"
```

Runners and *results* controllers should be extended with **users** service. This change must be accompanied by changes in the initialization functions.

The **struct** that represents the *runners* controller and initialization function will now look like this:

```
type RunnersController struct {
	runnersService *services.RunnersService
	usersService   *services.UsersService
}

func NewRunnersController(
	runnersService *services.RunnersService,
	usersService *services.UsersService) *RunnersController {

	return &RunnersController{
		runnersService: runnersService,
		usersService:   usersService,
	}
}
```

Identical changes will be visible in the results controller:

```
type ResultsController struct {
	resultsService *services.ResultsService
	usersService   *services.UsersService
}

func NewResultsController(
	resultsService *services.ResultsService,
	userService *services.UsersService) *ResultsController {

	return &ResultsController{
		resultsService: resultsService,
		usersService:   userService,
	}
}
```

At the start of each *runners* and *results* controller that handles routes with **GET** HTTP methods, the following code should be added:

```
accessToken := ctx.Request.Header.Get("Token")
auth, responseErr := rc.usersService.AuthorizeUser(
        accessToken, []string{ROLE_ADMIN, ROLE_RUNNER})
if responseErr != nil {
        ctx.JSON(responseErr.Status, responseErr)
        return
}

if !auth {
        ctx.Status(http.StatusUnauthorized)
        return
}
```

As we can see, at the start of the function, we will read the access token from HTTP headers, and call the service layer to check if the user is *authorized* to perform the desired operation. If the user is not allowed to perform the operation, a response with HTTP status *401 (Unauthorized)* will be returned to the client.

For all other methods, code at the start will be almost identical with one small change, role *runner* will be removed from the list of *authorized* roles:

```
auth, responseErr := rc.usersService.AuthorizeUser(
        accessToken, []string{ROLE_ADMIN})
```

The next layer, the **service layer**, will be less affected by security changes because the *controller layer* will cut off all *unauthorized* users.

Service layer

For the **users** service new file, **usersService.go** will be added to the **services** packages (*Figure 10.5*):

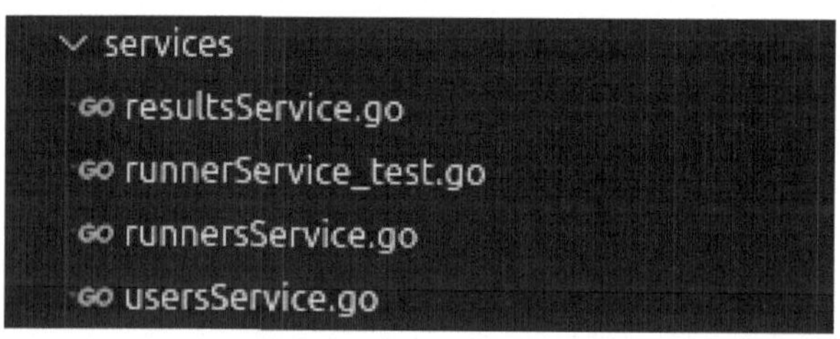

***Figure 10.5**: Services packages*

The **struct** that represents the **users** service will only contain a representation of the users repository. This will be initialized through **NewUsersService()** function. Three more public methods, **Login()**, **Logout()**, and **AuthorizeUser()**, and one private function **generateAccessToken()** will also be part of the **users** service:

```
package services

import (
        "encoding/base64"
        "fmt"
        "net/http"
        "runners-postgresql/models"
        "runners-postgresql/repositories"

        "golang.org/x/crypto/bcrypt"
)

type UsersService struct {
        usersRepository *repositories.UsersRepository
}

func NewUsersService(
        usersRepository *repositories.UsersRepository)
        *UsersService {

        return &UsersService{
                usersRepository: usersRepository,
        }
}

func (us UsersService) Login(username string,
        password string) (string, *models.ResponseError) {
        ...
}

func (us UsersService) Logout(
        accessToken string) *models.ResponseError {
        ...
```

```
}

func (us UsersService) AuthorizeUser(accessToken string,
       expectedRoles []string) (bool, *models.ResponseError) {
       ...
}

func generateAccessToken(
       username string) (string, *models.ResponseError) {
       ...
}
```

We can start with **Login()** method. It will receive a *username* and *password* and check them at the start. If one of those fields is *empty*, a proper error will be returned. Even if we validate *username* and *password* separately, we should never return a message that will contain information that only one is invalid. *Why?* As this can help potential intruders break into our system. *How?* They can try random usernames, and they will receive the *Invalid username* message; the moment they receive the *Invalid password* message, they will know that they figured out the username.

After *validation,* we can call the users repository to find the ID of the user whose credentials are. If the received ID is *empty,* the credentials are *invalid,*and we should return the proper error. In other cases, we will generate a token based on username (we can also use ID instead), write it into the database, and return it to the controller layer:

```
func (us UsersService) Login(username string,
       password string) (string, *models.ResponseError) {

       if username == "" || password == "" {
              return "", &models.ResponseError{
                     Message: "Invalid username or password",
                     Status:  http.StatusBadRequest,
              }
       }

       id, responseErr := us.usersRepository.LoginUser(
              username, password)
       if responseErr != nil {
```

```
            return "", responseErr
        }

        if id == "" {
            return "", &models.ResponseError{
                Message: "Login failed",
                Status:  http.StatusUnauthorized,
            }
        }

        accessToken, responseErr := generateAccessToken(username)
        if responseErr != nil {
            return "", responseErr
        }

        us.usersRepository.SetAccessToken(accessToken, id)

        return accessToken, nil
    }
```

Method **Logout()** will check the received access token, return an *error* if the token is *empty,* and invalidate the token through the repository layer function:

```
    func (us UsersService) Logout(
        accessToken string) *models.ResponseError {

        if accessToken == "" {
            return &models.ResponseError{
                Message: "Invalid access token",
                Status:  http.StatusBadRequest,
            }
        }

        return us.usersRepository.RemoveAccessToken(accessToken)
    }
```

The last method, **AuthorizeUser()** will get the user role with the access token. In case that returned role is *invalid* (empty), *unauthorized error* will be returned. If the user's role is in the list of expected roles, a Boolean value, **true** will be returned, and the user will be granted access to the desired operation:

```
func (us UsersService) AuthorizeUser(accessToken string,
      expectedRoles []string) (bool, *models.ResponseError) {

      if accessToken == "" {
            return false, &models.ResponseError{
                  Message: "Invalid access token",
                  Status:  http.StatusBadRequest,
            }
      }

      role, responseErr := us.usersRepository.
            GetUserRole(accessToken)
      if responseErr != nil {
            return false, responseErr
      }

      if role == "" {
            return false, &models.ResponseError{
                  Message: "Failed to authorize user",
                  Status:  http.StatusUnauthorized,
            }
      }

      for _, expectedRole := range expectedRoles {
            if expectedRole == role {
                  return true, nil
            }
      }

      return false, nil
}
```

The private method, **generateAccessToken()** will generate a new access token based on the username. Function **GenerateFromPassword()** will **bcrypt** hash of provided string at the given cost. This *function* (as the name suggests) is often used for hashing passwords, but it can be used with *non-password strings*. At the end of the function, we will encode our hash in **base64** format:

```
func generateAccessToken(username string) (string,
        *models.ResponseError) {
        hash, err := bcrypt.GenerateFromPassword(
                []byte(username), bcrypt.DefaultCost)
        if err != nil {
                return “”, &models.ResponseError{
                        Message: “Failed to generate token”,
                        Status:  http.StatusInternalServerError,
                }
        }

        return base64.StdEncoding.EncodeToString(hash), nil
}
```

In the next section, we will see how to update the current database schema.

Setting up a database

Inside the **dbscripts** directory, we will add a new SQL file, **update_schema.sql** (*Figure 10.6*). Inside this script, SQL commands that create **users** table and related indices can be found:

***Figure 10.6**: Dbscripts directory*

The first line in the script file will install the PostgreSQL extension for *cryptographic functions*, these functions will be used for password storing. The only other new thing that we have not seen before is the usage of the **UNIQUE** constraint for the username column. This will forbid *duplicated* usernames, and prevent potential problems and mixing of data between users with the same usernames.

At the end of the script file, we will insert two users, one with role *admin* and one with role *runner*. Since we do not have a system to create new users through some API, this will do. These users will be used for manual testing:

```
CREATE EXTENSION IF NOT EXISTS pgcrypto;

CREATE TABLE users (
    id uuid NOT NULL DEFAULT uuid_generate_v1mc(),
```

```
    username text NOT NULL UNIQUE,
    user_password text NOT NULL,
    user_role text NOT NULL,
    access_token text,
    CONSTRAINT users_pk PRIMARY KEY (id)
);

CREATE INDEX user_access_token
ON users (access_token);

INSERT INTO users(username, user_password, user_role)
VALUES
    ('admin', crypt('admin', gen_salt('bf')), 'admin'),
    ('runner', crypt('runner', gen_salt('bf')), 'runner');
```

Before we can move forward, we should explain the concept of salt. **Salting** can be defined as a technique designed to protect passwords stored in databases. Salt is a *string of 32* or more randomly generated characters that will be added at the end of the password. After addition, the *password* and *salt* will be hashed.

Functions **`crypt()`** and **`gen_salt()`** are designed for hashing passwords. Function **`gen_salt()`** generates random salt and tells the **`crypt()`** function which algorithm to use. *Salt* and *password* will be combined, hashed with the selected algorithm, and stored in the database.

The following algorithms are supported by the **`crypt()`** function:

- **Blowfish (bf)**
- **MD5 (md5)**
- **Extended DES (xdes)**
- **Original DES (des)**

The SQL script file can be executed in **pgAdmin** with Query Tool in the same way as in *Chapter 7, Relational Databases and Repository Layer*. If the script is executed without any errors, our database is updated and ready. We can implement the repository layer now.

Repository layer

Code for the new repository will be placed in the **`usersRepository.go`** file inside repositories packages (*Figure 10.7*). Other repositories will not be affected by security-related changes:

Figure 10.7: Repositories package

The **`struct`** that represents the **`users`** repository will have only one field, a representation of the database layer. Methods from this repository will never be part of any transaction, so we do not need a field that holds the current transaction. **`Users`** repository will be initialized in **`NewUsersRepository()`** function:

```
package repositories

import (
        “database/sql”
        “net/http”
        “runners-postgresql/models”
)

type UsersRepository struct {
        dbHandler *sql.DB
}

func NewUsersRepository(dbHAndler *sql.DB) *UsersRepository {
        return &UsersRepository{
                dbHandler: dbHAndler,
        }
}

func (ur UsersRepository) LoginUser(username string,
        password string) (string, *models.ResponseError) {
        ...
}

func (ur UsersRepository) GetUserRole(
        accessToken string) (string, *models.ResponseError) {
        ...
```

```
}

func (ur UsersRepository) SetAccessToken(
        accessToken string, id string) *models.ResponseError {
        ...
}

func (ur UsersRepository) RemoveAccessToken(
        accessToken string) *models.ResponseError {
        ...
}
```

The first method, **LoginUser()** will execute the **SELECT** command, which will return the ID of the user if a user with provided credentials exists. We used the **crypt()** to store passwords, so we must use it for read also. It will know which salt and encoding algorithm to use. If returned ID is an *empty* string, we consider that the user does not exist or provided credentials were wrong, so the login attempt will *fail*:

```
func (ur UsersRepository) LoginUser(username string,
        password string) (string, *models.ResponseError) {

        query := `
                SELECT id
                FROM users
        WHERE username = $1 AND
        user_password = crypt($2, user_password)`

        rows, err := ur.dbHandler.Query(query, username, password)
        if err != nil {
                return "", &models.ResponseError{
                        Message: err.Error(),
                        Status:  http.StatusInternalServerError,
                }
        }

        defer rows.Close()

        var id string
        for rows.Next() {
```

```
            err := rows.Scan(&id)
            if err != nil {
                return "", &models.ResponseError{
                    Message: err.Error(),
                    Status:  http.
                        StatusInternalServerError,
                }
            }
        }

        if rows.Err() != nil {
            return "", &models.ResponseError{
                Message: err.Error(),
                Status:  http.StatusInternalServerError,
            }
        }

        return id, nil
    }
```

The next method, **GetUserRole()** will try to find a user with a matching access token. This is basically the main *authorization* method. The only difference between this and the previous method is the different **SELECT** command:

```
    func (ur UsersRepository) GetUserRole(
        accessToken string) (string, *models.ResponseError) {

        query := `
            SELECT user_role
            FROM users
            WHERE access_token = $1`

        rows, err := ur.dbHandler.Query(query, accessToken)
        if err != nil {
            return "", &models.ResponseError{
                Message: err.Error(),
                Status:  http.StatusInternalServerError,
            }
```

```
		}

		defer rows.Close()

		var role string
		for rows.Next() {
			err := rows.Scan(&role)
			if err != nil {
				return "", &models.ResponseError{
					Message: err.Error(),
					Status:  http.
						StatusInternalServerError,
				}
			}
		}

		if rows.Err() != nil {
			return "", &models.ResponseError{
				Message: err.Error(),
				Status:  http.StatusInternalServerError,
			}
		}

		return role, nil
	}
```

The third method **SetAccessToken()** will assign generated access token to the user with a matching ID, with the **UPDATE** command:

```
	func (ur UsersRepository) SetAccessToken(
		accessToken string, id string) *models.ResponseError {

		query := `
			UPDATE users
			SET access_token = $1
			WHERE id = $2`

		_, err := ur.dbHandler.Exec(query, accessToken, id)
		if err != nil {
```

```
                return &models.ResponseError{
                        Message: err.Error(),
                        Status:  http.StatusInternalServerError,
                }
        }

        return nil
}
```

The last method, **RemoveAccessToken()** will invalidate the access token by setting it to an empty string through the **UPDATE** command:

```
func (ur UsersRepository) RemoveAccessToken(
        accessToken string) *models.ResponseError {

        query := `
                UPDATE users
                SET access_token = ''
                WHERE access_token = $1`

        _, err := ur.dbHandler.Exec(query, accessToken)
        if err != nil {
                return &models.ResponseError{
                        Message: err.Error(),
                        Status:  http.StatusInternalServerError,
                }
        }

        return nil
}
```

The access token solution that we implemented here is not wrong but has one small flaw. The access token will be invalidated only when the user executes **Logout()** operation, if he never calls it token will be active forever. This can be fixed with the addition of a new database column, **expires_at**, that represents the *time stamp* when the access token will expire.

Some standard is to set expiration time by adding *15 minutes* to the time when the user has successfully logged in. So, each time when we check if the access token exists, we should also check if is not expired. Additionally, expired time can be increased with each successful authorization. You can try to implement this improvement as an exercise.

The database layer will not require any changes, so our application update is completed. But before we move to the next chapter, we should check one more thing.

Testing

If we open **Postman** and try to execute any API call, we will always receive a response with status *400 (Bad Requests)*, because we do not include a token in HTTP headers.

The access token can be acquired by creating new requests for login API.In the **Authorization** tab we should select **Basic Auth** from the **TYPE** drop-down list. By entering the *username* and *password* and pressing **Send** button, a request will be sent and an *access token* will be placed in the *response* body (*Figure 10.8*):

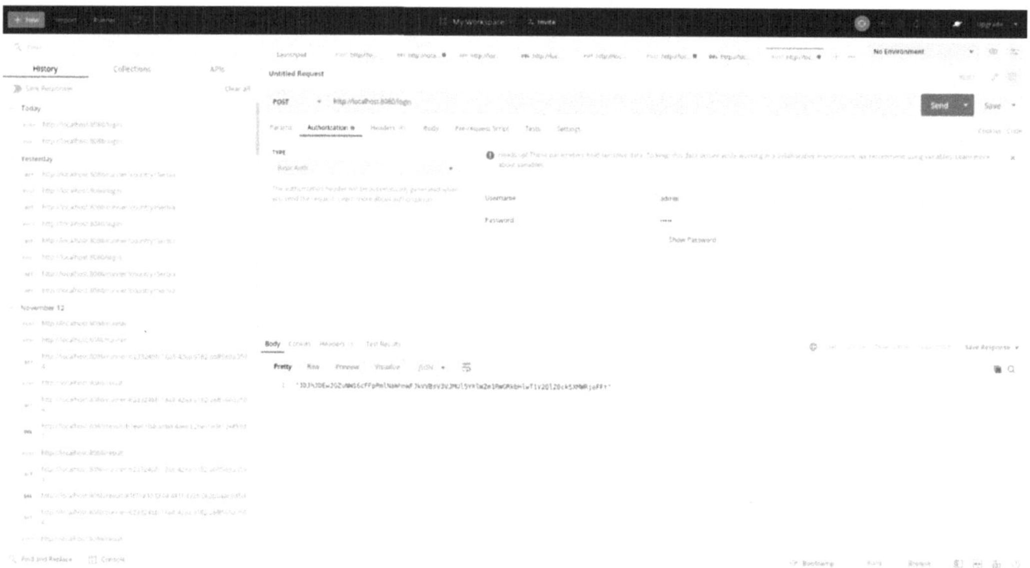

Figure 10.8: *Login with Postman*

Now for any other request, we should go to the **Headers** tab and add a token header with the value received in the *login* response. Now if we click on **Send** button, a proper response will be received (*Figure 10.9*):

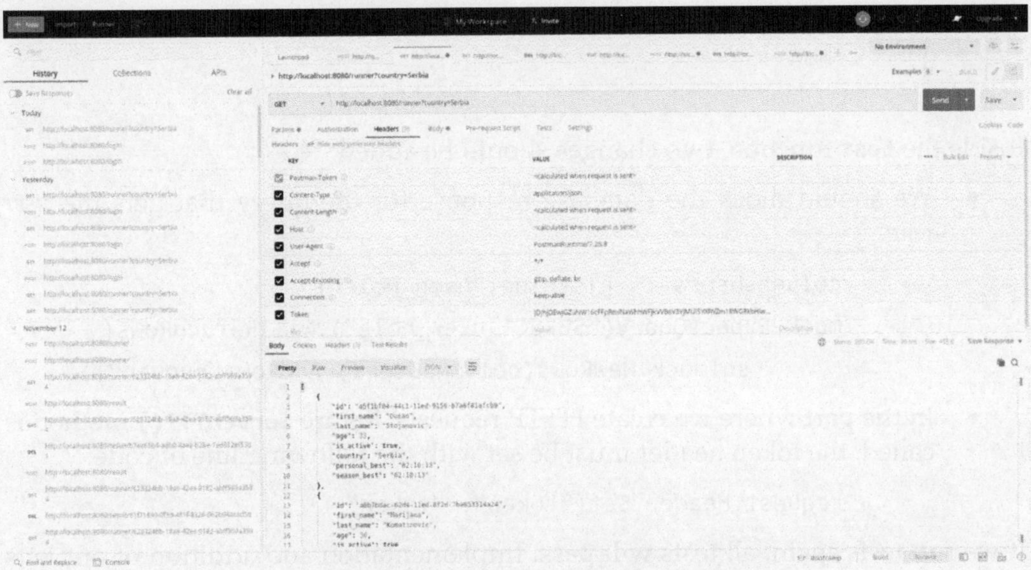

Figure 10.9: Using token in HTTP headers in Postman

Let us run the tests that we wrote in *Chapter 9, Testing*. Integration test **`TestGetRunnersResponse()`** will fail because the *access token* is not included, so the client will receive a *400 (Bad Requests)* response. This is one additional purpose of the test, if no tests fail when new functionality is introduced something is *wrong*.

First, the **`users`** service and **`users`** repository should be initialized inside the **`initTestRouter()`** function. This function will now look like this:

```
func initTestRouter(dbHandler *sql.DB) *gin.Engine {
        runnersRepository := repositories.
                NewRunnersRepository(dbHandler)
        usersRepository := repositories.
                NewUsersRepository(dbHandler)
        runnersService := services.NewRunnersService(
                runnersRepository, nil)
        usersServices := services.NewUsersService(usersRepository)
        runnersController := NewRunnersController(
                runnersService, usersServices)

        router := gin.Default()

        router.GET("/runner", runnersController.GetRunnersBatch)
```

```
        return router
}
```

Inside the **test** function, two changes should be added:

- We should mock the database response for the query that gets the *user* role:

  ```
  columnsUsers := []string{"user_role"}
  mock.ExpectQuery("SELECT user_role").WillReturnRows(
          sqlmock.NewRows(columnsUsers).AddRow("runner"))
  ```

- In the part where we create HTTP requests. Before **ServeHTTP()** method is called, the token header must be set with the following line of code:

  ```
  request.Header.Set("token", "token")
  ```

If we run tests again, all tests will pass. Implementation and addition of our fists feature are officially completed. *Our application is ready for deployment!*

Conclusion

Security is one of the most important topics in modern software development. It is also a very wide subject that can be covered with a lot more detail. Here, the idea was to introduce some basic concepts and get us familiar with them.

We introduced basic concepts of authentication and authorization, present some industry standards, and use these concepts in the application that was developed in the previous chapters. Obviously, there is a lot of space for improvement, the path to the perfect application is a continuous process.

Points to remember

- It is very important to insert one *superuser* with maximal permissions during initial deployment.
- It is good practice to create a system where usernames are unique, in order to avoid any sort of confusion.
- Never store passwords as plain text.

Multiple choice questions

1. Which authentication approach is the simplest?
    a. API keys
    b. OAuth 2.0
    c. Basic authentication
    d. HMAC
2. Where are the credentials placed for basic authentication?
    a. In HTTP headers
    b. In the body of the HTTP request
    c. As a query string
    d. All of the above
3. In which layer will authorization be performed?
    a. Database layer
    b. Repository layer
    c. Service layer
    d. Controller layer

Answers

1. c
2. a
3. d

Questions

1. How does the HMAC authentication approach work?
2. What are OAuth 2.0 grant types?
3. For what PostgreSQL extension `pgcrypto` is used?

Key terms

- **Authentication**: Process of verification of a user in a software system.
- **Authorization**: Process of verification that the user in the software system is permitted to perform a certain operation.

CHAPTER 11

Deploying Web Application

Introduction

We completed our application, and in this chapter, we will gradually learn how to deploy it. At the start of the chapter, we will take a deep look at Docker and learn how to Dockerize our application. After that, we will introduce Docker Compose, a tool for running multi-container Docker applications. In the next part of the chapter, we will deploy our web service to the **Google Cloud Platform (GCP)**. By the end of this chapter, we will set Kubernetes for automating deployment.

Structure

In this chapter, we will discuss the following topics:

- Docker
    - Setting up Docker
    - Docker commands
    - Dockerizing application
- Docker Compose
- Kubernetes
    - Setting up a local Kubernetes cluster
    - Kubectl commands
    - Deploying on Kubernetes
- **Google Cloud Platform (GCP)**
    - Setting up a database
    - Deployment of a web server application

Docker

During the deployment procedure, all dependencies must be installed in order for the application to run properly. For complex applications, something will often be forgotten and the application will not run as expected. It would be perfect if everything could be packaged together in one place and reused for deployment.

Well, it is possible. The **container** represents a software unit where code and all **dependencies** are packaged together. The application configured to run in the container is called **Containerized application**. We have two types of containers:

- Stateless container which does not read or store its state.
- Stateful container which reads and stores its state.

In practice, *stateless containers* are more common, especially for small services that only perform some sort of small calculation and proceed results to the next service. If for some reason, the container is restarted it will not have any history of the previous task, and it will literally be in its initial state.

Docker is the most popular platform that uses virtualization to deliver software in containers. Application containerized with Docker is often referred to as **Dockerized application**.

People often put an equal sign between Docker and Virtual Machine, but these terms do not represent the same thing. In *Figure 11.1*, we can see the differences between these two terms.

In order to run a virtual machine, the host operating system must have a **Hypervisor** or special software (or hardware) designed for that purpose. On created Virtual Machine, we must install the operating system, and now we can install our application Virtual Machine's OS (*Figure 11.1a*).

With Docker, the situation is less complex. If we have a host operating system with an installed Docker, we can run containers (with our application) on that machine (*Figure 11.1b*).

We should explain abbreviations from *Figure 11.1*:

- **OS: Operating System**
- **VM: Virtual Machine**
- **APP: Application**
- **DC: Docker Container**

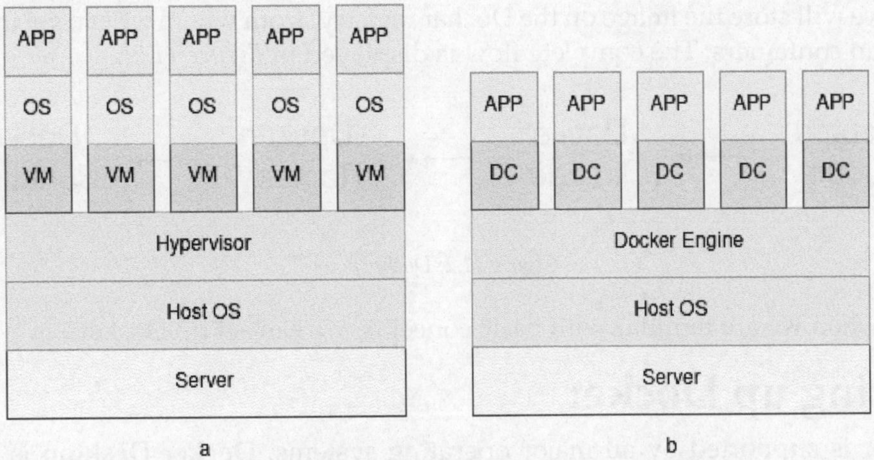

Figure 11.1: Differences between Docker and Virtual Machine

Before we can explain how to get from source code to Docker container, we should explain two Docker concepts. A **Docker image** represents a template for building containers, someone defines a Docker image as a stopped **Docker container** (and vice versa Docker container is a running image). To *transform* our source code to a Docker image, we will use **Dockerfile**.

Dockerfile is a configuration file that contains instructions on how to create a Docker image. Some of the most common instructions that can be found in Dockerfile are:

- **FROM**: First instruction in the Docker file, specifies the parent image from which our image will be built.
- **WORKDIR**: Creates a new working directory.
- **COPY**: Copies files from the machine to the container.
- **RUN**: Executes any command and commits results, mostly used for the execution of a command from the parent image. For example, if our parent image is some Linux distribution, we can execute any Linux command with **RUN**.
- **EXPOSE**: Exposes specified network ports.
- **CMD**: Specifies which command will be run inside the container, usually the last instruction in Dockerfile.
- **ENTRYPOINT**: Configures a container that will be run as an executable.

The **Docker registry** stores Docker images. Now that we are familiar with all terms, we can explain *Docker flow*.

First, we will use Dockerfile to create a Docker image from our source code. After that, we will store the image on the Docker registry, from where we can get images, and run containers. The complete flow is displayed in *Figure 11.2*::

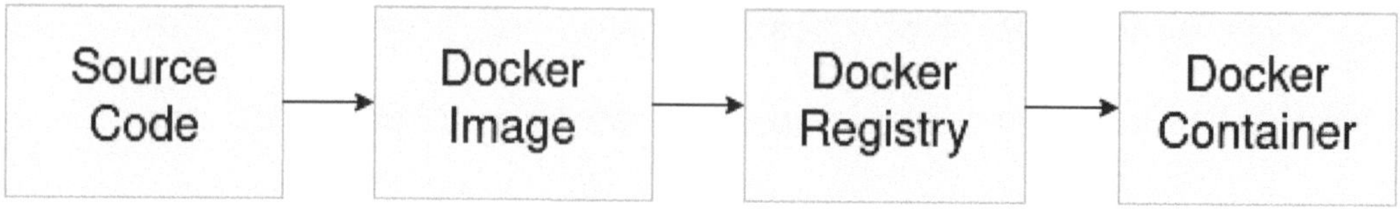

***Figure 11.2**: Docker flow*

Now when we are familiar with basic concepts, we can set up Docker.

Setting up Docker

Docker is supported by all major operating systems. **Docker Desktop** is a tool that allows us to build and run containerized applications. Installation files can be downloaded from the official website:

https://docs.docker.com/desktop/

For macOS, we should download the `dmg` file installer and open it. When the dialog is prompted, we should drag *Docker* icon (while that carries a stack of shipping containers) to the `Application` directory. When the installation is completed, Docker can be started by double-clicking on `Docker.app`.

Windows installer is a simple `.exe` file. After the download is completed, installation can be started by *double-clicking* on the installer file. When the configuration page is prompted, we should select or leave unselected the **Use WSL 2 Instead of Hyper-V** option. If Windows does not support *WSL* and *Hyper-V*, this option will not be offered. If we use only Docker on our OS, we can go with *WSL 2*, if we run another Virtual Machine, we should go with *Hyper-V*. When the installation is completed, Docker will be started by double-clicking on the *Docker* icon.

Linux installer comes in two forms, `rmp` file (**Red Hat Enterprise Linux** and **Fedora**) and `deb` file (**Debian** and **Ubuntu**). When the installer is downloaded, open the terminal, and execute the following command (in the directory where the installer is downloaded):

- Red Hat Enterprise Linux and Fedora:

  ```
  sudo yum install ./docker-desktop-4.14.1-x86_64.rpm
  ```

- Debian and Ubuntu:

  ```
  sudo apt-get install ./docker-desktop-4.14.1-amd64.deb
  ```

In previous command examples, the newest version of Docker Desktop is used. When the installation is completed, we can start Docker with one of the following commands:

- Red Hat Enterprise Linux and Fedora:

```
sudo systemctl start docker-desktop
```

- Debian and Ubuntu:

```
sudo service docker-desktop start
```

Now when Docker is set up, we can learn some basic Docker commands.

Docker commands

In this section, we will go through some of the most common Docker commands. All commands will be executed in the terminal/console.

Some of the most useful commands are:

- Information about Docker version:

```
docker version
```

- Information about the host (machine or service where Docker is running):

```
docker info
```

- List of running containers:

```
docker ps
```

  If we want to include all containers (currently and previously ran), we can use flag **-a**.

- List of Docker images, stored locally:

```
docker images
```

- Getting an image from **Docker Hub** (Docker registry provided by Docker):

```
docker_pull image_name:tag
```

  The **tag** usually represents a version of the Docker image. A special tag, **latest** will be used if **tag** is omitted. It will be applied to the most recently built Docker image. It is not a good practice to build Docker images with **latest** tag, or without **tag**; each image should have its own **tag**.

- Deleting local Docker image:

```
docker rmi image_name:tag
```

- Starting Docker container:

```
docker start container_name
```

- Stopping Docker container:

```
docker stop container_name
```

- Deleting Docker container:

  ```
  docker rm container_name
  ```

- Building Docker image:

  ```
  docker build -f name_of_dockerfile path_to_dockerfile
  -t image_name:tag
  ```

  Flag **-f** is used to specify the name of the Dockerfile, while flag **-t** is used to specify the *image name* and the *tag*. The **tag** is optional, if is omitted, the value **latest** will be set.

- Running Docker container:

  ```
  docker run -p host_port:container_port image_name:tag
  ```

  Flag **-p** is used to map exposed container ports to host (local machine in our case) ports.

For all commands, more flags can be used, but we show only the most important ones here. In the next section, we will see the usage of the **build** and **run** command with more details. Now we are ready to finally Dockerize our web service.

Dockerizing application

The first step in Dockerization will be the creation of a Dockerfile. We will create it inside the **root** directory of our project (*Figure 11.3*):

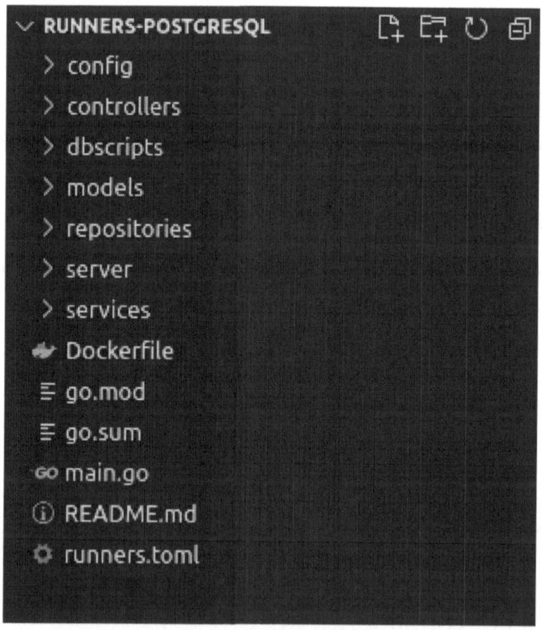

Figure 11.3: *Dockerfile*

Here we will provide the complete content of the Dockerfile, and explain it later, *instruction by instruction*:

```
FROM golang:1.20-alpine

WORKDIR /app

COPY . .

RUN go mod download

RUN go build -o runners-app main.go

EXPOSE 8080

CMD ["/app/runners-app"]
```

Instructions in Dockerfile will perform the following:

- Instruction `FROM` will define the base image. We will use the official image for *GO 19*, based on *Alpine Linux*, a small, and lightweight Linux distribution.
- Instruction **`WORKDIR`** will create a new working directory with the name **`app`**.
- Instruction **`COPY`** will copy the source code to the current working directory. Two points represent source and destination directories. Dot (`.`) represents the *current* directory, so in our case, we will copy the source code from the *current* directory on our computer (**`root`** directory of our project, where Dockerfile is) to the current *working* directory (directory **`app`** created with previous instruction).
- Instruction **`RUN`** will download all dependencies. If **`go.mod`** and **`go.sum`** files are not changed, dependencies will be cached.
- The second **`RUN`** instruction will build the Go application.
- Instruction **`EXPOSE`** will expose all necessary ports. In our case, only port **`8080`** will be used (for HTTP requests), so it should be exposed.
- The last instruction, **`CMD`**, will define what will be run when the container is started. In our case, we will run our application, built with the second **`RUN`** instruction.

Now when our Dockerfile is ready, we can build an image with the following command:

```
docker build -f Dockerfile . -t runners-app
```

It will take a couple of minutes before our image is built. When the build is completed, we can run the container with the following command:

```
docker run -p 8080:8080 runners-app
```

It seems that something is *not* good. If we check the log, we will see that the application failed to connect to the database:

```
2022/11/19 21:48:11 Starting Runners App
2022/11/19 21:48:11 Initializing configuration
2022/11/19 21:48:11 Initializing database
2022/11/19 21:48:11 Error while validating database: dial
tcp 127.0.0.1:5432: connect: connection refused
```

Problem is that our application is inside the container, while the database is on our local machine. The solution how to handle this issue depends on our operating system.

If we use Docker on Linux, we can run the container in *host networking mode*. In this mode, Docker will share the network namespace with the host machine and our application will successfully be started with the following command:

```
docker run --network host -p 8080:8080 runners-app
```

Host networking mode is supported only in Docker for Linux. For the macOS and Windows, we can use a special DNS name, **host.docker.internal**, which will resolve to the internal IP address used by the host. This DNS name should be used for the database connection string instead of localhost:

```
connection_string = "host=host.docker.internal port=5432
user=postgres password=postgres dbname=runners_db
sslmode=disable"
```

Interesting trivia, we can use *host networking mode* in run commands executed on macOS and Windows. No errors or warnings will be triggered, but our application will not work properly. The reason for that is that Docker on macOS and Windows uses Linux Virtual Machine, within containers will be run. When we use a *networking mode host*, Docker will share a namespace with a Virtual Machine, so from a command point of view, everything is *valid*.

Now when everything runs as expected, we can go back to **Postman** and try to call some API. Everything should work as expected (please be sure that the application is only running in a container).

Congratulations! Our first successfully Dockerized application. Now we can try to improve things a little bit.

Docker compose

In the previous section, we learned how to run a Docker container. But *what is the case when we should run more than one container?* We should create some script that will run multiple **docker run** commands. If we have complex commands with a lot of flags and options, it will be hard to maintain that script, also it would not be the most readable script.

Docker compose will allow us to run multiple Docker containers, by setting all parameters into a simple YAML file. In the current state of our application, we have only one container, but it is a good starting point for us to see how to create a Docker compose file. We will place the Docker compose file into the **root** directory of our project (*Figure 11.4*).

The first line in the Docker compose file is the version specification, in our case, we will use **version 3** (the current latest version). After that, we will define a list of **services** (containers) that we will run. The first line, after the **services** keyword, defines the container name, this name can be used as a network alias. For each container, we must define an image that will be used.

For macOS and Windows, we should map container and host ports, in the same way as with the **docker run** command. A short reminder, in order for the container to access the database on the local machine, we must use **host.docker.internal** in the configuration file:

```
version: “3”

services:

  runners-app:

    image: runners-app:latest

    ports:

      - 8080:8080
```

Indentation in YAML files is important! Structures in YAML files are determined by indentation, in most cases, errors, and mistakes related to Docker compose files are caused by the wrong indentation:

***Figure 11.4:** Docker compose file*

On Linux, we can use a *networking mode host*. This mode will automatically map all exposed container ports to the host ports. If we try to map them manually, an *error* will be triggered when we try to run containers, because port mapping and network mode will be in a collision. Docker compose file is a little different:

```
version: "3"
services:
  runners-app:
    image: runners-app:latest
    network_mode: "host"
```

Docker compose is automatically installed when Docker was installed, so we do not need to install anything additionally. We can start containers with the following command:

```
docker-compose -f docker-compose.yaml up
```

And stop them with:

```
docker-compose -f docker-compose.yaml down
```

As we can see these commands are more elegant than **`docker run`**. The YAML files are much more readable than long commands. Also, it is much easier to always use the same command and update the YAML file when it is necessary. So, it is a good practice to run containers through Docker compose instead of Docker.

We can send a couple of requests through **Postman**, to validate that everything runs correctly. If everything is fine, we can move to the next step, actual **deployment**.

Kubernetes

Kubernetes represents a system for the orchestration of containers, originally designed by *Google* and currently maintained by the **Cloud Native Computing Foundation** (**CNCF**). It supports all popular containers, including Docker. It is commonly stylized as **k8s**.

Before we learn how to use Kubernetes for deployment, we will list some basic concepts. In *Figure 11.5*, we can see a graphical representation of the relationship between these concepts for better understanding:

- **Node**: Physical or Virtual Machine that runs containerized applications.
- **Cluster**: Set of nodes.
- **Namespace**: Virtual cluster. Nodes from different physical clusters can be used in the namespace.
- **Pod**: The smallest and simplest object that runs containers.
- **Replica Set**: Set of pods that runs the same application.
- **Deployment**: Object that manages replicated applications.
- **Service**: Abstract used to expose deployment as network application:

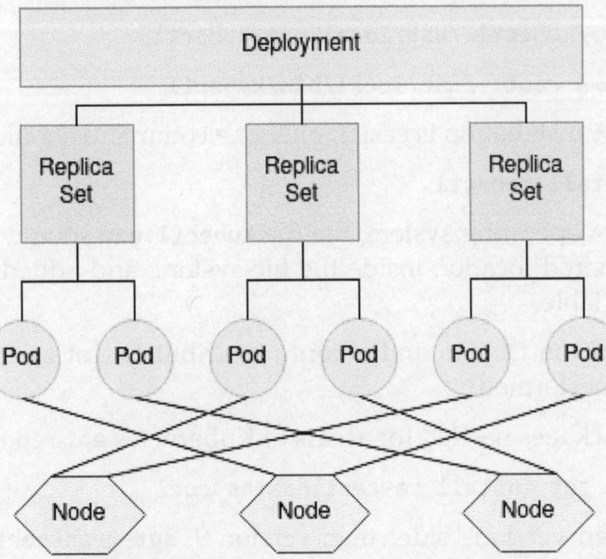

Figure 11.5*: Relationship between Kubernetes concepts*

Now, when we are familiar with basic Kubernetes concepts, we can set up a local cluster and deploy our application.

Setting up a local Kubernetes cluster

In order to set up and run the Kubernetes cluster locally (on our local machine), we must install two tools, **kubectl** and **minikube**. **Kubectl** is a command-line tool for the Kubernetes platform to perform API calls, while **minikube** is a tool for running Kubernetes locally.

First, we will install **kubectl**. Installation files for all operating systems (with instructions) can be found on the official website:

https://kubernetes.io/docs/tasks/tools/

We have two ways to install **kubectl** on macOS, with `curl` (short, for **Client URL**) command or with **Homebrew**. If we install **kubectl** with the `curl` command, we should perform the following steps:

1. Download the `kubectl` binary with the `curl` command:

   ```
   curl -LO "https://dl.k8s.io/release/$(curl -L -s
   https://dl.k8s.io/release/stable.txt)/bin/darwin/arm64/kubectl"
   ```

2. Make downloaded binary executable:

   ```
   ch mod +x ./kubectl
   ```

3. Move binary to a location on system `PATH` and assign root user as a *file owner*:

   ```
   sudo mv ./kubectl /usr/local/bin/kubectl
   sudo chown root: /usr/local/bin/kubectl
   ```

With Homebrow, installation is easier, only one command should be executed:

```
brew install kubectl
```

For the Windows operating system, the file `kubectl.exe` should be downloaded, placed in the desired location inside the file system, and added to the file `PATH` environment variable.

To install `kubectl` on Debian and Ubuntu distributions of Linux, the following steps should be performed:

1. Install packages needed for access to Kubernetes `apt` repository:

   ```
   sudo apt-get install ca-certificates curl
   ```

   For Debian versions older than version 9, `apt-transport-https` must be installed:

```
sudo apt-get install -y apt-transport-https
```

2. Download *Google Cloud* public signing key:

```
sudo curl -fsSLo /usr/share/keyrings/kubernetes-archive-keyring.
gpg
https://packages.cloud.google.com/apt/doc/apt-key.gpg
```

3. Add the Kubernetes `apt` repository:

```
echo "deb [signed-by=/usr/share/keyrings/kubernetes-archive-
keyring.gpg]
https://apt.kubernetes.io/ kubernetes-xenial main" |
sudo tee /etc/apt/sources.list.d/kubernetes.list
```

4. Install `kubectl`:

```
sudo apt-get install kubectl
```

For *Red Hat Enterprise Linux* and *Fedora*, the installation process is different, with only two steps:

1. Configure the package management system (`yum`):

```
cat <<EOF | sudo tee /etc/yum.repos.d/kubernetes.repo
[kubernetes]
name=Kubernetes
baseurl=https://packages.cloud.google.com/yum/repos/kubernetes-el7-
\$basearch
enabled=1
gpgcheck=1
gpgkey=https://packages.cloud.google.com/yum/doc/rpm-package-key.
gpg
EOF
```

2. Install `kubectl`:

```
sudo yum install kubectl
```

3. When the installation is completed, we can check it with the `version` command:

```
kubectl version --client
```

Docker Desktop can install its own version of `kubectl`, and add it to `PATH`. If we want to use the version installed with previous procedures, the Docker Desktop version must be removed from `PATH`.

Now we can install **minikube**. If we go to the official website:

https://minikube.sigs.k8s.io/docs/start/

We can see that it is available for different operating systems and architectures. The following architectures are available per operating system:

- **Linux**: x86-64, ARM64, ARMv7, ppc64, S390x
- **macOS**: x86-64, ARM64
- **Windows**: x86-64

In all commands used for demonstration of the installation process, we will use *x86-64 architecture.*

To install **minikube** on Windows, the latest release should be downloaded, in form of an `.exe` file. The downloaded file should be added to the `PATH` environment variable, and minikube is ready.

For macOS **minikube** can be installed with the `curl` command or with **Homebrew**. For `curl` installation, the following commands should be executed:

```
curl -LO https://storage.googleapis.com/minikube/releases/latest/
minikube-darwin-amd64

sudo install minikube-darwin-amd64 /usr/local/bin/minikube
```

The first command will download the installation file, the second one will install minikube.

This command will use Homebrew to install minikube:

```
brew install minikube
```

On Linux distribution, the `curl` command will download the installation file, while the second command will install minikube. The following command should be used, depending on the Linux distribution:

- Red Hat Enterprise Linux and Fedora:

```
curl -LO https://storage.googleapis.com/minikube/releases/latest/
minikube-latest.x86_64.rpm

sudo yum install ./minikube-latest.x86_64.rpm
```

- Debian and Ubuntu:

```
curl -LO https://storage.googleapis.com/minikube/releases/latest/
minikube_latest_amd64.deb
```

```
sudo apt-get install ./minikube_latest_amd64.deb
```

Installation can be checked with the version command:

```
minikube version
```

Our Kubernetes cluster is ready. Before we can deploy our application on it, we should familiarize ourselves with some basic **kubectl** commands.

Kubectl commands

Kubectl commands are used for the management of resources of Kubernetes clusters. Here we will show a couple of the most often-used commands.

The first command that we will see here is the **get** command. Command used to list Kubernetes resources. Here are a couple of examples, with different resources:

```
kubectl get nodes
kubectl get pods
kubectl get rs
kubectl get deployments
kubectl get services
```

Command **describe** shows details of the specified resource or group of resources. If we provide only resource type, details for all resources of the specified type will be provided. A group of resources can be described by providing a specific label for that group, with a **-l** flag. The following examples show the usage of the description command for *one specific pod*, *group of pods*, and *all pods*:

```
kubectl describe pods pod-01
kubectl describe pods -l version=v1
kubectl describe pods
```

Command create will create a new Kubernetes resource based on data stored in the file. Formats that can be accepted by this command are JSON and YAML:

```
kubectl create -f file_name
```

The same file can be used for the deletion of resources. Resource of a specific type can be deleted by *name* or *label*, or we can *delete* all resources of the same type with flag **--all**, as we can see in the following examples:

```
kubectl delete -f ./delete.yaml
kubectl delete pod pod-01
kubectl delete pod -l version=v1
kubectl delete pods --all
```

The last command that we will see here is the **scale** command. Will set up a number of replicas used to run the application. It is mainly used for deployment resources to increase or decrease the number of pods:

```
kubectl scale deployment deployment_name
-replicas=number_of_replicas
```

In the next section, we will use the commands learned here to deploy our application on Kubernetes.

Deploying on Kubernetes

Before we start with deployment, we will introduce a new concept. In order for our web server application to access the database, we must update our configuration file. The database will be on our local machine, while the web server application will run on Kubernetes.

Kubernetes cluster will run on different IP than our local machine, so we must use the local machine's address instead of localhost in the connection string. We can find the required address in the **Network Settings** of our operating system.

It is not practical to change the configuration file each time when we deploy our application on a different environment. It is good practice to have multiple configuration files and read one that holds the configuration for a specific environment.

We will create a new configuration file, **runners-k8s.toml** which holds configuration specific for the Kubernetes environment where **192.168.0.25** represents the address of my local machine:

```
######################################################################

# Database configuration

# Connection string is in Go pq driver format:
# host=<host> port=<port> user=<databaseUser>
password=<databaseUserPassword> dbname=<databaseName>

[database]

connection_string = "host=192.168.0.25 port=5432 user=postgres
password=postgres   dbname=runners_db sslmode=disable"
max_idle_connections = 5
max_open_connections = 20
```

```
connection_max_lifetime = "60s"
driver_name = "postgres"
###################################################################

# HTTP server configuration

[http]

server_address = ":8080"
###################################################################
```

We will introduce an *environment variable* that will be used for determining which configuration file should be read on application start. In our case, we can read the environment variable **ENV** and add it to the end of the default file name (**runners**). If the value is not set for the **ENV** variable, the default configuration will be loaded.

The private function **getConfigFileName()**, from **main.go** file, will use **Getenv()** function from the **os** package to read the value of the environment variable of the specified name and use that value to create a proper file name:

```
func getConfigFileName() string {
        env := os.Getenv("ENV")

        if env != "" {
                return "runners-" + env
        }

        return "runners"
}
```

This function will be used in the **main()** function:

```
config := config.InitConfig(getConfigFileName())
```

For our local run with the **go run** command or with the Docker run, we can use the default configuration. For Kubernetes deployment, we will set the value of the **ENV** variable to **k8s** and use Kubernetes-related configuration, *we will see how, soon.*

We can move forward. The YAML files will be used for the creation of Kubernetes resources. These files will be placed in the **kubernetes** directory inside our project (*Figure 11.6*):

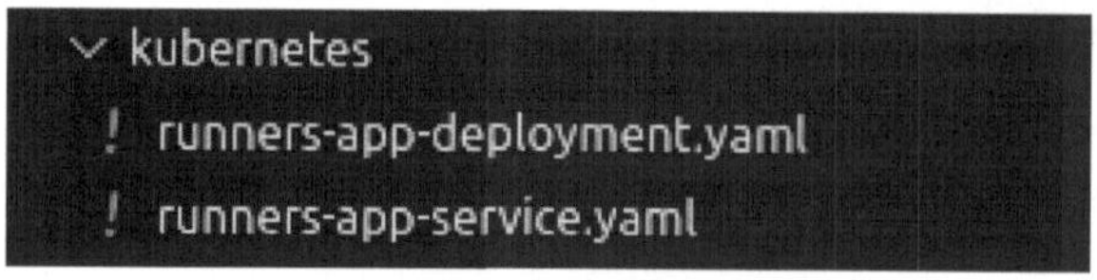

Figure 11.6: Kubernetes files

The first YAML file will be used for the creation of Kubernetes deployment. At the start of the file, we will define the API version, `apps/v1` in our case. For some older versions of Kubernetes `apps/v1beta2` must be used. In the second line, the kind of Kubernetes resource is defined, as we already mentioned we will create `Deployment`.

`Metadata` is used for the identification of resources, by *name*, or by *UID*. We will identify our resources by name (`runners-app`).

Under the `spec` section, we will define a specification for our `Deployment`. The `selector` will define a label that will be used to determine which resources are "under" `Deployment`. All pods that name starts with the specified label will be "`select`" as a part of `Deployment`.

A number of replicas will also be defined under the `spec` section. One pod is enough for now, but we can put an almost infinite number of pods under a single `Deployment`, we are only limited by the physical resources of the server where the Kubernetes cluster is running.

The last thing that we will have under the `spec` section is the `template` section. Here we will define the name under `metadata`. The *unique hash* will be added to that name to identify each pod. Under `spec`, we will set container specifications. Here, we will set the Docker image that will be used, container name, ports mapping, and values for environment variables. Here we will set the value for the `ENV` variable to `k8s`!

If the `imagePullPolicy` value is set to `Always`, Kubernetes will try to pull the Docker image from the official Docker registry. Our image is stored *locally* so we must set it to `Never` in order to prevent pull that will be unsuccessful and create some potential problems.

Here is the complete content of `runners-app-deployment.yaml` file:

```
apiVersion: apps/v1
kind: Deployment
metadata:
  name: runners-app
spec:
  selector:
```

```
    matchLabels:
      app: runners-app
  replicas: 1
  template:
    metadata:
      labels:
        app: runners-app
    spec:
      containers:
        - image: runners-app:latest
          name: runners-app
          imagePullPolicy: Never
          ports:
            - containerPort: 8080
          env:
            - name: ENV
              value: "k8s"
```

The second YAML file will be used for the creation of the Service. Again the first line will define the API version (**v1**), the second line will define the type of resource (**Service**), and the service name will be defined through **metadata**.

Inside the **spec** section, we will define the **selector**. In order to *wrap* **Deployment**, we should use the **Deployment** name here. Besides port mapping, we will define one more thing here, service **type**. The following service types are supported:

- **ClusterIP**: Service will be reachable only inside the cluster. This is the default service type.
- **NodePort**: Exposes all cluster nodes on the same port. Service can be reached outside the cluster with node IP and port.
- **LoadBalancer**: Creates load balancer and assigns a fixed IP address to the service. Service can be reached outside the cluster with the assigned address.
- **ExternalName**: The service will be exposed with an *arbitrary* name.

We will use **LoadBalancer** for our **Service**. Here is the content of the **runners-app-service.yaml** file:

```
apiVersion: v1
kind: Service
metadata:
```

```
  name: runners-app-service
spec:
  selector:
    app: runners-app
  type: LoadBalancer
  ports:
    - name: http
      protocol: TCP
      port: 8080
      targetPort: 8080
```

Now we can open the console/terminal and start our local Kubernetes cluster with the following **minikube** command:

```
minikube start
```

When **minikube** is started, we will hit our first problem. In order to detect and use locally stored images, **minikube** must use the same Docker daemon as local Docker. Depending on the operating system following command should be executed:

- Linux and macOS:

```
eval $(minikube docker-env)
```

- Windows (in PowerShell):

```
& minikube -p minikube docker-env --shell powershell |
Invoke-Expression
```

From this moment, all locally build images will be visible for minikube. We can move to the **root** directory of our project and execute the **docker build** command:

```
docker build -f Dockerfile . -t runners-app
```

If we check local images with **docker images** command, the **runners-app image**, with the tag **latest** should be listed. Now, we can use YAML files from the **kubernetes** directory to create resources. First, we will create **Deployment**:

```
kubectl create -f ./kubernetes/runners-app-deployment.yaml
```

We can check if pods are running as expected with:

```
kubectl get pods
```

The command output should be similar to this:

```
NAME                          READY   STATUS    RESTARTS   AGE
runners-app-5d86dc75b-btqn2   1/1     Running   0          112s
```

Now we can create a **Service** and check it with the **get** command:

```
kubectl create -f ./kubernetes/runners-app-service.yaml
kubectl get services
```

The output of the **get services** command shows the following:

```
NAME                TYPE          CLUSTER-IP     EXTERNAL-IP
PORT(S)             AGE
kubernetes          ClusterIP     10.96.0.1      <none>
443/TCP             13h
runners-app-service LoadBalancer  10.98.205.195  <pending>
8080:31780/   TCP   10s
```

Our service is in a pending state! Actually, this is not our mistake. The **LoadBalancer** service type is (at the moment) not supported by minikube. Execution of **tunnel** command will fix this issue:

```
minikube tunnel
```

Now if we check our services with the **get** command, the output should be different:

```
NAME                TYPE              CLUSTER-IP
EXTERNAL-IP         PORT(S)           AGE
kubernetes          ClusterIP         10.96.0.1
<none>              443/TCP           13h
runners-app-service LoadBalancer      10.98.205.195
10.98.205.195       8080:31780/TCP    7m16s
```

Our web server application is successfully deployed on Kubernetes. We can use external IP from the previous output (in combination with port) in **Postman** to test our application.

If something went wrong, we should analyze logs in order to find what caused the problem. In order to check logs, we should pass the resource name to the **logs** command. The following command will check logs on only Pod in our system:

```
kubectl logs runners-app-5d86dc75b-btqn2
```

If we are not comfortable with working in the console/terminal, we can use the Kubernetes dashboard. Before we start the dashboard, we should check, if *proper add-ons* are enabled. A list of all add-ons can be fetched with:

```
minikube addons list
```

If **dashboard** and **metrics-server** add-ons are disabled, we should enable them with these commands:

```
minikube addons enable dashboard
minikube addons enable metrics-server
```

Now we can start our **`dashboard`**:

```
minikube dashboard
```

The dashboard will be opened in the web browser (*Figure 11.7*). Here, we can use the graphical interface to perform different operations, like checking the statuses of resources, getting logs, scaling deployment up or down, and so on:

***Figure 11.7**: Kubernetes dashboard*

In the end, we will mention two useful **`minikube`** commands:

- Stopping Kubernetes cluster:

  ```
  minikube stop
  ```

- Deleting Kubernetes cluster with all locally stored Docker images created during the lifespan of the cluster:

  ```
  minikube delete
  ```

Now, we know how to configure and run Kubernetes locally. In the next section, we will discuss some options that can make our application globally accessible.

Google Cloud Platform

Google Cloud Platform (**GCP**) is a group of cloud computing services. These services run on the identical infrastructure that *Google* uses for internal products, like *YouTube*, *Gmail*, *Google Drive*, and so on.

With *Google Cloud*, we can use some of the free services. Most of the services described in this section are *not* free, and we need a billing account. A **billing account** can be defined as a *Google* account extended with credit card details and tax information.

A *free trial option* is also available, basically, this will create a billing account with *300$* in credit that can be spent over *three months*. Things that will be created in this section will cost around *5$*, maximum.

First, we will host our database on *Google Cloud*.

Setting up a database

Google Cloud offers a service that can host and run a relational database. On the side menu, if we select SQL, the **Cloud SQL Instances** page will be opened (*Figure 11.8*). Here, we should click on the **Create instance** button:

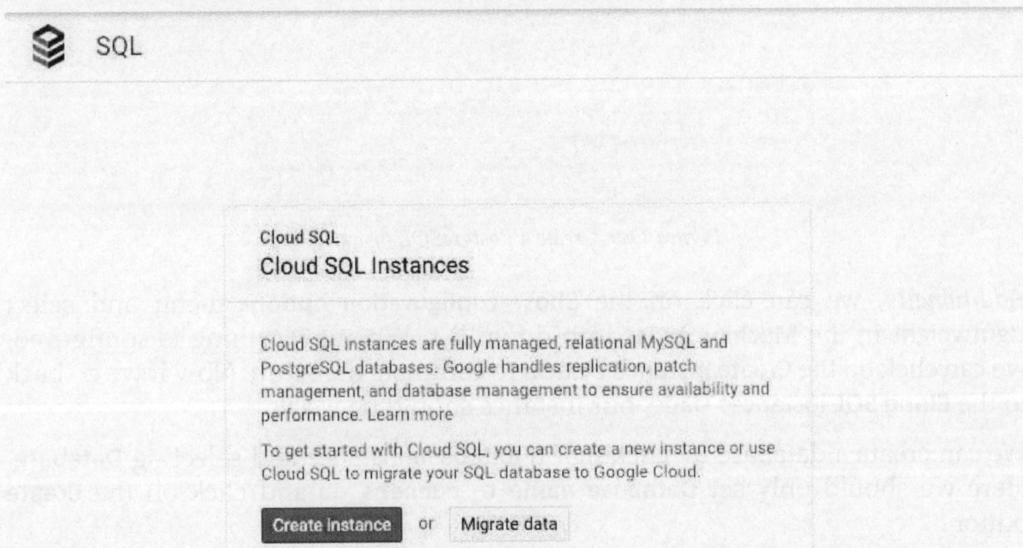

***Figure 11.8:** Cloud SQL instance page*

On the **Create a PostgreSQL instance** page (*Figure 11.9*), we will fill in **Instance ID** (**`database-instance`**), and **Password** for the default (**`postgres`**) user, and select the *PostgreSQL version*. Inside, **Choose region and zonal availability**, we should choose **Single zone** and select the closest region:

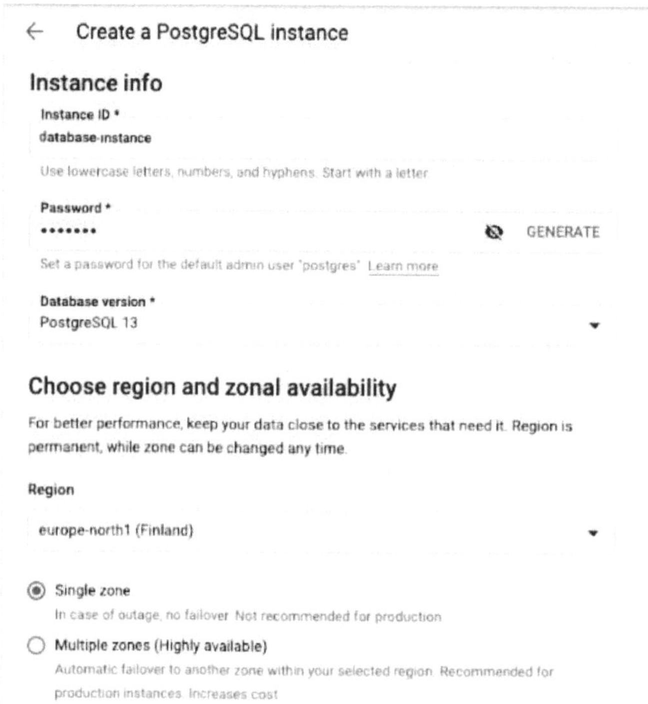

Figure 11.9: *Create a PostgreSQL instance*

Additionally, we can click on the **Show configuration options** menu and select **Lightweight** in the **Machine type** drop-down list. When everything is configured, we can click on the **Create instance** button to complete the setup. Now if we go back to the **Cloud SQL Instances** page, our instance should be *visible*.

We can create a database by clicking on **database-instance** and selecting **Database**. Here we should only set **Database name** to **`runners_db`** and click on the **Create** button.

From now on, we can check connection details, test connections, and use our scripts to initialize tables and indices and import data. The connection string from the configuration file in our project should be updated, or we can create a new one for the *Google Cloud* environment.

We can also create a *new database user* if the default one is not good or safe enough. Now we can move to the last step.

Deployment of a web server application

In order to deploy our web server application, first we should create a new project, by clicking on the drop-down list in the *header* toolbar (next to the *Google Cloud* sign) and selecting **New Project**. On the **New Project** page (*Figure 11.10*), we should set **Project name** (**`runners-app`**) and **Location (organization)** (we can leave it on default value – **No organization**). When everything is set up, we can click on the **Create** button:

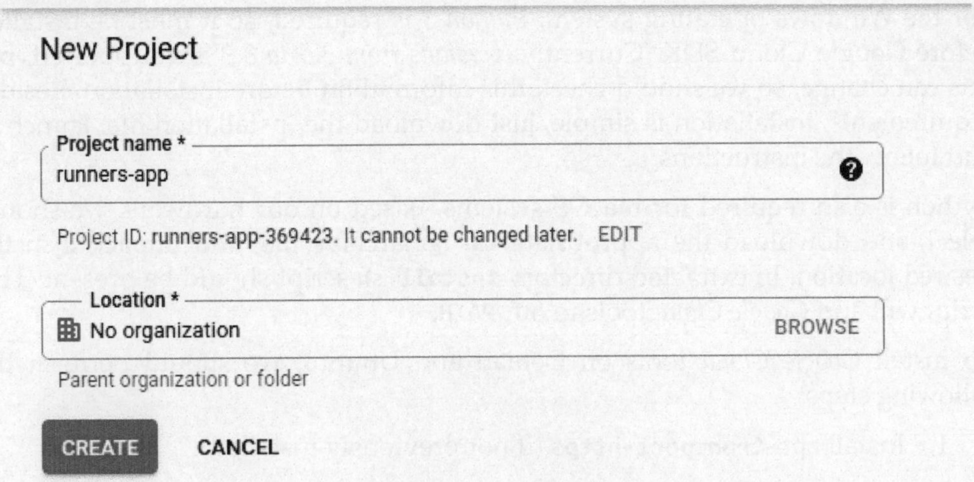

Figure 11.10: New Project page

Now, we will create a Kubernetes cluster by selecting **Kubernetes Engine** from the side menu, and then selecting **Clusters** (*Figure 11.11*). On the **Kubernetes Engine** page, if we click on the **Create cluster** button, the page for *cluster configuration* will be prompted.

Here, we can configure a name for our cluster, **zone** (it is a good practice to select a zone that is in the same region as a region that we selected for the database), **GKE (Google Kubernetes Engine)** version, and node pools. *Node pools* are very important, here we will select the number of nodes, how many CPU cores, and the memory we will use. If we do not select enough resources, our application will not be deployed, or it will not work as expected:

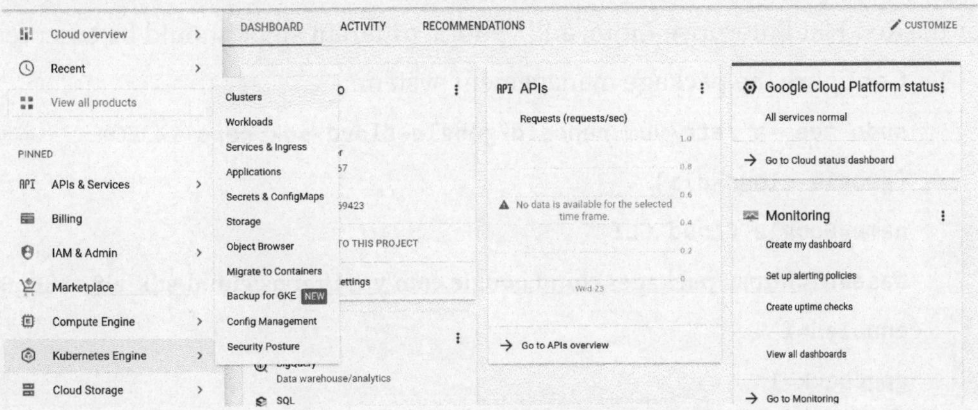

Figure 11.11: Creating Kubernetes cluster

We can access our Google Cloud cluster from our local machine, we just need to install Google Cloud SDK. It is supported by all operating systems.

For the Windows operating system, *Python 3* is required, so it must be installed before Google Cloud SDK. Currently, *versions from 3.5 to 3.9* are supported, but this can change, so we should check this information before installation. Besides requirements, installation is simple, just download the installation file, launch it, and follow the instructions.

Python is also required for macOS systems. Based on our hardware, we should select, and download the appropriate **tar.gz** archive file, and unpack it in the desired location. In extracted directory **install.sh** script should be present. This script will add *Google Cloud* tools to our **PATH**.

To install *Google Cloud* tools on Debian and Ubuntu, we should perform the following steps:

1. Install **apt-transport-https** (if not previously installed):

   ```
   sudo apt-get install apt-transport-https ca-certificates gnupg
   ```

2. Add *the gcloud CLI distribution URL* as a package source:

   ```
   echo "deb [signed-by=/usr/share/keyrings/cloud.google.gpg]
   https://packages.cloud.google.com/apt cloud-sdk main" |
   sudo tee -a /etc/apt/sources.list.d/google-cloud-sdk.list
   ```

3. Import the *Google Cloud public key*:

   ```
   curl https://packages.cloud.google.com/apt/doc/apt-key.gpg |
   sudo apt-key --keyring /usr/share/keyrings/cloud.google.gpg add -
   ```

4. Install:

   ```
   sudo apt-get update && sudo apt-get install google-cloud-cli
   ```

For the Red Hat Enterprise Linux and Fedora, different steps should be executed:

1. Configure the package management system:

   ```
   sudo tee -a /etc/yum.repos.d/google-cloud-sdk.repo << EOM
   [google-cloud-cli]
   name=Google Cloud CLI
   baseurl=https://packages.cloud.google.com/yum/repos/cloud-sdk-el8- x86_64
   enabled=1
   gpgcheck=1
   repo_gpgcheck=0
   ```

```
gpgkey=https://packages.cloud.google.com/yum/doc/rpm-package-key.
gpg
EOM
```

2. Install:

```
sudo yum install google-cloud-cli
```

When the installation is completed, we should initialize *Google Cloud SDK* with the following command:

```
gcloud init
```

Now we should set up our local **kubectl** to access the *Google Cloud Kubernetes* cluster, instead of **minikube**. First, we should obtain access credentials:

```
gcloud auth login
```

When the **Sign in with Google** page is prompted in a web browser, we should choose our *Google account* and click on the **Allow** button.

The existing **kubectl** configuration will be updated with credentials and *Google Cloud* cluster configuration:

```
gcloud container clusters get-credentials standard-cluster
--zone europe-north1-a --project runners-app
```

Here, we will use the **zone** and **project** name from the *Google Cloud Kubernetes* cluster that we previously set up. We are now connected to our remote Kubernetes cluster. From this moment, we can use the **kubectl** command that we used for local deployment to deploy our application *Google Cloud*.

Google Cloud also offers **Container Registry**, where we can push our Docker images and use them for deployment. In order to use it from our local machine, we must update the Docker configuration:

```
gcloud auth configure-docker
```

Now we can use the **docker push** command to push our images into a remote repository. We should update our Kubernetes YAML files to use images from the repository.

Whit this we completed our deployment procedure. Here are a few more small notes at the end.

It is a good practice to delete all services if they are created just for some testing or learning. This will prevent any unnecessary costs. For potential problems and more information follow the official *Google Cloud* documentation:

https://cloud.google.com/docs

Similar solutions from other companies are **AWS (Amazon Web Services)** and

Microsoft Azure. The solution often depends on the used technologies. For example, if our system works with **DynamoDB**, a database management system developed by *Amazon*, it is logical to deploy our system with *AWS*.

Conclusion

In this chapter, we learned how to containerize our application by using Docker and deploy it by using Kubernetes. At the end of the chapter, we provide some basic information and guidelines about *Google Cloud* solutions and how to use them to expose our application to the outside world.

In the next, last chapter, we will see how to monitor our application in order to prevent any potential problems.

References

- https://docs.docker.com/desktop/
- https://kubernetes.io/docs/tasks/tools/
- https://cloud.google.com/docs

Points to remember

- It is a good practice to pack applications and all dependencies together, in one place, if possible.
- Docker compose will allow us to run multiple Docker containers, by setting all parameters into a simple configuration file.
- The choice of application hosting solution (*Google Cloud, AWS, Microsoft Azure*) often depends on the used technologies.

Multiple choice questions

1. Which instruction is often the first one in Dockerfile?
    a. `FROM`
    b. `RUN`
    c. `COPY`
    d. `CMD`

2. How the smallest and simplest Kubernetes object is called?
    a. Node
    b. Cluster
    c. Pod
    d. Replica Set
3. For what Google Cloud can be used?
    a. Docker images repository
    b. Database hosting
    c. Container management with Kubernetes
    d. All of above

Answers

1. a
2. c
3. d

Questions

1. What are the differences between stateless and stateful containers?
2. What are the differences between Docker and Virtual Machine?
3. What is a Kubernetes namespace?

Key terms

- **Container**: Software unit where code and all dependencies are packaged together.
- **Docker**: The most popular platform that uses virtualization to deliver software in containers.
- **Kubernetes**: System for orchestration of containers.
- **Google Cloud Platform (GCP)**: Group of cloud computing services.

CHAPTER 12

Monitoring and Alerting

Introduction

In this last chapter, we will learn how to perform operations that follow after our application becomes available for users. At the start of the chapter, we will take a deep look at **Prometheus** and learn how to monitor our application. After that, we will use **Grafana** to visualize metrics picked up with **Prometheus** on the **Grafana** dashboard. At the end of the chapter, we learn how to create alerting rules and send an alert when a potential problem occurs.

Structure

In this chapter, we will discuss the following topics:

- Prometheus
  - Prometheus query language
  - Setting up Prometheus
  - Custom Prometheus metrics
- Grafana
  - Setting up Grafana
  - Creating Grafana dashboard
- Alerting

Prometheus

When our system is deployed and released (in production, is also a commonly used term for this situation) we should monitor it in order to prevent potential service-breaking problems. Examples of some common problems are:

- System runs out of memory
- CPU over-usage
- Database is down
- Part of the system is down

We can also set the *alerting system* to inform us when some system parameters, also known as **metrics**, are close to the *critical value*.

Prometheus is a free open-source monitoring toolkit. It is mainly used with containers, but it can be used with traditional (bare metal) servers.

Prometheus server performs metrics-related tasks and has three main components:

- **Retrieval**: Pulls metrics from targeted services.
- **Storage**: Stores metrics.
- **HTTP server**: Accepts and executes queries.

Metrics are *text-based* and *human-readable*. Each metric has the following attributes:

- **Type**: Represents the type of the metric, one of the supported types.
- **Help**: Is a simple metric description.

Prometheus supports three metric types:

- **Counter**: Counts how many times some event occurs. Value can go only *up*.
- **Gouge**: Represents the current value of the specific metric. Value can go *up* and *down*.
- **Histogram**: Samples observations and counts them in configurable buckets. Request duration and response size are some examples of observations. We will see in some examples later how we can use a histogram as a *timer*, to measure how long some events lasted.

As we mentioned before, Prometheus pulls metrics from targeted services. *Targeted service* must expose metrics through the HTTP endpoint (**/metrics** is the default endpoint). In order to perform that task, the targeted service must have an **Exporter**, tool that will read metrics, convert them to Prometheus format, and expose them.

Pull is a much better tactic than push. With **push**, targeted service must take care of metrics and push them to metrics service. *This can overload the metrics server!* With **pull,** the metrics server takes care of metrics and controls when they will be pulled, avoiding overload.

In the next section, we will see how to query metrics.

Prometheus query language

Prometheus Query Language, or shortened **PromoQL**, is a query language designed to work with Prometheus metrics. It can be executed on the Prometheus *Web User Interface*, or on some external tool that supports Prometheus metrics (we will see this later in this chapter).

Result of PromoQL expression can be one of the following types:

- **Instant vector**: Set of time series containing a single sample for each time series, all sharing the same timestamp.
- **Range vector**: Set of time series containing a range of data points over time for each time series.
- **Scalar**: Numerical floating-point value.
- **String**: String value, currently not in use.

Instant vector and range vector are pretty confusing terms. So we should try to explain it a little bit more. All Prometheus metrics are related to some *timestamp*. **Time series** can be defined as a series that maps a timestamp to recorded data. Or to simplify things a little bit more, **instant vectors** are used for *alerting*, while **range vectors** are used for *visual representation*.

With an *instant vector selector*, we can select a set of time series and a single value for each time stamp. For all examples in this section, we will use the fictional metric **`http_requests`**. The simplest selector is the one where only metric names will be provided. This selector will select all-time series that has the matching metric name:

```
http_requests
```

We can filter results by appending comma separated list of labels from curly brackets. In our example, the **`http_request`** metric will have a label method that represents the HTTP method. The following selector will select all-time series that have matching metric name and label values (all **`POST`** requests):

```
http_requests{method="post"}
```

Besides **equal** (=) we can use other matching operators:

- **Not equal** (!=)
- **Regex-match** (=~)
- **Not regex-match** (!~)

We can also match label values to the list of values separated by a *vertical bar*:

```
http_requests{method=”post|put|delete”}
```

For the *range vector selectors,* we use the *time duration* set in square brackets at the end of the selector. This value specifies how far back-in-time values should be fetched for the all time series. The following example will select all recorder values in the last `5 minutes` for all time series that have matching metric name and label values:

```
http_requests{method=”post”}[5m]
```

Time duration is represented with a numerical value(s) and one of the following time units:

- **Millisecond** (ms)
- **Second** (s)
- **Minute** (m)
- **Hours**(h)
- **Day** (d)
- **Week** (w)
- **Year** (y)

We can also combine time units, for example, *90m* and *1h30m* both can be used for a *time duration* of *90 minutes.*

Inside PromoQl queries, we can use arithmetic, comparison, and logical operators as well as some functions. The function `rate(rv range-vector)` that calculates the *per-second average rate* is one of the most important ones. It is mainly used in combination with counter-metrics. This example returns the per-second average rate for HTTP `POST` requests measured over the *last 3 minutes*:

```
rate(http_requests{method=”post”}[2m])
```

If we combine the `rate()` function with the aggregation operator (`sum`, `min`, `max`, `avg`, and so on), we should always first take `rate()` and then `aggregate`.

Now that we are familiar with the basic concepts of PromoQL, we can set up Prometheus.

Setting up Prometheus

In order to avoid unnecessary *Google Cloud* costs, we will again run everything on the local machine. First, we should set up our local Prometheus server.

Prometheus is available for all modern operating systems. On the official web page:

https://prometheus.io/download/

We can find and download archives in **`tar.gz`** format for Linux and macOS and in **`.zip`** format for Windows. When the download is completed we can extract the archive to the desired location.

Inside the extracted directory, we should find a file with the name **`prometheus.yml`**. This is a configuration file that has four main sections:

- **Global section** where we can set how often Prometheus will scrape metrics from targets.
- **Alerting section**, where **`alertmanager`** can be set up. Alert manager will fire alerts to configured channels (*slack, email,* and so on).
- The **rule_files section**, where rules for the metrics and alerts will be triggered when the rule condition is met. For example, we can trigger an alert when our system uses more than *500 MB of memory*.
- The **scrape_configs section**, where we will set targets that will be monitored.

For our case, we can use the default configuration and just set up a target. We will pull metrics from the service that will run on localhost, but we should choose the port. Our service will accept HTTP requests on port **`8080`**, it is good practice to use a different port for the metrics endpoint. Prometheus server will use port **`9090`** for its own HTTP server, so we can use port **`9000`** for the metrics endpoint.

Our Prometheus configuration should look similar to this:

```
global:
  scrape_interval: 15s
evaluation_interval: 15s

alerting:
  alertmanagers:
    - static_configs:
        - targets:
          # - alertmanager:9093


rule_files:
  # - "first_rules.yml"
  # - "second_rules.yml"

scrape_configs:
  - job_name: "prometheus"
```

```
static_configs:
  - targets: ["localhost:9000"]
```

Now we can run the Prometheus server, from the console/terminal with the following command:

```
./prometheus -config.file=prometheus.yml
```

Our Prometheus server is ready, now we can create some metrics, and add them to our web service.

Custom Prometheus metrics

In order to export Prometheus metrics, our system must have a proper **Exporter**. Implementation for Go programming language, known as a **client**, can be downloaded with the following command:

```
go get github.com/prometheus/client_golang/prometheus
```

First, we will initialize Prometheus. All initialization is in the **server** package, so we can add a new file, **prometheus.go**, and place the initialization function inside (*Figure 12.1*):

***Figure 12.1**: Server package*

Inside **InitPrometheus()** function, we will define a path for the metrics endpoint (**/metrics**) and start listening for requests on port **9000**. Here is the complete content of **prometheus.go** file from **server** package:

```
package server
import (
        "net/http"
        "github.com/prometheus/client_golang/prometheus/promhttp"
)

func InitPrometheus() {
        http.Handle("/metrics", promhttp.Handler())
        http.ListenAndServe(":9000", nil)
}
```

Inside the **main()** function, we will call **InitPrometheus()** function, but because method **ListenAndServe()** will block and wait for the requests, we must call it in a new goroutine. In that way, the main goroutine will handle HTTP requests, while the *subroutine* will handle metrics.

This code segment should be added, between database initialization and initialization of the HTTP server:

```
log.Println("Initializing Prometheus")
go server.InitPrometheus()
```

We can define our custom metrics in **metrics.go** file, inside the **metrics** package (*Figure 12.2*). We will demonstrate how to use *regular counters*, *counters with labels*, and *timers*. **Gauges** are similar to counters, in the way they are defined and used, so we will concentrate on counters:

***Figure 12.2:** Metrics package*

All *custom* metrics will be defined inside the **var** block of **metrics.go** file:

```
package metrics

import (
        "github.com/prometheus/client_golang/prometheus"
        "github.com/prometheus/client_golang/prometheus/promauto"
)
var (
        ...
)
```

First, we will learn how to define and use a simple counter metric that will count all HTTP requests. The counter is created with **NewCounter()** function that receives options, or name, and help (description) in our case:

```
HttpRequestsCounter = promauto.NewCounter(
        prometheus.CounterOpts{
                Name: "runners_app_http_requests",
                Help: "Total number of HTTP requests",
        },
)
```

Now when the counter is defined, at the start of each controller function we should increment its value:

```
metrics.HttpRequestsCounter.Inc()
```

Metrics can have labels assigned to them. In the following example, we will count all responses from the get runner API, but we will use a label that represents HTTP status to track metrics for different statuses.

For the definition of the counter with labels, we will use the **NewCounterVec()** function that will receive a list of labels, besides options:

```
GetRunnerHttpResponsesCounter = promauto.NewCounterVec(
        prometheus.CounterOpts{
                Name: "runners_app_get_runner_http_responses",
                Help: "Total number of HTTP responses for " +
                        get runner API",
        },
        []string{"status"},
)
```

In the **GetRunner()** method from the **runners** controller, we must increment this counter, and set the *proper label value*. We can use **Status** from the **ResponseError** model or set the *label value* directly if it is known.

Here is a new code for **GetRunner()** method where the counter is *incremented* and proper labels are set:

```
func (rc RunnersController) GetRunner(ctx *gin.Context) {
    metrics.HttpRequestsCounter.Inc()

    accessToken := ctx.Request.Header.Get("Token")
    auth, responseErr := rc.usersService.AuthorizeUser(
        accessToken, []string{ROLE_ADMIN, ROLE_RUNNER})
    if responseErr != nil {
        metrics.GetRunnerHttpResponsesCounter.
            WithLabelValues(strconv.Itoa(
            responseErr.Status)).Inc()
        ctx.JSON(responseErr.Status, responseErr)
        return
    }

    if !auth {
        metrics.GetRunnerHttpResponsesCounter.
            WithLabelValues("401").Inc()
        ctx.Status(http.StatusUnauthorized)
        return
    }

    runnerId := ctx.Param("id")

    response, responseErr := rc.runnersService.
        GetRunner(runnerId)
    if responseErr != nil {
        metrics.GetRunnerHttpResponsesCounter.
            WithLabelValues(strconv.Itoa(
            responseErr.Status)).Inc()
        ctx.JSON(responseErr.Status, responseErr)
        return
```

```
        }

        metrics.GetRunnerHttpResponsesCounter.
            WithLabelValues("200").Inc()
        ctx.JSON(http.StatusOK, response)
    }
```

In the end, we will learn how to use the timer. Here we will use **NewHistogram()** function that will accept options (**Name** and **Help**):

```
    GetAllRunnersTimer = promauto.NewHistogram(
        prometheus.HistogramOpts{
            Name: "runners_app_get_all_runners_duration",
            Help: "Duration of get all runners operation",
        },
    )
```

Timer usage is a little bit more complex than counters. The new timer will be created, while the observer provided through function arguments will observe the duration in *seconds*. In order to use the metric defined in the **metrics** package, we should use **ObserveFunc()**, a function that will adapt *regular* functions to work as observables.

We will use an anonymous function to *wrap* **Observe()** function from the **prometheus** package. Function **Observe()** will add a single *observation* to the histogram. This code should be placed at the start of the **GetRunnersBatch()** method from the **runners** controller:

```
    timer := prometheus.NewTimer(
        prometheus.ObserverFunc(func(f float64) {

        metrics.GetAllRunnersTimer.Observe(f)
    }))
```

When the function is *completed,* we should stop the timer. We can accomplish that with defer statement and **ObserveDuration()**, a function that will record the duration passed since the timer was created:

```
    defer func() {
        timer.ObserveDuration()
    }()
```

Now we can run our application and fire a couple of HTTP requests from **Postman** in order to generate values for our custom metrics. Now if we open a web browser and go to **`http://localhost:9000/metrics`**, metrics will be displayed (*Figure 12.3*). We should find our custom metric at the bottom of the page:

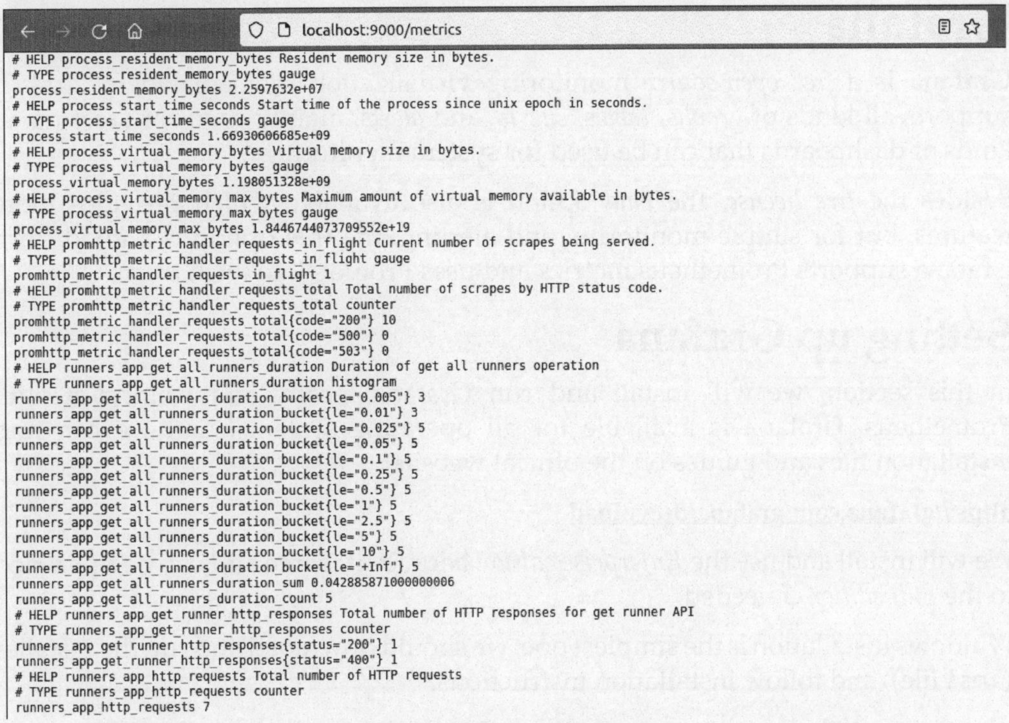

***Figure 12.3**: Prometheus metrics*

If we go to **`http://localhost:9090/graph`**, Prometheus *Web User Interface* will be prompted (*Figure 12.4*). Here, we can execute PromoQL queries, check metrics values, or test queries before it will be used in some external tool:

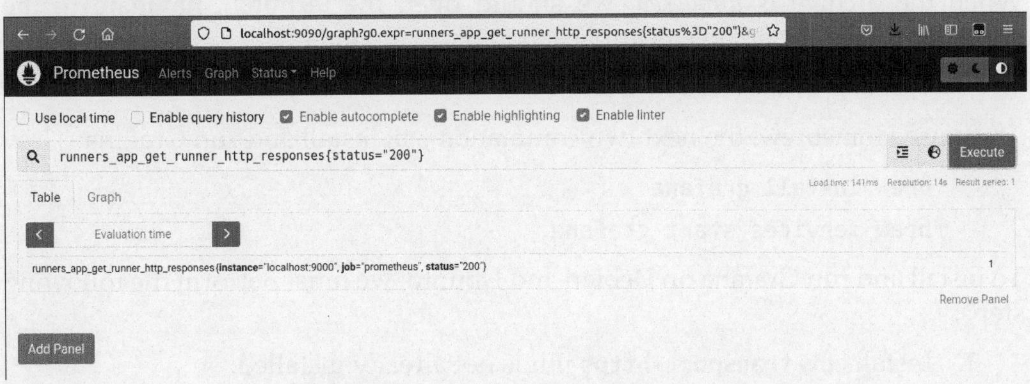

***Figure 12.4**: Prometheus Web User Interface*

Now we know how to create custom metrics and get their values. Everything we learned in this chapter, so far is not visually appealing. This can be fixed with some external tools.

Grafana

Grafana is a *free open-source* monitoring visualization tool created in *2014*. It supports all kinds of *graphs, tables, charts,* and *alerts,* mainly used for creating all kinds of dashboards that can be used for system monitoring.

Besides the *free license,* the *paid* option is also available which provides more features, but for simple monitoring and alerting, the free option is a good start. Grafana supports Prometheus metrics and uses PromoQL to fetch them.

Setting up Grafana

In this section, we will install and run Grafana locally and connect it with Prometheus. Grafana is available for all operating systems, and we can find installation files and guides on the official website:

https://grafana.com/grafana/download

We will install and use the *Enterprise edition* because it is free and can be upgraded to the *Full edition* if needed.

Windows installation is the simplest one, we should download and run the installer (`.msi` file), and follow installation instructions.

For the macOS we have two options, `curl` or `Homebrew`. For `curl` installation, we execute the following command that will download the `.tar.gz` archive:

```
curl -O https://dl.grafana.com/oss/release/
grafana-7.1.5.darwin-amd64.tar.gz
```

When the archive is *unpacked,* we should open the terminal, navigate to the directory where the archive is unpacked and run Grafana with:

```
./bin/grafana-server web
```

If we use Homebrew, the next two commands will install and run Grafana:

```
brew install grafana
brew services start grafana
```

To install and run Grafana on Debian and Ubuntu, we must perform the following steps:

1. Install `apt-transport-https` if it is not already installed:

```
sudo apt-get install -y apt-transport-https
```

2. Import Grafana public GPG key:

```
sudo apt-get install -y software-properties-common wget
sudo wget -q -O /usr/share/keyrings/grafana.key
https://apt.grafana.com/gpg.key
```

3. Add repository (create list file):

```
echo "deb [signed-by=/usr/share/keyrings/grafana.key]
https://apt.grafana.com stable main" |
sudo tee -a /etc/apt/sources.list.d/grafana.list
```

4. Install the latest Grafana version:

```
sudo apt-get install grafana-enterprise
```

5. Run Grafana:

```
sudo service grafana-server start
```

For Red Hat Enterprise Linux and Fedora, installation steps are different:

1. Configure the package management system (**yum**):

```
cat <<EOF | sudo tee /etc/yum.repos.d/grafana.repo
[grafana]
name=grafana
baseurl=https://rpm.grafana.com
repo_gpgcheck=1
enabled=1
gpgcheck=1
gpgkey=https://rpm.grafana.com/gpg.key
sslverify=1
sslcacert=/etc/pki/tls/certs/ca-bundle.crt
EOF
```

2. Install the latest Grafana version:

```
sudo yum install grafana-enterprise
```

3. Run Grafana:

```
sudo systemctl start grafana-server
```

If we go in our web browser to **http://localhost:3000 Grafana**, the login screen should be prompted (*Figure 12.5*). Here, we can enter *superuser* credentials **admin/admin** and click on the **Log in** button. Port **3000** is the default one for Grafana, but it can be changed if necessary. If any other dialog prompts after logging in, we can click on the **Skip** button:

Figure 12.5: Grafana login screen

Now, we can connect Grafana with Prometheus. If we select **Configuration** (*Gear* icon in side menu) and **Data Sources**, an empty **Data Source** configuration tab should be *prompted* (*Figure 12.6*). Here we should click on the **Add data source** button and select **Prometheus**:

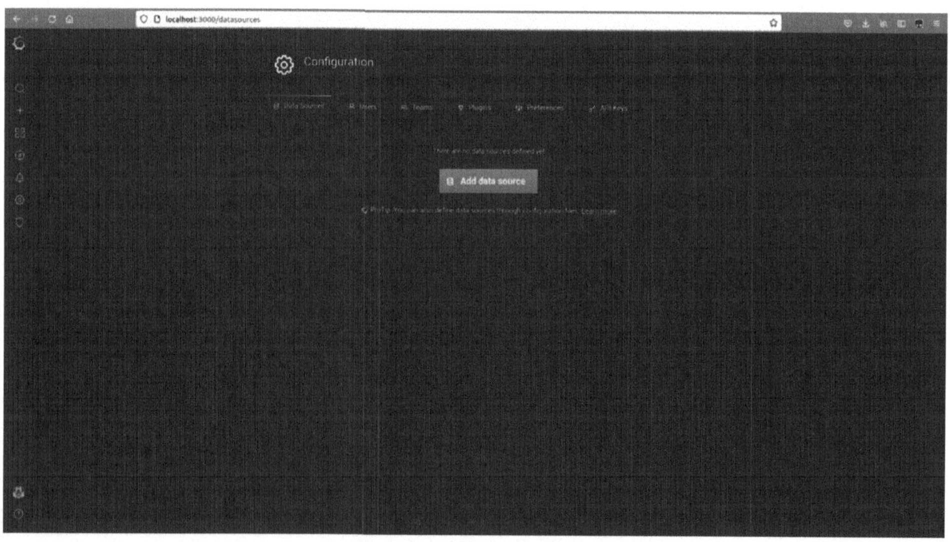

Figure 12.6: Data source tab

On the **Settings** tab (*Figure 12.7*), we can enter the data source **Name** and **URL**. For the name, we can choose `Prometheus`, while the URL will be the address of our local Prometheus server (`http://localhost:9090`). If the configuration is *valid*, when we click on the **Test and Save** button, a *green* pop-up with a **Data source is working message** will be displayed:

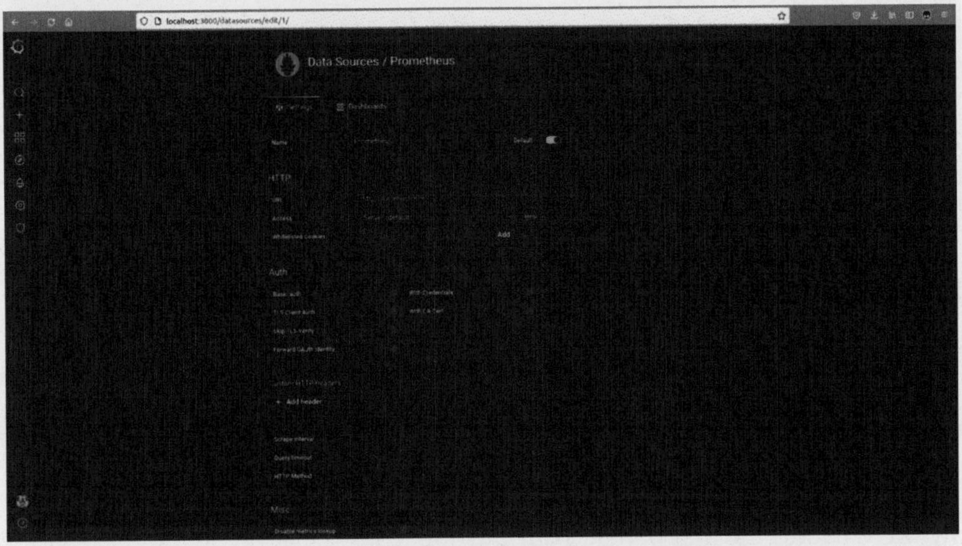

***Figure 12.7**: Data Source / Prometheus settings*

Grafana is configured and ready, we can create our first dashboard.

Creating Grafana dashboard

Finally, we can create our Grafana dashboard, by selecting *Create* (*plus* icon on the side menu) and **Dashboard**. A new, empty dashboard will be presented and we can first change some default settings by clicking on the *gear* icon from the *menu* bar at the top of the screen (*Figure 12.8*):

***Figure 12.8**: Dashboard settings icon in the menu bar*

On the **New dashboard / Settings** screen (*Figure 12.9*), we can configure many parameters. For our needs, we can use default options for most options, and just set a name for our dashboard. `Runners Dashboard` is the appropriate name, so we can enter it and click on the **Save dashboard** button.

On the prompted dialog, we can enter some message to serve as a reminder of what is *changed* and click on the **Save** button:

Figure 12.9: *Dashboard settings*

Now, we will add the first panel to our dashboard by clicking on the *Add panel* icon from the menu bar (*Figure 12.10*):

Figure 12.10: *Add panel icon in the menu bar*

The first panel that we will create will display the total number of received HTTP requests (*Figure 12.11*). On the right side of the screen (in the **Panel** tab), we should select **Stat** for **Panel** type and enter `Number of Requests` for the **Panel title**.

Below "preview" of our stat panel, we can find a form where we should insert PromoQL queries. To fetch the total number of received HTTP requests, we must get the current value of the request counter, with a simple query:

```
runners_app_http_requests
```

When the panel is completed, we can click on the **Apply** button:

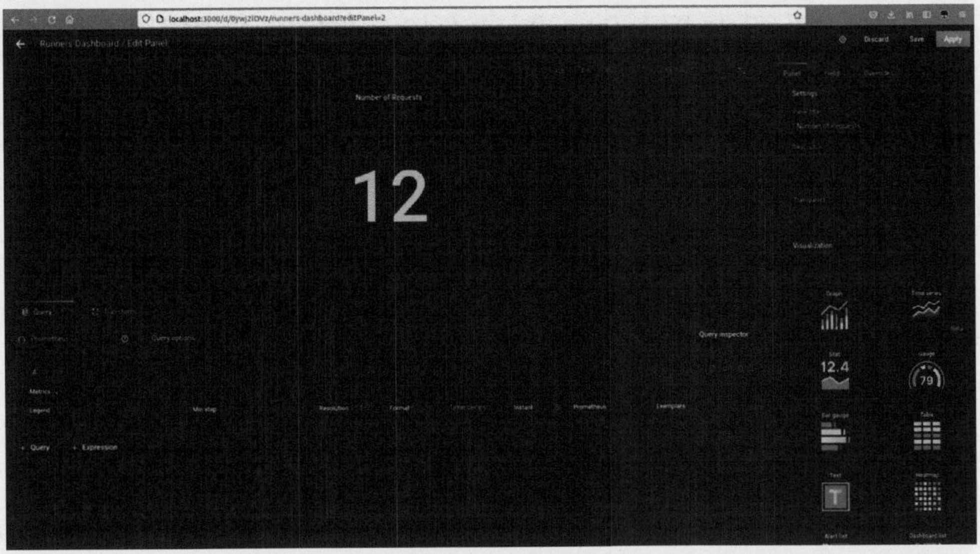

***Figure 12.11**: Stat panel*

The second panel will display the rate of HTTP responses for the *get runner* operation, separated by HTTP statuses (*Figure 12.12*). In the **Panel** tab, we will enter **`Get Runner HTTP Responses`** and select **Graph** for **Panel** type:

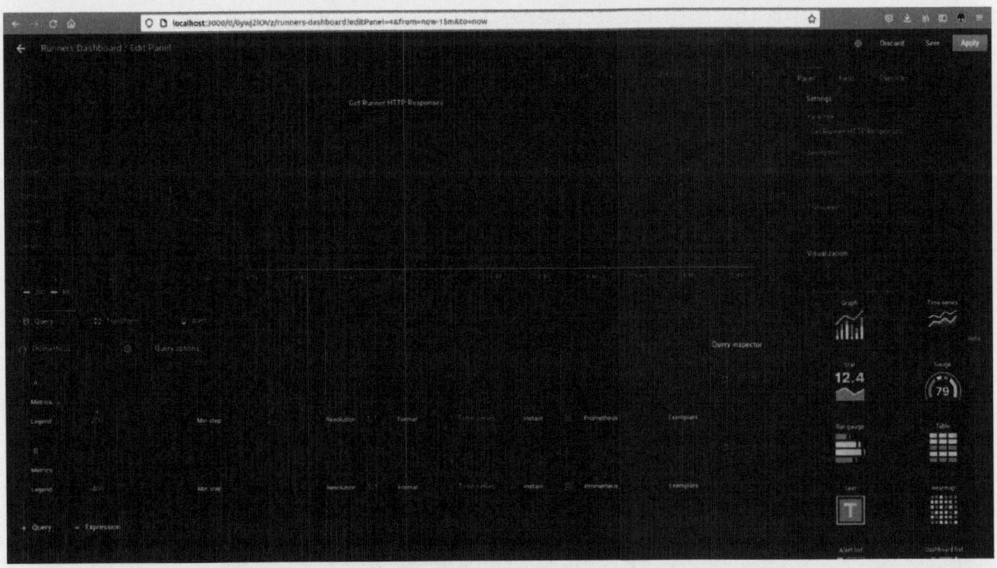

***Figure 12.12**: Graph panel*

In our example, we will have only two different statuses, **`200`** and **`401`**. We can fetch all status **`200`** responses with the following query:

```
rate(runners_app_get_runner_http_responses{status="200"}[2m])
```

For the *time-based panels*, we should use the **rate()** function. If we try to use metric without **rate()** Grafana will show display data, but a *warning* will be displayed after the query.

We covered status **200**, but *where to put the query for status 401?* We need one more query form. It will be created if we click on the **+ Query** button. Now we can use the second query:

```
rate(runners_app_get_runner_http_responses{status="401"}[2m])
```

On each query form, we have the input field **Legend**. Value from that field will be used in the panel's legend.

Before we can move to the *third* and the *last* panel, we must explain the term **bucket**. When the timer measures the duration, the result will be placed into the appropriate bucket. For example, we have three buckets for **100ms**, **200ms**, and **300ms**. If the measured duration is less or equal to **100ms** it will be placed in the *first* bucket if it is less or equal to **200ms**, but higher than **100ms** it will be placed in the *second* bucket, and so on. If the duration is higher than **300ms** it will be placed inside the so-called *infinite* bucket. We can define values for the bucket, or we can let Prometheus do that for us, as we did.

For the *third* panel, we will again select **Graph** type and enter **Get All Runners** for the panel name. Here, we can display the sum of rates for all buckets of get all runners timer, with the following query:

```
sum(rate(runners_app_get_all_runners_duration_bucket[2m]))
```

Now we can click on the **Save dashboard** button (*floppy disk* icon), and the dashboard is completed and ready (*Figure 12.13*):

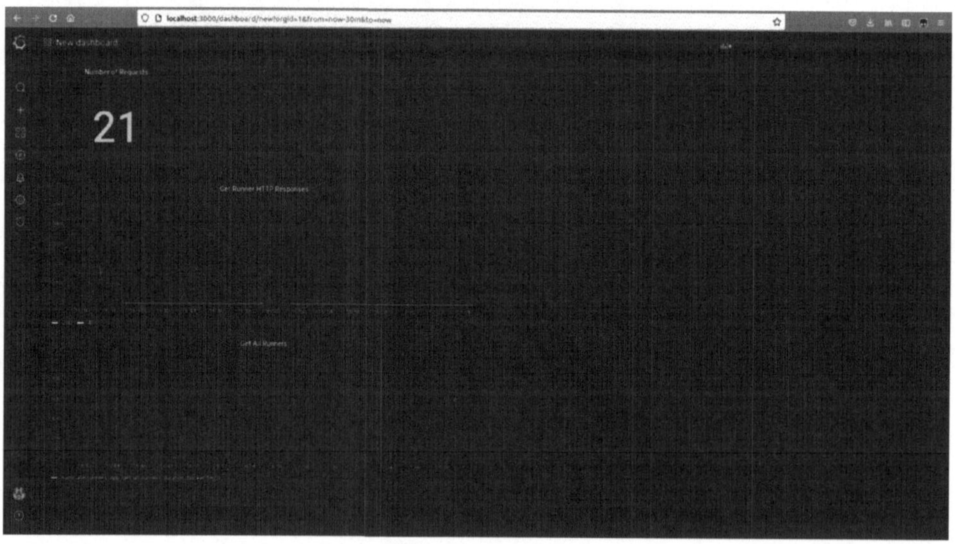

***Figure 12.13**: Runners dashboard*

Before we move forward, we should learn one more trick. We can create variables that can be dynamically used in PromoQL queries. First, we will click on the **Dashboard settings** button and then select **Variables** from the side menu. This action will open the **Variables** page (*Figure 12.14*):

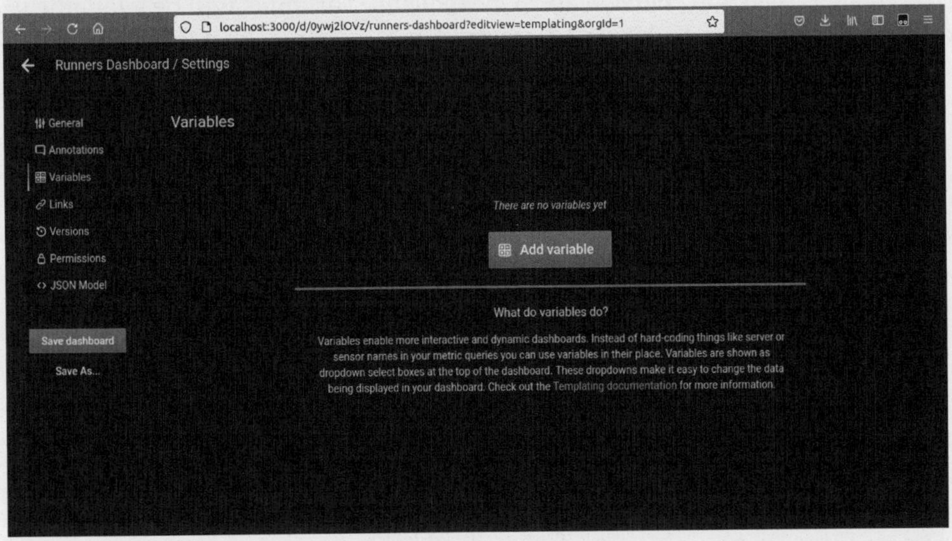

***Figure 12.14**: Variables page*

If we click on the **Add variable** button, the **Variables > Edit** page will be prompted (*Figure 12.15*). Here we can define the *name, label,* and *data source* for our variable. We can set `Status` for variable **Name**, and **Label**, and we should use **Prometheus** as a **Data source**:

***Figure 12.15**: Variable edit page*

All values for a specified variable can be fetched with the following query:

```
label_values(runners_app_get_runner_http_responses, status)
```

In our concrete example, we will fetch all values for the label status related to metric **runners_app_get_runner_http_responses**. Variables will be available in the drop-down list on our dashboard (*Figure 12.16*):

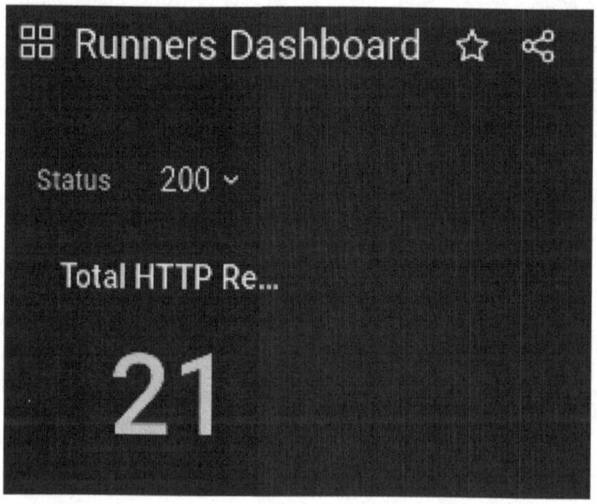

***Figure 12.16**: Variables*

Variable **status** can be used in queries in the following way:

```
rate(runners_app_get_runner_http_responses{status=”$status”}[2m])
```

We only have one topic that should be discussed before all tasks related to our web server are completed.

Alerting

As we have already seen, it is possible to set alerting rules in Prometheus. We can define alerting rule as a condition based on some Prometheus expression.

Here is a rule example, where an alert will be triggered when a number of HTTP responses with status **500** pass **1000**:

```
groups:
  - name: high number of internal errors
    rules:
    - alert: InternalErrors
      expr: runners_app_get_runner_http_responses{status=”500”} >
            1000
      for: 5m
      labels:
```

```
        severity: warn
      annotations:
        summary: High number of internal errors
```

Most of the statements from the previous rule have logical meanings, but we should explain a couple of them in more detail. The **for** statement defines how long Prometheus will wait from the moment the condition is first met until the alert is *triggered*. This will prevent the alert from being triggered in cases when the condition is met only for a couple of moments and avoid unnecessary panic. We can also attach a set of labels and annotations to the rule that can be used to provide more details, like *description* and *severity level*.

We can put all rules into a file and set it in the **rule_files** section of Prometheus configuration:

```
rule_files:
  - "./rules.yml"
```

Now if we restart Prometheus and open **http://localhost:9090/alerts** in a web browser, we can see our rules (*Figure 12.17*). Symbolically, *red* color represents alerts where the condition is *met*, while *green* represents that the condition is *not* met and everything is *fine*:

***Figure 12.17**: Prometheus alerts*

We can also set up an alert manager, to send messages to selected channels when the alert is *triggered*.

Conclusion

In this chapter, we learned how to monitor our application and trigger alerts when a potential problem occurs. With the completion of that task, our journey is over. *Congratulations we made it to the end!*

But we must be honest in the end, the development cycle is never over. Our application still has a lot of space for improvement. For example, we can introduce a better security model, write more tests, or maybe introduce new functionality.

I hope you enjoyed it. *Till the next meeting, goodbye.*

References

- **https://prometheus.io**
- **https://grafana.com/grafana**

Points to remember

- When the system is deployed and released it should be monitored in order to prevent potential service-breaking problems.
- For the time-based Grafana panels, the `rate()` function should be used.
- In cases when alerting condition is met only for a couple of moments, it is good practice to prevent the alert from being *triggered*, in order to avoid unnecessary panic.
- The development cycle is never over, there is still a lot of space for improvement.

Multiple choice questions

1. What is not the main component of the Prometheus server?
    a. Retrieval
    b. Exporter
    c. Storage
    d. HTTP server
2. Which component of the Prometheus server accepts and executes queries?
    a. HTTP Server
    b. Storage
    c. Retrieval
    d. None of above
3. The result of PromoQL expression can be one of the following types. Which one is currently not in use?
    a. Range vector
    b. Instant vector
    c. String
    d. Scalar

Answers

1. b
2. a
3. c

Questions

1. Which metric types are supported by Prometheus?
2. What is PromoQL?
3. How Grafana variables are used?

Key terms

- **Prometheus**: Open-source monitoring toolkit.
- **Grafana**: Open-source monitoring visualization tool.

Index

Symbols

A

B

C

H

N

O

P